Józef Piłsudski
Hero of Poland

by
Antoni Lenkiewicz

Józef Piłsudski: Hero of Poland
By Antoni Lenkiewicz
translated by Peter Obst
Cover design by Jan Kostka
This edition published in 2019

Winged Hussar Publishing, is an imprint of

P/KE & POWDER
PUBLISHING GROUP, LLP

Pike and Powder Publishing Group LLC
1525 Hulse Rd, Unit 1   1 Craven Lane, Box 66066
Point Pleasant, NJ 08742 Lawrence, NJ 08648-66066

Cover by Gabriela Paciorek.
Back cover by Wojciech Kossak

Copyright © Antoni Lenkiewicz
ISBN 978-1-94543-084-8
LCN 2019947550

Bibliographical References and Index
1. Piłsudski, Józef Klemens 1867 - 1935 2. Poland. 3. Biography

Pike and Powder Publishing Group LLC All rights reserved
For more information on Pike and Powder Publishing Group, LLC,
visit us at www.PikeandPowder.com & www.wingedhussarpublishing.com

twitter: @pike_powder
facebook: @PikeandPowder

This publication has been supported by the © POLAND Translation Program

Thanks to The Poles in America Foundation their support as well as The Polish Heritage Society for the cover art by Gabriela Paciorek.

List of Contents

Antoni Lenkiewicz

Introduction to the 2002 Edition of the Józef Piłsudski Biography

I was a Piłsudski admirer even before birth, because my parents were great fans of the Marshal. My mother's grandfather – Teofil – was brother of Jarosław Dąbrowski (1836-1871). Before Józef Piłsudski helped to recreate an Independent Poland, he had gained the respect of the Dąbrowskis by giving high praise to Jarosław in his first lecture on the January Uprising[1] (February 13, 1912).

Jarosław Dąbrowski was an individual who was at the head of events. A man who was more energetic, bolder and enterprising. Unfortunately, he was arrested before the outbreak of the uprising and had to sit it out in prison.

For me, outside of readings about Piłsudski, which I pursued actively and devoured, I only got to know the Marshal and his activities fully during the Solidarity decade (1980-1990). It was during this time that I understood that if we continue to present ourselves and think about our history as a series of defeats, and wait for outside help, we would never recover our independence and conditions for decent life and growth.

During my activities within NSZZ Solidarność (1980-1981), and later in prison where I was held in "internment," I realized that my lectures about Piłsudski were the most popular and informative. These would inspire Solidarity activists much younger than I and imparted or restored their faith in the possibility of an eventual victory.

Immediately after being released from internment, which in my case lasted from December 13, 1981 to December 23, 1982, I started to arrange the materials and notes to write a popular history about the Marshal. This would be in time for the 50th anniversary of his death, which in 1985 would be commemorated with great fanfare and resulted in a popular revival of our hopes for independence. The writing turned out to be the straightforward part. It was not as simple as having it published in the underground. In this regard, help came from the Radio Free Europe in 1984, when my book about Piłsudski was being read daily from the typed manuscript.

In 1985, my book appeared in "underground circulation." It was published in turn by the publishing initiative "Aspect," "Fighting Solidarity," "Libertas" publishing, and by the "Silesian Confederation," where I was the director. For my activities in promoting Piłsudski, I paid the price with nine months of imprisonment (from 11 November 1985 to 11 August 1986). The Marshal became a prominent figure not just in the Confederation of Independent Poland but in all the regions where Solidarity was active.

In a few dozen Catholic churches around Poland, excluding Legnica which was the main base for the Warsaw Pact, plaques were installed to mark Piłsudski's achievements as the recreator of an Independent Poland and a victorious leader in the war against Bolshevik Russia.

After 1990, people's interest in Piłsudski started to fade, but knowledge about him was still not fully accessible, and the possibilities of using this information had only started to open up. There were several reasons for this. Among them was the general feeling of weariness, disillusionment with the post-communist reality, and the fact that Lech Walesa made frequent references to the Marshal. Then there were those who for years had fought against Piłsudski's reputation with great vehemence but now, under new circumstances, decided to utilize his connections to socialism and the left.

On the patriotic side, the two great de-popularizers of Piłsudski were Jerzy Giedroyc and Piotr Wierzbicki, who kept repeating insistently that *Poland cannot be governed from the grave*; neither the one at Wawel castle nor the one at Bródno.[2] In this way, Wierzbicki cut himself off from the Piłsudski tradition, as well as that which would allow one to learn political philosophy from the many valuable writings of Roman Dmowski.

The effect was terrible. Despite the symbolic references to Piłsudski's and Dmowski's graves, there could have been positive effects from applying their ideas and principles. Instead, Poland was governed by terrified post-communists who could only poison the political atmosphere through their servility toward foreign powers or by lack of faith in our own strength, without which the possibility for action in difficult circumstances of our existence in the twenty-first century is seriously diminished.

On 14 October 2001, somewhat late but not without benefit, Polish Television started to broadcast a series of programs about Piłsudski. Watching the series, I felt moments of disappointment, but the conviction "better late than never" and "better a little than nothing" grew stronger.

In the final reckoning, one can say that Andrzej Trzos-Rastawiecki, known for such programs as "Enigma," a film about Stefan Starzyński, "Pielgrzym," "A Polish Pope," and "Scenes from the Life of the Ruling Establishment," did not disappoint his audience's trust. The underlying difficulty is in the fact that those who know little about the Marshal's life and accomplishments can get lost in the material. To fully know the great figures of our times, serial television programs are not enough. We must learn as much as we can about our heroes, read much, think about it, and discuss.

Overall, the series has the great ability to create interest in Marshal Piłsudski and compel those who are looking for answers to reach for a book about him on the 135th anniversary of his birth. At the beginning of the third millennium, the words of Piłsudski are still topical and important:

The many years of servitude have stopped our development and spoiled many of our efforts. Now all citizens of a free Poland must use this time of peace, make a great effort of will, and increase their level of work to quickly catch up with the rest of the world and stand as an equal in the great family of free nations. ... When I think about the tasks that await to be accomplished by Poland, I would like to take the intensity of work which would then permeate Poland, give all the ability to organize conscientious and honest work.

When the current generation learns about the life, deeds, and thoughts of Piłsudski, they can believe in themselves and the possibilities that stand before us. These are the conditions necessary for individual and collective successes.

Antoni Lenkiewicz

Introduction to the 1987 Edition – In Service to Truth and in Tribute to Piłsudski

I finished writing the first version of the book, *Józef Piłsudski – Life, Deeds, Thoughts*, in 1983, right after I was released from internment which, in my case, lasted from December 13, 1981 to December 23, 1982.

The situation inside the country and the conditions for writing were abnormal. During the time of the internments, I was cooperating with a Piłsudski inspired publication, *Wiadomości Bierzace* (Current News). Nearly the entire editorial team was arrested in December of 1982. Together with my brother Tadeusz, we continued to publish *Wiadomości Bierzace*. It was very absorbing work which brought us in close contact to the subject - Józef Piłsudski. There was a strong social need and a conviction that the best way to improve our political thinking was to return to Piłsudski's traditions.

I understood it as a calling to write and publish – outside of censorship – a popular book about the life, deeds, and thinking about the recreator of Independent Poland. I had been collecting books on the subject and had rough notes for the book. The entirety had to be worked over, edited, completed, and re-written on a typewriter.

As the basis for the dates of events, I decided to use *Kronika życia Józefa Piłsudskiego 1867-1935.* by Wacław Jędrzejewicz. This book was published by the Polish Cultural Foundation in London. I borrowed a copy from a friend and lived with the fear that the book would be confiscated by the Security Service (SB) if they surprised me while I was writing. So that this fear would not become fact, I attached a string to the book and would lower it out the window whenever the SBs knocked at my door. This method was effective in preserving the book. It was another matter with my notes. Twice, significant portions of the writing were taken away. District Attorney Czesław Kremis stated that, *the texts in question are not evidence in a criminal case but will not be returned to the suspect.*

Despite the unfavorable conditions, the "work" about Piłsudski was written faster than any of my historical-literary books (Kopernik, Pułaski, Łukasieński). In addition, the popularity of this book exceeded my wildest expectations. Many typed versions and their xeroxed copies circulated and multiplied in an extraordinary manner. Even before editions were published by "Fighting Solidarity" and "Aspect," the text of *Józef Piłsudski – Life, Deeds, Thoughts* was read on the air in 1984 by

Radio Free Europe.

Then, I decided that I would write a larger and better book about Piłsudski. Years passed and conditions changed. The number of available sources about Piłsudski grew along with writings about him. At the end of the 1980s, censored and uncensored publications aimed at the general reader differed very subtly, in a way difficult to notice, which is very important. A specific example of this is the long monograph about Piłsudski by Andrzej Garlicki. This book by a communist propagandist maintains an appearance of being scholarly but is an evil and harmful work. Not all will be able to recognize the many "half-truths" in Garlicki's work, which always amount to full-blown lies.

In accordance to the desires of his communist handlers, Garlicki set his main goal at undercutting and repainting Piłsudski's reputation and legend. The method is such that even when Garlicki cites facts that are essentially true, he uses them to build a false picture. When the author presents Piłsudski as a comrade – a member of the socialist party – the less informed, and such is the majority of Polish readers, were given a falsehood.

One of Garlicki's perfidious techniques is to cite, out of context, opinions about Piłsudski given by: Arski, Berbecki, Ciołkosz, Denikin, Gietrych, Grabski, Jabłoński, Konopczyński, Kuropieski, Jan Lipecki (a lampoonist hiding under the name of Irena Pannenkowa), Popiel, Reka, Studnicki, Fr. Warszawski, Witos, Zdanowski, and even Żeromski who at the beginning of WWI believed those who said that Piłsudski was bargaining with Polish blood in the interest of Austria and Germany.

Unfortunately, Garicki did not limit himself to citing false documents (Arski) and statements from which one is to believe that Piłsudski wanted to establish a dictatorship and destroy parliamentary democracy in Poland. Especially expressive and underhanded is a fragment cited from the "Diaries" of Zdanowski from 14 July 1930. False, and also naïve, is Garlicki's statement that, *at the end of 1929 only the revolutionary left – using the class criteria of analysis – had formulated a correct assessment of the situation and drew practical conclusions from it.* (p. 263)

It does not have to be explained that the relationship of communists to Piłsudski was very conflicted, and how damaging it can be to our culture when they lay claim to his greatness. To prevent this danger and keep my promises, which I repeatedly gave to listeners to my lectures about Piłsudski and to readers of my writings, I decided not to wait until a time came when I could write a perfect book about the Marshal.

Correcting and quickly supplementing that which was possible to correct, I present to my readers not a final work but only the next edition of *Józef Piłsudski – Life, Deeds, Thoughts.* In this way, I would like to continue to serve truth and take part in the nation's tribute that rightly should be given to Piłsudski and those who worked with him. I believe that in giving him tribute, we should not limit ourselves to mindless praise of his great accomplishments, but rather, take possession of them and use them as tools for use now and in the future.

It behooves me to explain that my work of popularizing Józef Piłsudski is tainted by "tendentiousness." I do not believe that in interpreting Polish history we should be constrained by so-called "objectivity." The lack of objectivity is not and cannot be falsification. The lack of objectivity should mean only, and only this, that our own homeland is closer to us than someone else's homeland. The Polish political left keeps telling us that one cannot love one's own nation more than any other, because this is a symptom of "nationalism" or even "chauvinism." These people know no better because they are steered by servility to other powers or suffer from a keen sense of inferiority acquired during years of servitude.

My tendentiousness on the matter of Piłsudski is based in the fact that I am not looking for a hole in the cloth of history, while from the life, deeds, and thoughts of our great marshal I extract, first of all, that which is instructive, inspirational, and useful in our present-day activities.

As far as his Polish policy is concerned, Piłsudski continued the romantic-insurrectionist traditions of the best kind, but also those that were the most reasonable. There was no other way open to him. The question "To fight or not to fight?" led to the alternative "To be or not to be?" Was not Piłsudski a nineteenth century anachronism, at odds with positivism, the widely understood socialism, and with all of modernity?

Accusations of this kind were often made against Piłsudski, but these were undisguised statements that merely revealed the smallness and shallowness of those who uttered them. In its best guise, Piłsudski's romanticism expressed itself in a heroic stance – so that in opposition to all external circumstances, he would not resign from the loftiness of his aims, the people's right to freedom, and the right of nations to independence.

In realizing his aims, Piłsudski was masterful in his realism, practicality, and infinite patience. He was wedded to the rich principles of Polish culture – as understood within the framework of Western-European tradition. He could not only feel deeply but think and act in a remarkable way.

Piłsudski did not have luck with biographers. He deeply regretted that he could not recognize himself either in texts written about him with praise and appreciation or in those that were filled with hate and venom. He thought that eventually he might write a truthful biography about himself. The Marshal did not have the strength and time. We say this with sorrow and the feeling of great loss, but this statement is not altogether true.

If one would go to the trouble of studying all the works written by Piłsudski, one would have to reach the conclusion that those texts contain about seventy percent of a great biography. In my work, I intentionally used many quotations, as it served the goals I set for myself: to serve truth and to popularize the life of the Marshal. He deserves a tribute in view of his historic accomplishments, and the book will also serve to build morale and uplift the spirits of my often totally lost and helpless countrymen.

Antoni Lenkiewicz

Chapter 1
In Family Life and School

The genealogy of the Piłsudski clan is not easy to establish. Information about the progenitors on both the maternal and paternal sides is very unreliable. But one cannot refute the ties between the Piłsudskis and the Ginets (which surname Piłsudski used in 1903). It was also mentioned in Bronisław Piłsudski's obituary.

Staying with only that which can be verified, it can be established that one of the forebears of Józef Piłsudski was Jan Kazimierz Giniatowicz vel Rymsza-Piłsudski (1614-1710). His son Roch Mikołaj used only the Piłsudski surname and the crest "Kościerze" or the "notched arrow."

Roch was the steward of Wołków, married to Malgorzata Pancerzyńska, sister of the Bishop of Vilnius. Roch's son was Kazimierz who held the post of Alka administrator. He married twice and had many children which somewhat clouds the family tree.

It is known that Piotr Piłsudski and Teodora nee Butler were the grandparents of the future marshal of an Independent Poland. His father – Józef Wincenty Piotr – was born in Rapszany in 1833. His marriage to the nine years younger Maria Billewiczówna took place on 23 April 1863 on her estate in Tenen. The couple were involved in insurrectionist activities. Józef was a commissioner of the National Assembly for Rosień county. Maria distinguished herself by transforming the family estate into a true insurrectionist base – with an arsenal, supply warehouse, and hospital.

After forty-four skirmishes that took place around Tenen, the Piłsudskis had to flee. Fortunately, they were able to make it to Vilnius, and then to one of the family estates in Zułowo[3] near Święciny. There on 5 December 1867, their fourth child, our hero, was born.

His older sisters were Helena (1864-1917) and Zofia (1865-1935), who later became the wife of Boleslaw Kadenacki. His older brother was Bronisław (1866-1918). Among his siblings were: Adam (1869-1935), Kazimierz (1871-1941), Maria (1873-1921) – the wife of Cezary Juchniewicz, Jan (1876-1950) – minister of the treasury and president of the Polish National Bank, Ludwika (1879-1924) – wife of Leon Majewski, Kacper (1881-1915), and the twins Piotr and Teodora who died as infants.

On 15 December, with the road known as the "Napoleonic tract" buried in snow, the child was taken to the parish church in Sorokopole. In honor of his father, the boy was named Józef; and to memorialize the saint of day of his birth, he received the middle name Klemens.

In nearby Święciny was an ancient manor house warped by time that was the particular object of pride for the local populace. In 1812, Napoleon stood in front of this house and watched his Grande Armee march east. "That year, who would have seen him in our land," they said, repeating after the bard. After the war was lost, Lithuania lost even its historic name. Under the tsarist domination, this was a backward depressed country, where a state of war was nearly permanent. This is how the Russians subjugated other nations.

The specific barbarity of this method was described by Adam Mickiewicz[4] in the IX Book of his *Pan Tadeusz*. Yet, what was perpetrated by Moscow's General Governor Michail Muraviev surpassed the worst nightmares of the bards. Years later, Piłsudski wrote in his text *Bibula*: *the impression of the murderous rule imposed by Marawjew was so fresh and awful that people would shiver at the sight of his service uniform.*

Of all the men who died during the January Insurrection, sixty percent of them were from Lithuania. Muraviev's role is described aptly by the sobriquet "Hangman." In his practical way, he ordered that the scaffolds not be taken down – *Let them stand and wait for the next series of executions.*

The persona of Józef Piłsudski senior was interestingly described by Andrzej Masiewicz, an inhabitant of Zułow.

He was a magnificent man. How could one compare to Józef, or any of his sons? He was a great man, passing from his forbearers. He was extremely strong. He walked the fields in a way that a man riding a horse could not keep up. Putting his hands behind his back, he would walk submerged in thought. If you had business with him, it was best not to approach him then, another time would serve.

Well educated and talented - he knew contemporary agricultural sciences well and was involved in many businesses. He started a turpentine plant in Zułowo, a flour mill, a sawmill, and a brick works. Unfortunately, he did not have the necessary patience to realize these undertakings. With great passion, he started in on new ideas, but they did not bring financial rewards. He was well read, loved music, played the piano, and even composed music.

In describing his parents, in a conversation with Artur Śliwiński, Piłsudski stated that he got his talents from his father and his character from his mother.

Mother was an unrepentant patriot; she did not even try to hide the pain and disappointment she felt when the insurrection failed. Of course, she raised us with a special stress on the necessity of continuing the fight with our homeland's enemy. From the earliest years, we were acquainted with the works of our bards, especially the censored and forbidden works. We learned Poland's history, and they bought only Polish books. But this patriotism had no specific social direction. Among our bards, my mother liked Krasiński best, but from an early age I was fascinated with Słowacki,[5] who was my first teacher of democratic principles.

National ideals, embodied in the works of our great poets – Piłsudski continued - *were a type of bible for us. We had them hidden at home and in the evenings would gather to hear mother read ... I still remember the psalm: "There will be a Poland, in the Lord's name," with which we always ended these secret family meetings.*

The family-home conditions in which young Józef, nicknamed Ziuk,[6] spent his childhood were summarized by Pobóg-Malinowski in his seminal work on Józef Piłsudski.

A large wooden manor – inside, twelve sizeable rooms, portraits of the progenitors on the walls; outside, surrounding the manor, numerous farm and industrial buildings; in front of a glassed-in walkway, a great lawn, beyond it a gate with the family crests; on the left of the lawn – fruit orchards and gardens. The narrow but deep Mera River flanks the manor with a picturesque half-circle. Two streams flow into the river, the Paprotka and Zułówka - the first serves to fill a large and deep pond with tall slender trees on its banks. Along the Mera is a second orchard and a beautiful avenue lined with fir trees. In addition, stands of old linden trees fill the space between the manor and river. Another picturesque place was a wooded hill near the river. Beyond the manor farm was a forest that was impassable in its interior. Within this forest, a few kilometers from the manor, was hidden the large Lake Piorun.

On 4 July 1874, the property caught fire and burned, causing the entire family to relocate to Vilnius. For little Ziuk, it was a painful experience. Up to that time, the Piłsudski children had their own household tutor and forbidden books, which their mother read to them in the evenings. Now he had to learn in a Russian-run middle school (*lyceum*). The Russian teachers sought to suppress the independence and self-worth of their students. Lessons were conducted in Russian, any mention of Poland was filled with contempt, history was falsified, Russian culture was praised, and gratitude was demanded for Poland being governed under the scepter of the Tsar. In answer to the question, why Polish could not be used in school, the teacher answered angrily: "You eat Russian bread, you have all the privileges of Russian citizens under the law, and you would not want to speak the beautiful Russian language?"

Ziuk would often hear words of encouragement from his mother: *What to do, what to do, son? You will grow up and you will get revenge. Now, learn and learn.* Later Piłsudski would write,

The time I spent at school was for me a time spent in prison ... there would not be a vellum sheet large enough to write down all the constant, humiliating statements made by the teachers, and the denigrating of everything that I held with love and respect ... In such an environment, hate for the Tsarist system and its oppression grew from year to year. Impotent rage would strangle me often, and I felt the shame of not being able to do anything to strike back at the enemy, burn my cheeks while having to endure in silence as my self-respect was trampled, and false and disparaging words were said about Poland, Poles, and our history. These were the emotions of depression, belonging to a slave, who could be crushed by the masters like a bug under their heel. This lay on my heart like a stone. The years I spent in the middle school I count as the worst years of my life.

Ziuk started his "political" activities in 1880. Together with his older brother Bronisław, he started to publish (in small quantities) an illegal publication called *Gołąb Zułowski* (*The Zułów Dove*). They filled the columns of this little paper with texts of insurrectionist songs and hymns, poetry from *Spiewy Historyczne* by Niemcewicz, and later with their own texts which were written versions of family stories from the Insurrection.

In an interview given to Mieczysław Lepecki, Piłsudski said, *When I was seven or ten years old, I decided that when I turned fifteen, which to me seemed to be the pinnacle of maturity, that I would start an uprising and chase the Russians out of Podbrzezie.*

An important document about the life of the Piłsudski family during those years is Bronisław's journal, started on 24 January 1882 and closed on 20 January 1884. Day after day, with diligence, Bronisław recorded everything that went on in the house, in school, and among his friends. We see from this record that Ziuk often played truant from school because he was bored or his patriotic feelings were offended. Bronisław cautioned Ziuk about this, for there could have been severe consequences, but these warnings were for nothing because "Ziuk was always a risk taker." He endured many hours of detention after school in an empty classroom or even under a special school arrest, but in general, Ziuk was very lucky.

Bronisław described it as follows.

When he ran away from lessons, he had double luck, he was able to avoid the unhappy consequences and on the street he would meet someone nice. ... When he did not know the lesson, he was called to the board just as the bell announced recess. ... And luck followed him outside of school. He had incredible success with the girls.

In connection to this statement is passing mention of brunette Stefcia and blonde Zosia, together with information that Ziuk was able to impress the entire family by beautifully reciting long fragments from Słowacki and Mickiewicz, following that up with imitations of various people dancing, making them cry with laughter.

The brothers loved each other despite "arguments" and "passing storms." In the evenings, when in bed, they would analyze their activities and "shed light" on misunderstandings. The course of these conversations, which Bronisław really liked, was always dependent on Ziuk's mood. Often, he would end any comments addressed to him with some short sentence, but sometimes he would open up his soul - speaking with great convictions about the flaws of his own character. Bronisław would always deny such, for he could not stand to hear things of this kind.

From 1882, the conspiratorial activities of the two brothers took place within the self-education circle "Spójnia." During the group's meetings, they studied Poland's history and discussed socio-political problems. Among their favorite and frequently read authors were: T. T. Jeż, E. Orzeszkowa, B. Limanowski, but first of all was Henryk Sienkiewicz.[7] We learn that during this time, Ziuk *listened eagerly and practically imbibed books, especially if they were historical.*

Much was said then about how "Narodna Wola" was fighting against the Tsarist regime. The Poles were quiet. The older generation said, "The Insurrection was a crime. We cannot dream of Polish independence; we must accept reality and not spit into the wind."

Among the intellectual trends that reached Vilnius from St. Petersburg was socialist ideology. The Russian Socialists, and people who saw value and reason in socialism, concentrated on condemning the bourgeoisie and said much about "the rotten European west" which did not have the virtues of the Russian nation. Some Poles uncritically embraced the slogans of Russian socialism, and as a result became totally Russified.

On 1 September 1884, at age 42, Maria Piłsudska died. Ziuk was 17 and started his last class in the middle school. The death of a moth-

14

er of ten children was a cruel stroke for the entire family. The way Ziuk lived after the death of his mother was diametrically different. This was especially visible in his activities within the "Spójnia." Earlier, as noted Bronisław, "he would often skip the sessions, he preferred to read alone, and often walked on Świetego Jerzego Street, or went to see his aunt."

In autumn of 1884, Ziuk started to work within "Spójnia" with dedication and great energy. In time, he surpassed the very diligent Bronisław and the other participants – showing himself as a leader for the first time.

Ziuk passed his maturation exam in Vilnius, and Bronisław moved to St. Petersburg. On 23 June 1885: *Pupil of the VIII class, Klemens Józef Piłsudski, of the Roman Catholic religion, nobleman... is awarded this certificate of maturation, no. 995.*

Chapter 2
Exiled to Siberia

After lengthy family discussions, and more from contrariness than conviction as he later stated, Ziuk decided to study medicine at the university in Kharkov. His studies went well, and in December 1885, he was taking his first exams. At that time, he came into contact with activists of the "Narodna Wola," but the programs they advocated did not entice him to join that organization.

In March 1886, large scale protests took place at the university on the twenty-fifth anniversary of the "emancipation of the serfs." Among the one hundred and fifty students arrested at the time was Piłsudski (he was punished with a six-day arrest). After successfully finishing his first year of studies, he decided to transfer to the university at Dorpat (now Tartu in Estonia). There were many Poles studying there. His life and plans were greatly complicated and started to move in a totally different direction. Like most Poles of his generation, he was against terrorism as preached and practiced by "Narodna Wola," but this did not protect him from the terror of the Tsarist police which treated all Poles as potential enemies and persecuted them with exceptional doggedness.

Bronisław Piłsudski finished his studies in St. Petersburg at this time. It is difficult to tell if he was indeed a member of "Narodna Wola." He never confirmed this himself. One undisputable fact is that together with Lenin's older brother, Alexander Ulianov, he was tried for preparing the assassination of Tsar Alexander III. It is also a fact that a certain Michal Kanczer, who was sent to St. Petersburg on a mission connected to the assassination, gave the address where Ziuk lived. When the plotters were arrested, Kanczer broke. In his confession, he told about his trip to Vilnius and the man who put him up for the night.

On 10 March 1887, Józef Piłsudski was arrested and held in a former monastery where Adam Mickiewicz and the heroes of *Dziady* (*Forefathers' Eve*) were also imprisoned. In mid-April, he was taken to the Fortress of St. Peter and Paul in St. Petersburg. In that prison, Piłsudski also met up with traces of Polish history, because nearly one-hundred years earlier, Tadeusz Kosciuszko and Ursyn Niemcewicz were held there.

The trial of these unlikely assassins was carried out in a manner typical of Russian despotism. All fifteen were summarily condemned to death. Lenin's brother (Alexander Ulianov), who was only twenty-one years old, ended his life on a scaffold. Bronisław Piłsudski (brother to the future Marshal of independent Poland) was not accused of any specific crime, and on this basis, his death sentence was commuted to fifteen years exile in Sakhalin. Later, he became an ethnographer of worldwide renown.

Bronisław's descendants are still living in Japan. His grandson, Kazuyausu Kimura, is full of admiration for Poland and has repeatedly visited the country of his grandfather with daughter Kanako. Dr. Antoni Kuczynski, a professor at Wrocław University, is a tireless researcher of the life and accomplishments of Bronisław Piłsudski.

Józef Piłsudski had no other evidence against him, aside from the fact that he let Kanczer stay overnight in his apartment. But that is all the Russian authorities needed to apply a severely repressive verdict. On 20 April 1887, he was condemned to five years of Siberian exile. He was twenty years old, and in his youthful imagination, he had prepared himself for great actions; but before he could begin, he would spend the best years of his life isolated and away from Polish society.

Despairing over his situation but also inspired by romantic role models, he sought relief in poetry. On 24 May 1887, he wrote a letter to his father in the form of a poem. Most Piłsudski biographers question the authenticity of this letter and skip over it in silence. Those authors, like Andrzej Garlicki, cite this "poem," do it with sour commentary and false interpretation: *This letter was written by a 19 year-old boy ... broken, without the certainty of goals, faith in the rightness of his actions, and in the purpose of the sacrifice.*

I personally believe that the poem is really Piłsudski's. From the literary aspect it is an imperfect piece, but we can see in it the influence of Słowacki and deep thought, totally unlike that which Garlicki draws from the text. Those who are interested can look it up in a book by Stefan Hinezy, *Pierwszy Żołnierz Odrodzonej Polski* [*The First Soldier of Reborn Poland*].

In the crude poetry written by young Piłsudski, there is a definite announcement of a creative combination of romantic goals with the positivist means for their realization. Bohdan Urbankowski in his *Filozofia Czynu* (*Philosophy of Action*) aptly commented: *Piłsudski's poem is an expression of disbelief in methods ... he is not disillusioned about the greatest national values, neither in the light of universal human values ("the sacred human rights") nor in the value of individual deeds.*

It was a sad meeting of a father with two sons in a prison cell. Before being sent into exile, Piłsudski was taken to the Moscow "Butyrka" prison. After Kharkov, Vilnius, the Fortress of St. Peter and Paul, and the investigative arrest in St. Petersburg, this was his fifth place of incarceration. Did he think, at the time, that during his lifetime he would see a dozen more such prisons?

The Russian revolutionary Burtsev[8] (the one who after many years would gain fame for unmasking Azef[9]) wrote at that time this description of Ziuk: *Young, with a boyish appearance, with a barely visible moustache, had a reputation as one of the toughest prisoners at Butyrki. Together with Homoluk, he was housed in the so-called "clock tower" and to spite the guards would sing the national anthem and other Polish songs.*

On 25 May 1887, their journey started. Around 60 persons, shackled in chains, were pushed into a barred railcar. The train took them to Nizhny Novgorod (present Gorki). A river boat took them on the Volga and Kam Rivers to Perm, then via Irtysz and Obi to Tomsk. The segment from Tomsk to Krasnojarsk was made on foot. Here it is worthwhile to cite Burcev's memoirs: *The young man walked among the prisoners in his grey soldier's coat, following the wagons with the sick, despite the fact that as a nobleman, he had the right to a place on the wagon.*

The place designated for Piłsudski's exile was Eastern Siberia, more specifically, Kierensk on the Lena River (about 1,000 kilometers north of Irkuck). They reached Irkuck on 4 October and stayed in the local prison waiting for the Lena River to freeze over. Piłsudski recorded the experiences from that prison stay in the colorful and humorous story, *Bunt więzienny w Irkucku [Prison Mutiny in Irkuck]*. The cause of the mutiny was a beating administered to one of the inmates. Piłsudski stood up in his defense and was struck with a rifle butt by the prison guard. His front teeth were knocked out and he was put on trial. As a minor, since he was not yet twenty-one, he was given three months of imprisonment. When the prosecuting attorney objected, the sentence was increased to six months.

In his memoir, Piłsudski wrote: *I don't know how the criminality of our actions was proven in court, because we all refused to take part in the legal comedy and we refused any defense. … A week after the trial, December 13, we crossed the Lena, and only a year later did I receive the verdict of the court, which in its generosity doubled the punishment, giving me a six-month jail term. I served it out in Kierensk, the place of my exile.*

In addition to the information about Piłsudski himself, his memoirs are excellent comparative material for the readers of *The Gulag Archipelago* by Alexander Soldzienitzen. Despite the obvious criminality of the Tsarist government, in comparison to the Soviet system, exile under the Tsar was almost idyllic. Each exile received 10 rubles per month for his upkeep. They lived in small villages among the locals and in the splendid natural environment of Siberia. They had no specific duties imposed by the administrators. They could wander on the taiga, hunt and do anything that they considered appropriate, with the exception of going out too far from their place of residence.

In Kierensk, Piłsudski made friends with the family of Stanisław Lande. He was a socialist sentenced to twelve years of prison, which was then changed to exile. At the beginning of 1889, the wife of Stanisław Lande, Felicija, was joined by Leonarda Lewandowska, who was also sent into exile for her improper attitude toward the Tsarist system. Ziuk then was twenty-two years old, she was a few years older. Love in the Siberian waste turned out to be natural for young hearts. When Leonarda (called Leosia or Olesia by Ziuk) ended her exile on 19 March 1890, she settled in Odessa and they wrote letters to each other. The letters (thirty have been preserved) are an extremely important source that shows us personal attributes, thoughts at the time, and the worries and concerns that young Piłsudski had about the future.

In a letter from 4 May 1890 he wrote: *The river started to flow this year. On April 30, it started to move and since yesterday has been flowing steadily, so today it is nearly free of ice. The breaking of the ice was not important, and I must say that it did not interest me much, not wishing to recall that last year I was waiting and watching for the Lena to move in this time period. Do you remember? Do you remember how I sat up entire nights with you waiting for the river to become passable?*

A letter from 5 November had a different tone - *It should be understood that one can dream, I dream about doing literary work, but for that one must study much. But in general, practically, I cannot imagine my life in Poland, and this is somewhat frightening. Understand, that I do believe in my own strength and talent, but from another point of view, who does not, despite this, we still have many who fail...*

In the following letters, Piłsudski mentions his plans for a literary career: *I started several items and now threw it all away, so understand I am rather bothered for this reason. I wanted to finish it in Siberia, but now I doubt that something would come of it. ... Please, dear, forgive me that today I write so little, but it is late, and I got up early to get some food for dinner.*

Besides Piłsudski's memoirs and his letters to Leosia, another source of information about the conditions in which he lived and matured during his Siberian exile are letters to his true and adoptive aunts (Lipmanowna, Masłowska, Bokosztówna) and especially to his loving sister Zofia and to his brother Bronisław, who was also in exile.

Daily chores, connected mainly with keeping alive, were tiring to Ziuk who was a "practical" man. He was irritated by idly wasted time and then he would accuse himself of the inability to use his talents and his unusual destiny, which he believed in since his youth.

He wrote to Leosia: *You ask what I am doing? Oh my God. I rise in the morning, I go to Awerburg's, and stay there until evening. Thank God, there is much work. Then I return home, drink my tea, walk around the room, and think of You, remembering the best times. Then I think a little about the future, read a bit, and fall into bed. And that is all.* The above mentioned Awerburg was a merchant who employed Piłsudski to conduct his correspondence and keep his account books.

The climate in Kierensk was very bad for his health. As a result of sickness and efforts undertaken by Stanisław Lande and friends, Piłsudski was allowed to change his place of exile by the governor. He was sent to the village of Tunka about two hundred kilometers south of Irkutsk, which had a better climate. His near catastrophic state of health in Kierensk improved dramatically in Tunka.

It could be said without exaggeration that the five-year exile in Siberia shaped Piłsudski's character and views. With Russians – exiles who were undoubtedly representatives of the best people in that nation – he coexisted and conversed on various topics, but the political discussions bored him. Later he wrote: *All of them are identical imperialists, not excluding the revolutionaries. ... Centralism is part of their thinking, always striving for absolutism. They cannot stand diversity; they cannot reconcile differing views – these weaken their will and imagination to such a degree that they cannot combine differences into a unified reality and reject the necessity for socially conscious organizations. That is why there are so many anarchists among them. It is a strange thing that among the Russians I cannot find any republicans. Weakness of spirit, apathy, surrender without fighting against violence – these are the basic attributes of that nation. ... Only here, when I could peacefully think over everything that I had experienced, I became the person I am. Chiefly, I was able to rid myself of the remains of Russian influence. ... Then in Siberia, where without any culture, social factors appear without camouflage, in their nakedness, I saw how the machinery of the Tsarist system works and how it influences human life in Russia. I came to fully hate this Asiatic monster, which is barely covered by a European veneer.* Among the books which Piłsudski studied while there were works of Spencer and Marx.

From among the Poles in exile with him, undoubtedly the greatest influence on Piłsudski had Bronisław Szwarce (1834-1904). He had spent seven years in the most terrifying of the Russian prisons, the Szlisselburg Fortress. He met Walerian Łukasinski (1786-1868) there. Szwarce[10] was a member of the Central National Committee before the outbreak of the January Insurrection and stayed faithful to the conviction that the only realistic program of activity for the Polish nation was to prepare for an armed uprising. In one of the letters from Siberia written by Piłsudski was the following statement - *Szwarce is a sympathetic man, a bit too old to be my friend, but I have exceptionally pleasant conversations with him, since he has seen much and read more.*

It can be accepted then, that the idea of an active struggle was formed during his Siberian exile. In this way, Piłsudski became a link between the January Insurrectionists and the new generation of fighters in the Polish Socialist Party and the Legions. The creative interaction between Piłsudski and Bronisław Szwarce turned out to be long lasting. They met in Lwów in 1896. Piłsudski asked him to write a cycle of articles about the unsuccessful insurrection for the *Przedswit* publication. Szwarce never completed the assignment. He was too old and embittered, but by saying: "the generation of grandsons must survive and overcome disaster", he foretold the future.

The Marshal's parents Maria Piłsudski (nee Billewicz) (1842 – 1884) and Józef Wincenty Piłsudski (1833 – 1902)

Józef Piłsudski (left) and his brother Bronisław (right) around 1870

Józef Piłsudski as a student at the Wilno Gimnasium, 1882

Several people in the self-education circle of "Spójnia," circa 1885. From the left, Szwengruber, Bronisław and Józef Piłsudski, and Busz

Description
Age: 19, born 1867
Height: 1 m 75 cm (5 ft 8in)
Face: clear
Eyes: Grey
Hair: Dark
Whiskers: Light blond
Eyebrows: Dark blond
Beard: Dark blond
Mustache: Light blond
Nose: Normal
Mouth: Normal
Teeth: Not all of them
Chin: Round
Particular Characteristics:
1) Face clear, the eyebrows come together over the nose
2) At the end of his right ear is a wart

(Left) A Russian polic document from 1887 titled: "Criminal of the state Józef Piłsudski".
(Right) a translation of the Russian Police document

(Left) a drawing by Zdzisław Czermański depicting Józef Piłsudski on his way to his Siberian Exile.
(Right) Leonarda Lewandowska – the first love of Ziuk, whom he knew from his exile in Siberia

Chapter 3
In the Polish Socialist Party (PPS)

Piłsudski returned to Vilnius on 1 July 1892. He had a long beard, an ex-otic suntan, and missing front teeth. He had changed so much that when he called out to a friend, actually a relative, *How are you Zygmunt?* the man said, *I don't remember you, sir? Could this be a mistake?* Piłsudski replied, *There's no mistake, but I see I must introduce myself; I am Józef Piłsudski.*

One of the political salons in Vilnius was led by Maria Koplews-ka-Juszkiewiczowa, the daughter of a well-known physician and a divor-cee from a very rich husband. Taking advantage of her social position and having cover under the Russian administration, this Lovely Lady (as she was popularly known) conducted conspiratorial activities, inviting to her salons outstanding persons from among the patriotically oriented Poles. Among her circle were: Dominik Rymkiewicz, Maria Paszkowska, Leon Wasilewski, and Stanisław Mendelson. Frequent guests from Warsaw were Ludwik Krzywicki, Jan Ludwik Popławski, Kazimierz Pietkiewicz, and Aleksander Sulkiewicz. From Mitawa (now Jełgawa) would come Ro-man Dmowski, who was forced to relocate there.

There is a view that all future disagreements between Piłsudski and Dmowski started because of their competition for the hand of the "Lovely Lady." This, of course, is an exaggeration. It is a fact, though, that Piłsudski married Maria, and that Dmowski was also in love with her and never married.

At a convention in Paris, which lasted from 17 to 23 November 1892, the Foreign Society of Polish Socialists was founded. In March of 1893, representatives of the Society founded the illegal Polish Socialist Party (PPS) in Warsaw. This party was joined by the socialist group from Vilnius that included Stanisław Medelson, Stanisław Wojciechowski, and Józef Piłsudski.

During 1893 and the following years, Piłsudski published many articles in *Przedświt*. In issue no. 8, which appeared in August 1893, there was an article entitled: "A Stance Toward the Russian Revolutionaries."

The links of a chain with which the Tsarist regime has bound us are also a natural bond that connects our efforts in the struggle, directed at shaking off the ignoble shackles, but the struggle with the Tsarist regime is not our full political program. The PPS has in its program the demand for establishing an independent and democratic Poland.

The editorial board of *Przedświt* informed the readers that this article was the official position of the PPS in reference to Russian revolutionary groups.

During the last days of June and the first days of July in 1893, the initial group meeting of the PPS took place in the forest outside of Vilnius. Among the many important resolutions, there was one that referenced the publication of an official newspaper, *Robotnik (The Worker)*, by the Polish Socialist Party. The group that was to make this happen included Józef Piłsudski. Preparations lasted a year. At the beginning of July 1894, the printing press arrived, purchased by Stanisław Wojciechowski[11] in Leipzig (for one hundred and twenty-five rubles) and sent by a London based firm to Konigsberg, from where it was smuggled to Lipniszek (fifty kilometers from Vilnius).

The machine clacks a bit, but this too can be fixed. ... In any case we thank you for this thresher, wrote Piłsudski to London in mid-July 1894. Piłsudski was first in his dedication to the work. He wrote, edited, and set type, then distributed the printed issues around Poland, spoke to workers and peasants, and organized the party. To get a measure of this undertaking, one should know that two printers during an hour of intense work could produce fifty issues of the publication, where the average total printing amounted to two thousand newspapers. The entire output was then taken (by Piłsudski and future president of Poland Stanisław Wojciechowski) to meeting points, handing them over to other members of the conspiracy for distribution. The illegal newspaper was carried in two suitcases – a light colored one and a dark one. Jokingly they were referred to as the "Blonde" and the "Brunette."

We dress quickly, grab the packages with the latest issue of the Robotnik, and leave the print shop, beginning the uncertain trip to meet the regular recipients of the publication. A momentary pause, and the carriage wheels start clattering. One of us returns home with a slight worry in his heart, the other, a bit disturbed, thinks if this time he will pass through the Vilnius Rail Station in Warsaw, a place that was always under the eye of the police.

This is how Piłsudski remembered his activities after years had passed. He traveled not only to Warsaw and Łódź but also to St. Petersburg, Moscow, Kiev, and Odessa.

Robotnik became a moral and political authority. Everyone who was interested in preserving the dignity of men and Poles feared being placed on the "blacklist" of people cooperating with the Tsarist authorities. The brutal Russian government terrorized Poles. Turning the "Land of the Vistula" into a place strictly Russian seemed a near done thing. Meanwhile, in the first issue of *Robotnik*, Piłsudski, announced that Polish independence was one of the main and realizable tasks of the PPS.

It is a national necessity to prepare for an armed struggle for Poland. The future and welfare of the workers are tightly bound to the recovery of Polish independence. A Free Poland is a worthy goal in a fight for life or death. It is a duty of the working people to adopt this goal as their own and make it a reality. No one would agree to die in a struggle for a pay raise of ten kopecks. We must show the people a worthy goal. The future of Poland depends on the involvement of the greatest number in this work.

Piłsudski was opposed to overvaluing the role of the economic factors: *The policy of humility, especially with the Russian government has never brought any benefits to the working masses ... Humility and passivity lead only to the strengthening and solidifying bondage ... To date the struggle confirmed our conviction that the organized power of our enemies must be opposed by a unified strength of the workers.*

Piłsudski would frequently write about economics and the class struggle, but even more often about the nation and traditions. In opposition to a contemporary trend, Piłsudski's articles contain no trace of enmity toward religion, or even anti-clericalism; instead there are frequent and unequivocal statements praising Catholicism.

Piłsudski was infuriated by all the frequent appearances of servility and compromise. In September 1897, Tsar Nicholas II came to Warsaw and was greeted with pomp by Zygmunt Wielopolski. In an article written at the time, Piłsudski stated: *Today we do not have the ability to speak to the Tsar in a language that he alone can understand – the language of strength and force. We must stand as mute witnesses to the welcoming performances and the servility of those who push forward to show the Tsar their faithful servitude. We must remain unbending toward our united foes, and fight with greater energy, prepare and concentrate our strength, until there comes a time in the streets of Warsaw when the enormous voice of a rising people rings out: Death to despots! Away with slavery! Long live a free Polish people!*

One of Piłsudski's colleagues (Józef Dąbrowski) characterized him as follows: *Wiktor, known as Ziuk to his closest friends, and Żuczek to his lady friends, was then thirty. His height was average, the posture leaning slightly; short, dark, thick hair styled in a "buzz cut" as it was impossible to comb. His face surrounded by a thick pointed beard, with a bushy moustache and protruding, nearly pouting lips – that is his contemporary portrait. First of all, one is struck by his gaze. The eyes seem understanding and peaceful, looking out from under thick brows, set deeply and looking out on the world as if from concealment. "Wiktor" spoke in a domineering way, with great confidence in himself and his opinions. Though very sincere, he is able to hold all at a distance. As an activist, he impresses one with his strength of will and self-control. To a large degree, he has the primary and most important trait of a leader – he treated his political moves like a game of chess, which he liked enormously. If some alignment did not work out, he would abandon it and work out a new one.*

The print shop for the *Robotnik* was first housed in Lipniszki near Vilnius, then in Vilnius itself. Later, it was in Łódź at 19 Wschodnia Street. In Lipniszki, six issues were printed, the last dated 24 December 1894. Aleksander Sulkiewicz moved the printing press to Vilnius. At the time, Józef Piłsudski was at the First Convention of the Foreign Polish Socialist Society, which took place in Zurich.

In Vilnius, the closest colleague of Piłsudski in editing and printing the Robotnik was Stanisław Wojciechowski, who later became a president of the Polish Republic. In his memoir he wrote: *Piłsudski wrote the introductory articles and duplicated the composed text whenever I was involved in composing.*

In 1896, Piłsudski spent several months in London, and while there, took part in the 2nd Congress of the Socialist International. His life during those years of conspiratorial activity is little known. Even when he lived in Vilnius, he could not see his family who were under constant surveillance. To throw the watchers off the track, his letters were routed through various European countries and even America. The major evidence of Piłsudski's enormous work done at the time were articles published regularly in *Robotnik* and *Przedświt*, and the many mentions of his organizational activities.

From October 1893, he was a member of the Central Workers' Committee of the PPS. Among his responsibilities were such things as financial resources, relations with the Russians and other national groups, liaison with students, and cooperation with the press.

Did Piłsudski have a private life, did he take time off, or did he ever rest? One can take it for granted that the constant travel to Warsaw, Vilnius, Kovno, Kraków, Lwów, St. Petersburg, Zurich, Geneva, Moscow, Kiev, and Odessa; his writing, editing and organizational activities; supplying paper and distributing finished issues; meetings; consultations; and conversations totally filled his time.

But there had to be some other private times, some absolutely private contacts and meetings, because in spring of 1899, he became serious about marrying the already mentioned "Lovely Lady." There were problems in realizing the marriage because Maria was a divorcee, and divorce was not approved of by the Catholic Church. So the appropriate legal arrangements were made in the Reformed Evangelical Church, and within that denomination, Józef Klemens Piłsudski married Maria Juszkiewiczowa nee Koplewska in the village of Paproć Duża near Łomża, on 15 July 1899.

Shortly after the nuptials, the Piłsudskis, using the name Dąbrowski, settled in Łódź were the editorial office of the *Robotnik* was relocated. This is where their intensive work went on and where the Polish Socialist Party started to grow in strength. A record of a kind was the fact that clandestine publication continued for seven consecutive years without being discovered by the authorities. Yet, eventually it had to end. Their exposure was unexpected, and as is usual, quite accidental. The Piłsudskis had a visitor from the Central Workers' Committee of the PPS – Alexander Malinowski. Apparently, he was "tailed" because on the same night, 21–22 February 1900, the apartment with the secret printing press was raided by police and operatives of the Tsarist "Okhrana." The search of the apartment lasted until noon of 22 February and yielded unequivocal evidence. Maria and Józef were arrested. First, they were kept in the Łódź prison until 17 April, and then were taken to the 10th Pavilion of the Warsaw Citadel.

It was not easy, Piłsudski said, *to organize such a difficult thing, and it would not be easy to organize such an activity again.* Piłsudski breathed with relief on learning several weeks later that thanks to the efforts of his coworkers, the next issue, number 36 of the *Robotnik,* was published. The situation was serious. Piłsudski was facing a lengthy period of interrogation and then eight to ten years of hard time was the usual punishment for such a "crime" under the Tsar.

The leaders of the PPS decided to undertake an action in order to free "Wiktor." Escape from the Citadel was nearly impossible. Some stratagem had to be employed to get him moved to another location. This had to be an illness, one whose cure could not be affected at the prison hospital in Warsaw. They turned to the brilliant psychiatrist – Dr. Rafal Radziwiłłowicz, who gave them a set of instructions. First, there had to be the appearance of a mental agitation, manifested on seeing prison guards with refusal by the inmate to consume meals, due to fear of poisoning. Because of the dreadful fast, the prisoner's state to health started to worsen and this caused concern among his captors. "For the good of the investigation" the prisoner had to be in decent health. They were counting on being able to catch other conspirators, and a trap was prepared in Łódź.

Among the experts called into the case was a decent Russian doctor named Ivan Szabasznikow. Despite some suspicions of a sham, he decided that it was necessary to place the prisoner under observation, and the only hospital of the right kind was in St. Petersburg. The desired goal had been achieved. On 15 December 1900, Piłsudski was taken from the Citadel to the Hospital of Nicholas, the Miracle-Worker, in St. Petersburg.

The mastermind behind the escape was Alexander Sulkiewicz. It was also a lucky break that the administrator of the hospital was Dr. Otton Cze-szczott. Directly involved in the escape was another Pole, the young and well-situated physician, Władysław Mazurkiewicz. Thanks to his father's influence with then governor of St. Petersburg, General Kleigels, he was assigned to do his internship at the mental hospital.

In his memoirs, Piłsudski wrote: *It was a very miserable game. Aside from the hunger, which was very acute, they would send in some special and delicious meals which I had to refuse. In addition, simulating insanity, having to beware at all times of one's actions, composing and holding facial expressions and the necessity for nonsensical utterances, tired me to the extreme. Sometimes the expressions of perturbation elicited on my keepers by my behavior seemed funny to me.*

After several months, his keepers' watchfulness waned. When the decisive moment arrived, the night of 14-15 May 1901, Dr. Mazurkiewicz, gave orders to the guard after making his mandatory scheduled inspection of all the hospital wards and special cells where individual prisoners were kept.

This is a very interesting case, he said approaching Piłsudski's cell, *after you make your rounds, bring him in for testing in my office.* The guard did as ordered and per the regulations waited outside the door. After a long period of silence, he knocked; it turned out that the door was locked from within. As a result of the alarm, the door was forced. The hospital clothing on the floor, with remnants of freshly cut hair, explained the situation immediately. *He escaped. A clever, well organized escape by a dangerous prisoner*, said the commandant. *Who was on duty? Mazurkiewicz – I should have known; he is a Pole.*

The escapees left the hospital successfully, but this was not easy, and only a fortunate turn of events saved them from recapture. Sulkiewicz's help proved to be instrumental. That very night in uniforms and carrying documents of the customs office, they left for Rewla (present day Tallin). A little earlier, after eleven months of imprisonment in the Warsaw Citadel, Maria Piłsudska was released. The court decided that she was a "victim of love" and could not denounce her husband. They met at the Czysta Łuża manor in Polesie. There they rested and waited for the intense police search after the escape to subside.

On 20 June, Piłsudski wrote his first (after the escape) letter to Jędrzejowski in London. *I will not write much, first of all I lack the inclination, and then I hope that after a short while I will see you in person. Meanwhile, I want to tell you that I am endlessly glad that I was, so beautifully, able to remain among you.*

In order to discuss many matters before re-entering into conspiratorial work, the Piłsudskis decided to go to London. They started out in mid-November 1901. Their route took them through Katowice and Poznań. They stopped in both cities for a while to meet activists from the PPS and get an idea as to the state and situation within the party. At the rail station in London, they were greeted by Jędrzejowski, Filipowicz, and Wasilewski. They took a small room at 67 Colworth Road, in Leytonstone, a far suburb of London. The building housed a center of the PPS manned by emigrants. This is where *Przedświt* was printed, the newspaper with which Piłsudski had longtime ties.

The stay in London was to have been a time of rest after fifteen months of imprisonment and faking insanity, but Piłsudski could not be inactive. He gave lectures on Polish insurrections that failed to win independence to workers' clubs, while at meetings organized by the Jewish Bund, he spoke about the situation in Russia. The Russian publication *Swoboda* (no. 2) in Geneva printed his long article entitled "The Self-Appointed Rulers of Poland." Piłsudski stressed Polish aspirations for independence and expressed the hope that "at least those Russians who are fighting for their own freedoms will learn to respect the desires and freedom of other nations."

The state of Piłsudski's health was not good, however. In one of his letters, he wrote, *I feel strange about my health, everything bothers me to the extreme, and even minor physical and mental efforts make of me a beaten man. In a word, the devil knows what has happened to me, the mechanism is starting to break down. Perhaps those idiotic mountains, where the doctor is making me go, will have a positive influence on me.* The place for his rest-cure was Fryburg in Switzerland, because Ignacy Mościcki lived there. Eventually these plans resulted in the Piłsudskis departing for Zakopane.

In one of the letters from Zakopane written to Jędrzejewski, he wrote, *You have no idea how lazy I have become these days. I don't want to read, or write, and often I don't even want to talk. Now I have justified myself by saying that there is no such cure where a man does nothing at all, and I console myself that when I leave Zakopane, everything will change. Meanwhile, the cure seems to be working.*

During this time, Ksawery Prauss and Jan Miklaszewski were arrested. There were other difficulties, due mainly to the distance separating the London leaders from the PPS in Poland. In that situation, Piłsudski decided not to worry about his health anymore and return to active service.

On 16 April 1902, he was in Kraków and then went to Vilnius. He also visited Kiev, where Feliks Perl edited and printed the *Robotnik.*

Piłsudski's escape was widely known, but he was not happy about such fame, especially when he realized that this could have a detrimental effect on his future conspiratorial work in Russian territories.

35

Chapter 4
War with Japan, A Dream About a Sword and Divisions within the PPS

In June 1902, the 4th Convention of the PPS took place in Lublin. Piłsudski made various organizational proposals, but these faced wide opposition. One of the more important organizational changes that he championed was to move the London-based "leadership" to Galicia. That oasis of freedom with blooming cultural life, seemed to Piłsudski to be the political "Piedmont"[12] for Polish independence-oriented activities. Stanisław Wyspianski's[13] play, *Wesełe (The Wedding)*,[14] the popularity of Żeromski's[15] novels, the "Racławice Panorama"[16] – were indicators that time had come - fired the imagination of youth and encouraged action.

It should be mentioned that in this time period, Piłsudski had established contacts with the creative community, especially Stefan Żeromski, and through him with Wyspiański, and these gave him hope for changes to occur. Bolesław Raczyński wrote the following in the Literary Supplement to the *Ilustrowany Kuryer Codzienny (Daily Illustrated Courier)* (No. 216, August 6, 1934):

> *Before the premiere of* Bolesław the Bold, *I visited Wyspiański at dusk to discuss the background music for the play. Wyspiański's wife informed me that "someone is with Stan and has been here for two hours discussing something important." I waited in the dining room, next to the studio, and when it got to be late, I rose to say my goodbyes to the wife and children. Then the door to the studio opened and Wyspiański called me in.*
>
> *I entered the dark room, lit as always by a candle (Wyspiański could not abide the light from kerosene lamps and the house was not wired for electricity). He was saying his farewells to someone, and that person exited via a door that led directly from the studio into the foyer. After shaking my hand, he sat down, as always, at his table, silent but in a strangely euphoric mood. From his expression, I saw that "something was up." After a while, he turned to me and said, "A moment ago I enlisted in the Polish army, which is being formed." I was startled and thought, "He's gone mad." But the writer of* The Wedding *explained, "I will be on the financial staff" ...*
>
> *For a long time, there have been rumors in Kraków, which probably also reached Wyspiański, about Piłsudski the conspirator, who was going about Kraków and putting ideas into the heads of the*

young men. The local society, just as pictured in The Wedding, *was composed of soulless dolls who could see moths and fleas but did not want to know that we had to take up arms... the soulless political establishment only wanted to bow low to the authorities in Vienna.*

The lack of spirit in Polish society bothered Wyspiański, who in his Warszawianka *[Varsovie], condemned the vacuity of the protagonists of the November Insurrection, who on the field of battle wrote poetry about heroism in their official portmanteaus. In* The Wedding, *he threw into the face of society, "For your moods, I tell you to your face, I pity you." Wyspiański's great spirit, on meeting Piłsudski who was just a nameless conspirator, felt in his artistic soul Piłsudski's greatness which would build Poland "not through moods, or moths and fleas," but "a real Poland" of blood and bone, made through the spilling of blood and breaking of bones on the battlefield. Wyspiański decided to enlist in Piłsudski's ranks.*

In the *Elegies*, Żeromski recalls March 1905: *In a small room, on the upper floor of the Jordanowka villa in Zakopane, Józef Piłsudski asked me if I could go to see Wyspiański and convince him of the necessity to sign an appeal that would call on the nation to make monetary contributions to buy arms for a Polish army being formed. If Piłsudski sent Żeromski to see Wyspiański about signing an appeal, then Wyspiański already had accepted the duty and joined the military organization, a secret conspiratorial organization ...*

The dominant political camp in Galicia was still the conservatives, the so called "Stańczyks,"[17] but more and more often this was a patriotic and enlightened conservatism. Living in Kraków on Podzamcza street with his wife and stepdaughter, Piłsudski often snuck into Warsaw and Łódź, keeping up contact with the organizations there. Because of his direct involvement he saw, before other PPS activists, the signs of a crisis forming within the conspiratorial organization. He summarized his observations and proposals in a lengthy memorandum to the Foreign Committee of the PPS dated September 14, 1903.

The situation has changed, but the PPS has not changed its methods and forms of working ... The awaking of life among society, the variety of potential which has grown, is something for which the PPS was not prepared. We have continued to repeat the old patterns staying on the beaten path and continued to utter the old idioms: independence, conspiracy, publishing - independence, conspiracy and so on in a loop... Naturally, sticking with a tested organization, relying on the flexibility and professionalism of various people, we can continue to tread the same paths, but this cannot be satisfactory for the long term ... Only we, I say we and the PPS and persons forming a living link between the past and present, who personify experience, influence, history – can we transform and adapt the socialist movement to new conditions. If we do not take this up and are not able to do it, I see a breaking-up of the socialist movement into many groups and the loss – in view of the disorder – of serious influence.

In the cited memorandum, Piłsudski indicated the necessity for acting in the following directions:

1. Unify the Socialist movement from all the three zones of partition and abroad.
2. Involvement in the widely understood cultural mission.
3. To increase, wherever possible, the visibility of party life.
4. Develop tactics for a mass movement.
5. Begin the preparation for an armed struggle for Polish independence, mainly against Russia, which is the most dangerous occupier.

In one of his letters, also from 1903, Piłsudski stated:

I have purged myself of the last of Russian influences and by recognizing more closely ... the representatives of the Russian administration, as well as Russian literature and publicity, I have stopped to overestimate the significance of the strength of a revolution in Russia. In this way, I have cleared the road to Western European influence ... I have seen the machinery of the Tsarist system and its effect on human life ... and I have grown to hate this Asiatic monster, covered with even more of a European veneer.

We cannot be victorious through publishing alone – Piłsudski repeated on all possible occasions, but this was a cry in the wilderness. The fashion among the contemporary socialists was to outshout each other with anti-war slogans. *Away with arms. Away with war. The working masses will be victorious without bloodshed, through their numbers, and will gain advantage everywhere taking power into their own hands.* No one wanted to hear or seriously discuss Piłsudski's proposals for forming a military organization and gathering arms.

Meanwhile, the Russo-Japanese War was approaching, and this changed the situation in a very basic way, because it could affect the whole of Europe. The war did indeed break out. The Poles drafted into the Russian army would have to fight and die in the Far East. For whom? And for what? *We should not permit conscription or at least interfere with it. It is nonsense and shame to go and spill blood somewhere far away for the Russian cause. For us to be led like cattle to Manchuria, when blood spilled here in fighting the occupier, in defense of our national honor, can give us incalculable benefits.*

Piłsudski's arguments only reached a few individuals. In Polish educated society, there was a spiritual lethargy, a fear of action. Phrases about the hopelessness of the Polish cause, facing reality, exercising good judgment, and preserving the core of the nation were constantly repeated. Piłsudski wrote a draft of an article stating the position of the PPS in reference to the Russo-Japanese War as he traveled back from Siedlce to Riga, where the Robotnik was being published. But this was toned down and even deformed.

Piłsudski was then director of military activities within the CKR (Central Workers' Committee) and had major hopes that the Russo-Japanese War would affect the Polish situation, and for some time even thought that it could escalate into a world war that would involve European countries. It was proposed to create a unified group of representatives that would include socialists from each of the three zones of partition and eventually transform it into an insurrectionist government. Among Piłsudski's ideas was one to establish co-operation with the Japanese government. The purpose of this cooperation would be to advance the Polish cause internationally and gain material support for the independence movement in Poland.

In Paris and London, PPS representatives made contact with the respective Japanese ambassadors, proposing "establishing a relationship with Poles as the natural enemies of Russia, who wish to take advantage of the present situation." In March and April of 1904, Tytus Filipowicz repeatedly met with Colonel Utsunomiya, the military attaché of the Japanese embassy in London, but decisions of a political nature could only be made in Tokyo.

In April 1904, in Kraków, the CKR passed a resolution on the matter of sending a mission to Tokyo. At the end of May, after overcoming various hurdles and difficulties, Piłsudski was in London. In his conversation with the Mikado's ambassador, he realized that the Japanese had an exceptional understanding of not only the Polish-Russian situation, but also of the conditions within Polish society.

At beginning of June, Józef Piłsudski and Tytus Filipowicz sailed for New York on the liner *Compania*. After a short stay in the United States (Chicago), they continued from San Francisco to Japan. Aboard the *Coptic*, Piłsudski composed his famous memorandum to the Japanese government. It is worthwhile to cite several of its passages.

Russia is a unified country only in a superficial sense, in truth it is not united at all. Most of that empire was constructed by conquest and by forcibly annexing nations and countries which theretofore conducted themselves differently from the Russian model. Differences in historical traditions and the memory of past and present violence further affects the disunity of the Tsarist Empire... The strength of Poland and its significance among the mosaic of countries making up the Russian Empire makes us bold to pick a political goal – to fragment the empire into its constituent parts and free those countries that were incorporated into that empire by force. We consider this not only as the fulfillment of cultural intentions for our homeland to be independent, but a guarantee for its further existence, for when Russia is shed of its conquests, it will be sufficiently weakened, becoming no longer a threatening and dangerous neighbor.

In the draft memorandum of an agreement between the PPS and the Japanese government, it was expected that Japan would provide monetary support to the opposition movement, arms to form a Polish Legion, and would advance on the international arena the question of recovering Poland's independence. The PPS was to supply volunteers to Japan along with propaganda and diversionary activities to impede Russian transport and mobilization. A separate protocol addressed the matter of organizing an intelligence service that would work on behalf the Japanese.

On 10 July 1904, the *Coptic* arrived in Yokohama, and the Poles were taken to Tokyo on the next day. Piłsudski's memorandum was translated into English and deposited with the Japanese Foreign Ministry on July 13th. That day, the main negotiations took place. A very polite Japanese general spoke excellent Russian. The discussion was nearly over when he stated that a totally opposing viewpoint was expressed by another Pole, who is now in Tokyo. *What is his name?* asked Piłsudski, *Roman Dmowski*, answered the general with a Russian accent. Quite by accident, they met him on a Tokyo street a few hours later. Several hours of discussion did not bring a reconciliation of views among the Polish leaders. Dmowski kept repeating his arguments about clear reasoning, geopolitical impossibilities, the German threat, the greatness of Polish culture, which in symbiosis with that of Russia, would serve to accomplish a great mission, and so on. Piłsudski defending himself against accusations of "martyrological romanticism" and not being realistic, demonstrated that "realism" cannot be based only on recognizing the power of others but, first of all, must be grounded in recognizing one's own needs and strength.

The conduct of the mission to Tokyo and its effects, were summarized by Piłsudski in his Corrections to History.

*Sometime in May of 1904, I was invited by the Japanese gov-
ernment to come to Tokyo for a conversation, which was not further
described in the invitation. I could have had others go but decided to
go myself. I did this because I thought that the most likely subject of
this conversation would be information of a military nature and on
such an important matter I did not wish to authorize anyone else. The
Japanese government would fund our trip there.*

*During the trip, while I crossed two oceans and the American
continent, I had sufficient time to think about how to comport myself
in Japan. I decided immediately that I could consent to providing intelligence only if Japan would agree to give us material aid with arms
and ammunition. I did not think that such an event, as a war conducted by Russia, could pass without affecting the Russian Empire and not
allow us Poles, with the help of a friendly power, to improve our own
situation. In accordance to the letter of recommendation given to me
by the Japanese representative in England, I had to present myself at
the Foreign Ministry in Tokyo and then conduct official talks with the
deputy leader of the Japanese General Staff. My conversation, where
I immediately put forth a request for Japanese material assistance,
did not yield any practical results, the only positive effect being that
Polish soldiers taken prisoner by the Japanese would be assigned to
separate groups – and there must have been many Poles who willingly gave themselves up.*

The effect that Roman Dmowski had on cooling Japanese willingness to help the Polish cause cannot be underestimated. The course of
that war was favorable to Japan without engaging any Polish assistance
in fighting the Russian Empire. During the time the Poles were in Tokyo,
swarms of newsboys were singing out the news of Japanese victories.
That part of Polish blood spilled for the preservation of the entirety and
sovereignty of the Russian Empire, had no significance to the Japanese.
Dmowski thought that something could be "bargained" from the Russians by such a sacrifice of blood, that it would save the country from
revolution and victimization. But more and more Piłsudski's program for
the necessity of an armed struggle against Russia was beginning to mature. Without forcing concessions, not only independence, but even an
expanded autonomy, could not even be imagined or dreamed.

At that time, Stefan Żeromski wrote his *Dream of a Sword – Above
you, Polish soldier, when you swing on the scaffold – when you are thrown
into the bloody ditch, with your heart pierced by bullets – when you are
dying of exhaustion on the Siberian steppe - there is no banner of a faraway
power. Beyond you, there is nothing. There is only the grave dug to swal-*

low your cadaver. Before you stand armies ... Into your bony hands, only
powerless in death, have thrust their dream of a knightly sword, so many
generations of youth.

This encapsulated many of Piłsudski's thoughts, which propagated the necessity of a national resistance against the naïve pacifism and
the belief in the ethos of Polish warrior spirit – the positive role of Polish
military force.

When I first visited the United States, in 1990, as a grantee of the
Piłsudski Institute in New York, I had the occasion to speak with the then
only honorary president of that institution, the still creative Gen. Wacław
Jędrzejewicz.[18] He made it possible for me to retrace the entire journey
that Piłsudski took in the United States – from New York to Chicago and
then to San Francisco. Wacław Jędrzejewicz thought that the Russo-Japanese War had a critical impact on Piłsudski's further activities, and its
effect was only seemingly insignificant. Wacław Jędrzejewicz spoke com-
petently on Japan, about its present importance, and enthusiastically, for
as a young colonel in 1925-1928, he was the Polish Military Attaché in
Tokyo. Thanks to these conversations, I learned many details about the
life and activities of Bronisław, brother to Józef Piłsudski.

Before his departure for Japan, in May of 1904, Piłsudski organized a command for street demonstrations, entrusting it to Bolesław
Berger,[19] known by the code-name "Kuroki." During October 17-20, a
consecutive conference of the CKR took place with the participation of
Piłsudski. He considered the current situation as extremely serious, one
demanding stronger tactics.

> *In this moment, when a turnover is possible, we are silent and by*
> *ourselves harm the Polish cause. Now, we cannot stay silent. Politics*
> *are not mathematics. One cannot calculate and account for every-*
> *thing ... We must adopt new tactics, even if it would lead to an insur-*
> *rection drowned in blood. It would be less costly than dying in place.*
> *Naturally, an organization must be prepared to do this.*

The task of the fighting groups was to protect the demonstrators
from the currently unobstructed attacks by the police. The first so protected demonstration was organized in Warsaw (Leszno district) on October 23, but full success and a breakthrough was achieved on 13 November 1904 (on a Sunday) during a demonstration on Grzybowski Square.
The demonstrators were opposed by the Russian army, which used its
weapons. Seven people were killed and twenty-seven were wounded, but
the demonstrators did not run and were not scattered. Shots were fired
at the soldiers and they were forced to retreat.

(Left) Maria Juszkiewicz (nee Koplewska) the first wife of Józef Piłsudski
(Right) Józef Piłsudski in 1899

(Top) The activist group of the PPS in London, 1896. From the left seated: Ignacy Mościcki, Bolesław Antoni Jędrzejowski, Józef Piłsudski and Aleksander Dębski. Standing: Bolsesław Miklaszewski and Witold Jodko-Narkiewicz.
(Bottom) A police photograph taken after his arrest in Łodz, in 1900.

The Russo-Japanese War 1904-1905. "Fighting at the barbed wire at Port Arthur" – drawing published in, "Weekly Illustrated" (nr 38 in 1904)

(Left) Gen. Wacław Jędrzejewicz (1893 – 1993) and Antoni Lenkiewicz at the Józef Piłsudski Institute in New York in 1990. Gen. Jędrzejewicz talked about the mission of Piłsudski in Japan, about Bronisław Piłsudski, and about his own mission in Tokoyo during the years 1925 – 1928, when he was a military attaché in the second Polish Republic. (Right) Stanisław Wyspiański (1869 – 1907) who was active in the independence movement with Piłsudski.

The demonstration on Grzybowski Square had a great significance and caused Polish hopes to rise. Similar demonstrations took place in Łódź, Ostrowiec, Zawiercie, Starochowice, Ćmielów, and Częstochowa. There was no lack of condemnation from the loyalists. A peaceful co-existence with Russia was promoted by the National Democrats and had approval among that part of society which was afraid to make sacrifices. Piłsudski's ideas were described as adventurism or provocation by newspapers which condemned the demonstrations. "Japan and England pay for this," they wrote.

In the first months of 1905, Piłsudski was ill and spent time in Zakopane. Meanwhile, on 22 January, the so-called "Bloody Sunday" took place in St. Petersburg. Fr. Georgij Gapon, in employ of the Tsarist Ohrana, led a crowd toward the Blue Palace. The guards used firearms indiscriminately. About a thousand people were killed and twice as many were wounded. In answer to this bestiality, enslaved Russia reacted. Strikes broke out in many cities. The Polish socialists decided that the events in Russia are the beginning of a revolution and scheduled a general strike for January 27, 1905. In a few days, the strike was on in all the Polish cities in the Russian zone of partition. In Warsaw, and other cities, the army used firearms. There were many dead and wounded.

In writing to Stanisław Wojciechowski on January 30, Piłsudski had some critical remarks to make about this "revolution." *People here are universally celebrating and euphoric – it's a shame to say this, and I am angered. This is so childish and stupid. This assumption that Russia is in revolution – when it has already been crushed – this revolution led by Gapon – is no kind of revolution. It is simply laughable ... I blame myself that on hearing the first news about the St. Petersburg I did not go there myself ... But maybe it is better to get a clarification on the situation here, than there, where all news has been suppressed by censorship ... Either one has proper demonstrations or in the eventuality a general strike ... and then stop it on command. The impression made would be great ... Now, when I think what great things could be accomplished without involving major resources using this general unrest, the devil takes me. It happened - one must keep a calm expression in light of a bad game and think about saving the situation... Well, old man. We were there together and did not lose our heads. It's a shame that there remain so few of the old hands, like us. My wife went to get guns, so I'm alone.*

A general strike could not defeat an enemy government which was indifferent to the economic situation in the country. Instead, prisons were full of workers who struck. Hopes the socialists had that, through propaganda leaflets, the Russian soldiers would mutiny and stand with the strikers, proved to be in vain. Piłsudski knew the Russian mentality and knew the situation better than others. The Poles could count only on themselves and the vagaries of the international situation, which had to be used with great skill.

In February 1905, on the initiative of Józef Kwiatek[20] - one of the young leaders in the PPS who was slowly going communist and ended as a Bolshevik – a central conference was called together in Warsaw. Because of the "revolutionary" situation, this conference called itself the VII Convention of the PPS. The leadership of this convention was taken over by the so-called "younger" members on the political left, who gave precedence to economic factors, forgetting the importance of, then current, matter of Polish independence. In elections to the CKR, all the "older" members were voted out, except for Piłsudski, who did not take part in the convention, but still enjoyed great respect among the members. He too, saved the party from breakup, at least temporarily, explaining to the "older" faction that things were not as bad as they thought.

In a letter to Wojciechowski from 29 March, he wrote: *I do not consider this matter to be either so frightening or so harmful – it is mainly very unpleasant for personal reasons, and that is all ... As to the convention itself, it was already much advocated that a convention be called together ... I put it by mainly because of the unclear situation. Perhaps I am in fault for this, that I avoided and postponed this convention ... The committee for the convention was organized behind our backs and in this way the popular thought about the convention moved forward. I am convinced that if I had attended the convention, much of what happened would not have taken place ... I can only suppose but much of that which happened can be fixed, while other things are very good ... And I have no objection to having much of the work land on the backs of the younger men. But we, however, should go strongly in the direction of conspiratorial resistance, that's one, and to publish via the press, that's two.*

Piłsudski was still involved in the socialist movement and in this he was sincere, but his stance toward socialism was diverging from doctrine and was closer to Polish tradition, together with an appreciation for the significance of religion in culture. Adam Borkiewicz,[21] in his text entitled *Sources for a Biography of Józef Piłsudski [Źródła do biografii Józefa Piłsudskiego]*, correctly highlighted the situation from 1905 by calling attention to one of Piłsudski's statements that he made to his friends, "In addition to Marx's *Das Kapital*, I know another book, not less important, that is the *Trilogy* [by Henryk Sienkiewicz]."

Chapter 5
The Fighting Organization and the Revolutionary Faction

The definitive split in the PPS came a lot quicker than Piłsudski assumed. At the conference of the Party Council at the CKR (Central Workers Committee) which took place during 15-18 June 1905 in Józefów near Warsaw, the second scheduled presentation on the subject of tactics, Piłsudski stated: *I am personally accused of insurrectionist tendencies ... From the beginning of the [Russo-Japanese] war, the word "insurrection" was on many lips... Yet, today I am at a place where the so-called "insurrection" is not yet timely ... I am not in support of an insurrection; I am not the romanticist scarecrow which some make me out to be. Words not supported by action cannot be propagated. Revolutionary tactics should be based on inspiring all which would cause people to act.*

In his speech, Piłsudski, for the first time in public, used the words "young" and "old" to indicate the division in the party. As a result of the clear differences on their views and positions he resigned from the CKR. The party did not formally split, because Piłsudski was satisfied by the passing of the resolution regarding the Fighting Organization. At a subsequent meeting of the Party Council, which took place 15 October 1905, he was given the directorship of the Fighting Division, with a resolution giving autonomy to the Fighting Organization from the party leadership.

In 1906, internal relations within the PPS became even more complicated because of differences between the "young" and "old" members. In February, the 8th Convention of the PPS took place in Lwów. The question of party unity again hung on a thread. Piłsudski's personal success rested on the fact that he managed to defend the independence of the Fighting Organization (OB). The main task of the OB, defined during the convention, was to prepare leaders for a future military conflict. After tumultuous discussions, it was decided to keep the matter of independence on the agenda, with a qualifier that "Poland's relationship with Russia will be defined by the Warsaw constituent assembly in communication with the constituent assembly in St. Petersburg."

In May 1906, during an inspection of a weapons storehouse in Warsaw, Piłsudski met Aleksandra Szczerbińska, who had responsibility for the transport and storage of arms in the Fighting Organization. Aleksandra's impression from meeting Ziuk for the first time was recorded in her memoir and is worth mentioning.

I remember this picture quite well, when on that spring after-noon we stood among the rifles, baskets of Browning pistols, Maus-ers, and ammunition. I thought that here I saw a man whom Siberia could not break ... Before me stood a man of medium height, with wide shoulders, thin in the waist. He had a lot of grace and elegance in his motions ... His head was small, his ears were shapely, slightly pointed, his eyes were set back, thoughtful, penetrating, blue-gray. His animated face reflected almost every thought. But most interest-ing was the contrast between his right and left hand. The left hand was narrow and sensitive, shapely and delicate, ending in fingers that were nearly feminine. It was the hand of an artist. The right one was much larger, as if belonging to another man. Strong, even brutal, it had even squarely ending fingers; so strong that, it seemed, they could bend horseshoes. It was the hand of a soldier and man of action.

The conspiratorial work of thirty-nine year old "Wiktor" and twenty-four year old "Ola" [Aleksandra] turned into love in July 1907.

In the Kraków Trybuna (August 15, 1906), Piłsudski published an important article entitled "The politics of active struggle." He wrote: *One cannot break this power but by the sword. An armed revolution, but not as in Moscow, but sufficient to crush the government forces – that is a historic necessity which stands before us.*

With penetrating words and a great feeling for reality, Piłsudski presented the difficulties which are present in a program of this kind: *Today, to speak about a one-time, sudden armed insurrection ... is to admit to one's full ignorance of the positive conditions of the struggle, or rather use the insurrectionist slogans as meaningless phrases, which will only re-main as phrases ... but looking at history: there was no political current, no slogan, that at the beginning did not find condemnation, and always the strongest condemnation was given to the directions which later were vic-torious ... It is the same with the armed insurrection. Today it is considered utopian, later people will become used to the thought of it ... and the sooner we realize that we cannot get out of the present situation in any other way, only through armed struggle – then the better.*

During the days 19-22 November 1906, the 9th Convention of the PPS took place in Vienna. This convention saw the final fracturing of the party. The "young" section started the PPS-Left, removing the program for recovering Polish independence from its mission. The "old" section, headed by Piłsudski, continued the activities of the PPS-Revolutionary Faction. In March 1907, representatives of the faction were called to Vi-enna for what was recognized as the 10th PPS Convention. Under Piłsud-ski's influence, a four-point program was accepted.

1. The one system that is suitable for Poles is an Independent Democratic Polish Commonwealth.
2. This goal can be achieved only through armed struggle.
3. The ultimate expression of this struggle must be an armed insurrection against the Tsarist government.
4. The armed insurrection cannot occur without military training.

In a brochure entitled: *Practical tasks for revolution in the Russian zone of partition*, Piłsudski wrote: *Neither the independence of Poland, nor the conditions under which the Poles could fight in a western-European fashion, will not be given to us, and no one will fight for us. For our political and social goals, we must fight by ourselves. And this will not be a word-fight; not through the printed sheet, but with weapons in hand. We must oppose an organized force of the occupier, founded on the bayonets of his soldiers, with the armed force of the Polish people. The revolution for which we are preparing is the armed battle of the people against the army of the Tsar, which defends his rule. For the revolution to succeed, it must have multi-sided preparation, taking lessons from the sad experiences of the past – the Year 1863 ... we must instill the people with boldness and faith in the effectiveness of the struggle and draw the masses into it. We must form a resilient organization that would encompass the entire movement of the armed struggle. ... There are two kinds of peoples' wars: armed demonstrations and armed revolutions. The difference between the demonstration and the revolution is that in the first the goal is to create a certain impression, to call attention to the pitiful situation of the country and its people, not to win a victory. ... The strongest part of the revolution is the people and their willingness to fight.*

The Fighting Organization, which included around six thousand determined individuals, conducted a series of operations among which the most famous was the freeing of ten fighters from Pawiak Prison who were condemned to die. A great impression was made by the operation of 15 August 1906 – later known as "Bloody Saturday." In several cities, offices of the Tsarist Ochrana were demolished. In addition, several dozen especially "dedicated" policemen and provocateurs were executed. By taking up an active struggle with the Tsarist authorities, Piłsudski wanted to break the complex of Polish inferiority and wanted to, *instill the people with boldness and faith in the effectiveness of the struggle and draw the masses into it.*

There were losses in this uneven struggle. Stefan Okrzeja, Józef Montwiłł-Mirecki, and Henryk Baron were hung on the scaffolds of the Warsaw Citadel. The Tsarist authorities, and even part of Polish society, treated them as bandits. Many years passed before these fighters for independence received their just due. The Fighting Organization was a school for sacrificial patriotism and the first military organization since the time of the January Insurrection. It gave rise to future leaders of the riflemen's associations, the Legions, and the conspiratorial Polish Military Organization (POW), which in the final years of World War I was the main organization fighting for Polish independence.

In his excellent book, *Philosophy of Deeds (Filozofia Czynu)*, Bohdan Urbankowski noted correctly that Piłsudski was recorded in our national consciousness mainly and almost exclusively not as "Commandant" and "Father" but rather as "Grandfather" and "Grand Old Man." It is characteristic that among photographs of Piłsudski from the earlier time of his life, it is easier to find those which are connected to his Siberian exile or earlier conspiratorial involvement, than those which show him as a thin, elegant man about forty years old.

He then lived in Kraków together with his wife Maria at 18 Topolowa Street. Officially, he represented himself as a member of the literati, dressed nonchalantly in that fashion, and like other men of letters had a beard but was exceptional in his peaceful, moderate manner of living. Among his various activities, Piłsudski, at that time, devoted himself to the study of military matters. The January Insurrection, Napoleon's campaigns, the works of Karl Von Clausewitz, the Boer War (1899-1902), the Russo-Japanese War, and others became part of his impressive store of knowledge.

The study of military matters was continuously interrupted by ongoing activities and travel to Zagłębie, Warsaw, Vilnius, Kiev, Lwów, or Łódź. In the *Robotnik* (no. 226 from 4 February 1906), Piłsudski published an article entitled "How to prepare for armed conflict." He wrote: "All our victories we attribute to our moral strength, all our losses and disasters are due to the lack of physical strength."

In mid-1908, Piłsudski's stepdaughter, Wanda Juszkiewicz,[22] suddenly died. A young freedom fighter, then only twenty-seven years old, Walery Sławek was in love with her. The entire community, together with Piłsudski who was very attached to his stepdaughter, sincerely mourned her unexpected passing at an early age.

Activities of conspiratorial and military nature in the PPS suffered because of a chronic lack of funds. Unfortunate incidents happened because of the lack of a few rubles to pay for a carriage or a safe place.

It was discovered that twice per week, every Tuesday and Saturday, a special car on the Warsaw-St. Petersburg train carried cash from the tax offices to a bank in Moscow. The Fighting Organization had already accomplished several successful raids, but these yielded meager results – about forty thousand rubles total. Aware of this situation, Pił-sudski started to prepare to take serious action, one that – as he wrote to Jodko[23] – would solve their financial problems for a longer time. Piłsudski proposed to lead the operation himself, to silence those who were apt to claim that he risked the lives of others while staying safe himself. The preparations took a long time, but the resulting effect was impressive.

In connection with this operation, which took place at the Bezda-ny train station (twenty-five kilometers from Vilnius), Piłsudski wrote the following letter during the first days of September 1908, which describes the motivation for his actions.

To Felix,[24] or whomever writes my obituary. Dear Friend. At one time you promised that you would write a beautiful obituary when the devil chooses to take me. Now when I go on a raid from which I may not return, I sent to you this note as my obituary writer, with a small request. I do not intend to dictate to you how you should sum up my life and work. No. In this you are entirely free to do as you will, but please do not make of me the "good officer" or a "weeping sentimentalist" that is, a dedicated man, stretched on the cross for the good of humanity, or something of that sort.

At some point I was like that, but it was during my cloudy and turbulent youth. Now, it is all behind me forever, and that weeping, and crucifixion has gotten under my skin, and when I saw it among our intelligentsia, it was weak and hopeless. I fight and die only because this cesspool, which is our life, I cannot endure, and it offends me. Do you understand – it offends me as a man, a man who has dignity, unlike a slave. Let others play at tending the flowers of socialism or Polishness, or whatever else in this cesspool (not even a toilet) atmosphere. I cannot do this. This is not sentimentalism or weeping, it is not the machine for social evolution, or anything else; it is just being a man.

I want to succeed. Without fighting and going into harm's way, I'm not even a wrestler, but only a beast driven with a stick or whip. I hope you understand me. I am driven by neither despair nor dedication, but the desire for victory and the need to obtain resources for a future victory. My last idea, which I have not yet developed, is the necessity, under our conditions, to develop the facility to utilize physical power. I will use a description that is uncomfortable to the ears of "humanitarians" (funny how hysterical ladies can't stand the sound of nails scratching across glass but will take a slap across the face) – the function of brutal violence. I wanted to introduce this idea into my work in the last few years. I swore to myself that I would do it or perish. I had already done something in this direction, but too little to be able to rest on my laurels and start serious and direct prepara- tions for the fight. ...

Now I put it all on one card. And a few more words about this. I know that my one uncertainty is that I may die, and this fact I need to explain. I had sent so many people out into danger, so many went to the scaffold, so that if I die, it will be natural for those silent heroes to have the moral satisfaction to know that their chief did not shirk this work and did not use them as mere tools to do dirty work, leaving his own hands clean. That is one. The second – that it is of necessity. Hard coin. May the devil take it, how I despise it, but I prefer to take it as the prize in a fight than to collect it from the childish and cowardly Polish society – and since I don't have it and must get it for specific purposes.

I, who was called a fine individual and noble socialist, about whom even enemies never said anything evil out-loud, am but a man who did a few things for the good of the nation, now must stress the very bitter truth that in a society which cannot fight for itself, which shrinks before every blow aimed at its face, people must die even do- ing things that are not noble, beautiful, or great. Well that's it. Now a kiss, my boy, to you and all of you, old friends with whom we dreamed so much, lived even more, and loved well. Yours and theirs, Ziuk.

This letter, written to Perl or another editor whose job would have been to write the obituary, has a great depth and is among the most significant texts that was penned by the future leader of independent Po- land's rebirth. The critical assessment of Poland's moral condition was linked to a moral responsibility to take action, and a statement of bitter truth, *that in a society, which cannot fight for itself ... people must die.*

The first attempt to take the train was set for Saturday, 19 Sep- tember 1908. Because of some unforeseen difficulties, Piłsudski called off the operation. A week later (26 September), all was going according to plan. Among the seventeen fighters who went into action against the postal mail car, were four future prime ministers of the independent Pol- ish Commonwealth, namely: Tomasz Arciszewski, Aleksander Prystor, Walery Sławek,[25] and Józef Piłsudski. It was a game of poker and lives were at stake. Piłsudski called out that he would count to ten and then a bomb would be used to blow the door open. When he reached seven, he heard a voice: *We give up, we won't shoot.*

The operation could not last longer than forty-five minutes be- cause then the next train to Vilnius would come through. The loading of cash, bearer bonds, silver, and gold took a long time. Piłsudski kept an eye on the clock himself and finally gave the signal to go. They moved out in three groups, using different routes to reach designated points. The first group moved ostentatiously along the tracks. In order to call attention to this escape route, several shots were fired. The second group, with Sławek, Prystor, and Arciszewski, scattered with the intention of putting the greatest distance between themselves and the place where the action took place. The third group, that included Piłsudski, Momentowicz, and Świrski, had the most difficult task. They covered the longest distance in a carriage filed with money, weapons, and explosives. In Jedliny, about seventy kilometers from Bezdany, Aleksandra Szczerbińska was waiting for them.

The operation yielded over two hundred thousand rubles for the party. None of the fighters were killed or injured. By chance, Fiałkowski was arrested. The money was designated for assistance to the imprisoned and their families, for publishing and educational activities, but mainly to start work of military nature.

Piłsudski's participation in this "robbery raid" did have an influence on his health and mental outlook. Michał Soklonicki, who saw him immediately after Bezdany, wrote the following:

His health was damaged, he looked bad, and I was struck by the gloominess on his face. I also detected new appearances of hardness in the manner he approached me - As for the fighting organization, I decided to close it down.

The problems and worries faced by Piłsudski were many and very complicated, both in the personal and in the political sense. During this time, representatives of the Masonic Order contacted him (among them Rafał Radziwiłłowicz, Stefan Żeromski, and Andrzej Strug) counting on being able to gain the membership of an influential man. He refused, and his reasons, which are known from a much later conversation with Monsignor Tokarzewski, are very significant to his characteristic mental stance. *Could a priest who knows me well ever imagine that I would join a secret organization in which I was subject to orders without even knowing the persons who were giving them?*

The priest could not imagine such a situation or bring up any sensible reason that would support Piłsudski's becoming a Mason, but this has no effect on rumors that are still repeated until the present day.

Piłsudski's state of health continued to be poor. Despite this, he continued to work and took part in many meetings. He only asked that people not to visit him before ten in the morning. It was the rule then that ill and tired conspirators would go to Zakopane to recuperate. Stefan Żeromski said the following about his meeting Piłsudski in Zakopane.

It was proletarian misery. ... I found him sitting at a table playing solitaire. He was in his long underwear because the only pair of trousers he owned were at the tailor's being mended. ... The course of the solitaire game interested him more than a discussion. "I made a promise that if this solitaire game completes successfully, then we will have a Poland," he said. Such a dream about Poland in that ramshackle house and in underwear, shook me then.

When Piłsudski's state of health worsened, he wrote to Ola Szczerbińska: *My dear. I am rather severely ill. The preceding weeks have sapped my heart so that I had a light fever, then influenza (the grippe) struck me and did such damage that I can move neither hand nor foot or start any work or endure any emotion. I am for the time a damned invalid, in body and spirit. All my wonderful projects are shattered, and even writing this letter moves me so that I feel my heart palpitating.*

Among the many difficulties with which Piłsudski had to deal was the "tragic triangle" that he described in one of his letters. Maria knew about the presence and significance of Aleksandra Szczerbińska, but she would not consent to a divorce.

Piłsudski wrote to Ola: *My intention from the beginning was that any outcome be decided together, as the result of three interested parties. The decision in this matter, on your part and mine, is clear and plain, but the action of the third party is to oppose and hold on at any cost as not to reach the clear and plain conclusion. ... I am convinced that my steady and constant, but not violent, determination will do its work and feel that things are proceeding well. Many things have changed for the better toward reaching a mutual understanding. The crisis point, in my opinion, has passed, and now things are moving toward resolution.*

During the months and years after this letter was written, Piłsudski continued to live in Kraków with Maria, and their apartment was still the center of independence-oriented activities. Maria ran an open house and was liked and appreciated by the community. Only old Bolesław Limanowski wrote, not without reasons, that, *[Maria] Piłsudska is unendurable in her spiteful painting everything the blackest possible colors.* Piłsudski explained to Ola how it was impossible to settle these personal problems.

I cannot change my basic method of attempting to get an understanding in order to reach a mutual settlement of the legal formalities in the current relationships. Another way of acting would lead to difficulties that would throw a shadow on both our lives, is not acceptable.

Only with the start of the World War, did the crisis in the marriage with Maria led to a separation. After his return from Magdeburg, Piłsudski never went back to living with Maria, but complications connected with the marriage lasted until Maria's death on August 17, 1921.

The PPS-Revolutionary Faction was now only a formal political basis for Piłsudski's activities. In mid-1908, the Union of Active Struggle (ZWC) took on a major influence in his life. A major task in party relations was to break the resistance against the ZWC. Some of the activists in the Faction were of the opinion that building up a paramilitary organization meant that the party's program was being pushed aside. In fact, this fear was not without basis, and in some part was shared by Piłsudski, because he did not want to see the role of the party diminished. Of great importance to strengthening the position of Piłsudski within the party and gaining support for his concepts for its program was the 11th Convention of the PPS which took place 15-28 January 1909 in Vienna. The convention rejected the title "Revolutionary Faction" and returned to its previous name of Polish Socialist Party. During these discussions, Piłsudski took the podium often, and among others, advanced the thesis that, *an alliance even with a bourgeois party is possible if the necessity arises and will not have a detrimental effect on socialism.*

Accepting such a proposal would have obvious and serious theoretical and practical consequences in the future activities of the PPS, because it led to a unified, not class based, program of fighting for Polish independence. The convention accepted the necessity for further developing the paramilitary organization independently of the party. A resolution to establish a Party Council that would mediate between the CKR and the Convention as a group. The number of members in the CKR was dropped to three: Jodko, Filipowicz, and Piłsudski.

Doubtless, this was a great success for Piłsudski in his party activity. He needed to be in the leadership of the party, but it was never his goal - it was necessary so that he could orchestrate a bigger issue, the political game to win Polish independence. The sense and complications of this game were often misunderstood by his countrymen. It is undoubtedly a paradox that one of the most accurate assessments of Piłsudski's character is contained in a report written by the Austrian police in Lwów.

In Kraków, he started to propagate, by word and in print, the idea that to obtain Polish independence, one must move from talk and dreaming to the creation of a force and an organization that at the appropriate moment can take up a military struggle against Russia. Piłsudski, in making his plans for fighting Russia, wants to involve the entire nation, regardless of party affiliation or political convictions. He is moving beyond the tactics of the social democrats who have accepted his plans with incredulity and mistrust.

Chapter 6
The Union of Active Struggle (ZWC) and the Riflemen's Associations

In many conversations with his closest co-workers (Jodko and Sosnkow-ski[26]), Piłsudski came to realize by 1908 that there must be established a non-party military organization, *so that instead of the old, a new page would begin*. The effect of this line of thinking led to the founding of the Union of Active Struggle (ZWC). In the mission statement of the Union was written that its purpose is, *to conduct the preparation and education of leaders outside the borders of Russian territory and directors for a future armed insurrection in the Russian zone of partition.*

Sosnkowski was initially at the head of the ZWC, but soon was replaced by Piłsudski. Having recovered his health, he devoted his new supply of energy and devotion to this matter, creating a regular military school within the ZWC. In an article describing the program at the time, he wrote:

> It is not enough to educate a group of able professionals and create an officer cadre. In this society, we must awaken the love for and un-derstanding of military maters. ... All Poland must become a military camp in readiness. In this way, we can create a force and be victorious in the coming battle... Half-a-century of peace, the lack of our own army, a theory of organic work, the original anarchism of the wage earners that rejects the necessity of government for the nation, have created in us the most peacefully oriented society in the world... If we do not create an armed force and take part in the future war between Austria and Russia, we will cross ourselves out for a long time, and perhaps forever, from the ranks of living nations. The nations of Eu-rope will not respect us. Our neighbors will destroy us, take our land, and put us into eternal servitude.

On 5 October 1908, Emperor Franz Joseph I ordered that Bosnia and Herzegovina would be incorporated into the Austro-Hungarian Em-pire. Russia treated this as a threat to its influence in Serbia. Both empires started mobilization. It seemed that an armed conflict was unavoidable. The Germans declared they would aid Austria-Hungary, and this stopped Russia. The Russo-Austrian conflict was defused, but war was coming on inexorably. Piłsudski knew, as few did, that there would be a war in which Poland would regain its independence, and he did everything possible not to let this opportunity pass by. Other similar occasions had been lost through the lack of preparedness, by indecision and procrastination, or simply through common political stupidity.

Austria was trying every way to win the Poles over to its side in this dispute with Russia. Taking advantage of this situation, Piłsudski decided to try to obtain legal permission for organizing military units. As a result of these efforts, in 1910, several legal organizations were established: The Union of Riflemen in Lwów and the "Shooting Society" in Kraków. Piłsudski conducted lectures on the subject of the history of the January Insurrection, the PPS Fighting Organization, military geography of Poland, and practical training for the future war. He also took an active part in training in the field. Piłsudski's studies on the military found expression in his publications. In the December 1910 issue of Przedświt, there was a significant article entitled "Reform in the Russian Army."

A result of the many years Piłsudski spent studying the January Insurrection was a cycle of ten lectures entitled "An Outline of the Military History of the January Insurrection" given in the School of Socio-Political Studies in Kraków from 13 March to 17 May 1912. These lectures were the culmination of the many years Piłsudski devoted to the problems of the January Insurrection. These were not only a penetrating look at the previous work of many professional historians, who often uncritically accepted the testimony of traitors, but the most valuable lessons from past experiences had their source in the strength and the weakness of that national uprising. The source of its strength was the establishment of a National Government, which had great influence, as well as the establishment of a military school in Genoa. The weakness of the insurrection was a lack of good leadership, shortages in weapons, and many organizational flaws.

That insurrection flashed like scattered gunpowder, not as gunpowder tamped down in a gun barrel, said Piłsudski. His greatest respect was for the last dictator of the insurrection, Romuald Tragutt, who reorganized the army into four corps and created a clear hierarchical line of command. At the end of the lecture, he posed the question, *Could the insurrection have ended in victory?* The answer was a definite No! The help promised by Russian conspirators failed, and many "reds" were counting on it. Likewise, there was no aid from the west, on which the "whites" counted. Despite the conclusion that the insurrection was destined to fail, Piłsudski extracted the thing that was its strength – a legend and instruction for the living, who could not ever lose hope. Participants in the insurrection would have told me the things I tell myself – we did not die for nothing, and the lessons learned for you were earned through our deaths.

The Riflemen's Associations were established not only in Lwów and Kraków, but also in Przemyśl, Stanisłowice, Rzeszów, Tarów, Nowy Sacz, Stryj, Borysław, and Zakopane. These legal para-military organizations were subordinate to the ZWC. But some right-oriented, and even centrist, independence activists were distrustful of the Union of Active Struggle, fearing socialist radicalism. Seeing the general weakness in these military preparations, Piłsudski sought to find what linked and strengthened the individuals who hoped for independence. To accomplish this, he put much of his effort into overcoming mutual mistrust and prejudice.

At the end of April 1912, on Piłsudski's initiative, a conference was organized in Zakopane where activists from various parties, attitudes, and sides could take part. Giving the keynote speech on the state of Polish preparations for an armed conflict, Piłsudski had many bitter words for his countrymen. The main thrust is often cited: Poles want to have independence, but desire that this independence only cost them two groschen and two drops of blood. Yet independence is a commodity that is not only valuable, it is very expensive. In trying to move the minds and consciences, Piłsudski expressed regret that the nation had gone weak and given up, treating all the military efforts with a derisive-patronizing smile. Piłsudski regarded the effects and state of organization in a pessimistic way and stressed that this state will remain such, until we receive moral support from society.

The socialists connected with Piłsudski, Jodko and Daszyński,[27] spoke in a similar spirit, convincing the listeners that in the matter of the fight for independence, they stand firmly on the ground of national solidarity. An important outcome of the Zakopane conference was the creation of a Polish Military Fund (PSW). Bolesław Limanowski became honorary chairman of the PSW, and Walery Sławek became the administrative secretary. Beyond improving the always difficult financial situation the PSW contributed to the growth of the political base of the paramilitary organization. This applied to those groups which were under the direct control of the Union of Active Struggle, as well as those that were spontaneously created at this time. In his later memoirs, Piłsudski wrote: *During the year 1913, there was unprecedented growth in the paramilitary organizations. The count showed that we could no longer say there were only two: The Union of Riflemen and the Rifle Groups.*

Among the organizations which provided members for the future Polish army, a significant role was played by the Field Units of the "Falcon" movement, the Podhale Groups, the Bartoszow Units, and the Scouting Units. In the year 1913, during the 50th anniversary observance of the January Insurrection and the 100th Anniversary of the death of Józef

Poniatowski, Piłsudski did an inspection of these forces which amounted to over ten thousand members. They were composed of patriotically inspired youth, not only from the intelligentsia, but also from the working class and the rural areas.

The next initiative of the ZWC, after establishing the Polish Military Fund, was the creation of a Temporary Commission of Confederated Independence Parties. (KTSSN) On the bumpy road to uniting and coordinating the Polish desire for independence, this was another major step forward. At the first meeting of the commission, Piłsudski was named the commander-in-chief of all the units and shooting societies. Jodko was made secretary of the KTSSN.

An important document issued by the KTSSN was an appeal to Polish society:

The threat of war now hanging over Poland has moved and fired up all the instincts and emotions of the Polish nation. At the moment the war breaks out, the nation will be forced into a fearful position – Poles in the Russian army facing Poles in the Austrian army – to murder each other. This threat of war, all the uncounted sufferings and sacrifices that await us, will be our undoing and the destruction of our future if Poland bleeds for foreign interests. It must awaken and take up the cause to fight for its own rights, for its own future, and the independence of its people. Too long has servitude turned a great and numerous nation into three exploited and oppressed provinces, conquered by others, poor and weak. The destruction of Russian despotism on Polish land would create the possibility to a great workshop of work for the national welfare, the possibility of creating an autonomous economic organism, our future and our strength.

Who would not take up the fight at such moment, who would not desire to create his own freedom and a better future, those then would deservedly be subject to the enemy's abuse of the defenseless? Passivity and humility will not save Poles from the lawlessness, instead will be the justification for the enemy's harshest measures. To make active resistance possible, the fight to bring independence and freedom to the Polish nation, an organization that unites representatives of various Polish parties was formed. All the organizations represented in the Temporary Commission consider armed resistance - in the face of a war against the oppressive Tsarist regime – as the most likely, the only possible, course to be taken by an organization of the Polish people. The liberation of the Polish Kingdom from domination – this is our goal during the war of the great powers against Russia. We can win only through faith in our own power, we will get freedom only through our own acts, for which we must take responsibility. Those who want freedom must fight for it themselves!

This appeal was undoubtedly written with Piłsudski's participation. It called on Poles to create and support organizations readying
themselves for armed conflict and make contributions to the Polish Military Fund. The effects from this appeal were miniscule.

Piłsudski was under pressure since he, more than others, was
aware of the opportunity which a war among the great powers would
create for Poland. At the same time, he could see the passivity of Polish
society which has not yet matured to the level of these historical challenges. *There is nothing so hurtful as not being able to take advantage of
fortunate circumstances, and these are coming – they are within reach.*

In 1912, when Piłsudski was asked about the possibilities for victory among the nations involved in the future war, he said: *I believe that
Germany, because of its advanced technology, has a chance to defeat Russia.
But the resources and financial assets of England and France will defeat the
German power.* In this way, Piłsudski did not appear to be pro-German
or pro-Austrian, as his accusers would later claim. The universal war,
for which Poles believing in God and independence prayed for since the
times of Mickiewicz,[28] was becoming more and more likely.

On 18 October 1912, the First Balkan War[29] broke out. Bulgaria, Montenegro, Greece, and Serbia declared war on Turkey. Hostilities
concluded on 30 May 1913, but peace did not last long, as the Russians
continued to maneuver in order to gain dominance in the Balkans. On 29
June, the Second Balkan War started. The aid given by Russia to Serbia
only caused a worsening of Russo-Austrian relations.

The course of the war and its significance to Polish independence-oriented organizations, their expectations and political thought on
this matter, found expression in an interview given by Piłsudski to Józef
Hłasko. The interview was published in the *Kurier Litewski [Lithuanian
Courier]* in Vilnius on 25 February 1913. "We must come out as a self-reli-
ant military force, which as the war is extinguished and the warring sides
are weakened and tired, can influence the outcome."

Walery Sławek, in a special report to the Piłsudski Historical Institute, supplemented the above cited fragment with Piłsudski's comments, which were given during the interview, but could not be published
because of censorship. He forecasted the defeat of Russia and a favorable
situation for the realization of Polish yearnings for independence.

In connection with an article, "Austrian Disorientation" by Zygmunt Balicki,[30] one of the leaders of the National Democracy party, Piłsudski published a retort "Mr. Balicki's Orientation," in *Naprzód [Forward]* on
30 July 1913. In it, he rejected, with humor flavored with bitterness, the
idea that the KTSSN[31] was inspired by the Austrian intelligence service.

In organizing intrigues and plots against Piłsudski's pro-independence activities, the Russian counter-intelligence service was much superior to the Austrians. It was able to reach into its ally France, and even the United States and Canada. The tools in use to maintain Tsarist rule - misinformation, outright lies, defamation, insinuation, provocation - were handled with great mastery acquired from hundreds of years of practice. Since Polonia[32] was prone to disagreements, such methods were successful, creating mistrust for the riflemen's society movement and depressing the donations flowing into the Polish Military Fund.

In 1913, despite the avalanche of work associated with the military organization, Piłsudski managed to organize his lectures on the January Insurrection and publish them in Poznań as a book entitled *22 January 1863* [*22 stycznia 1863*]. The book was illustrated with drawings by Edward Rydz, a student of Leon Wyczółkowski at the Kraków Art Academy and Piłsudski's outstanding colleague in the ZWC and the Riflemen's Societies.

From the prison in Aleksandrovsk near Irkutsk, Piłsudski received a burned-on-wood picture showing Prometheus breaking his shackles. In his thank-you for the gift he wrote: *It is one of the most valued awards I have received for anything I have ever done.* One should realize that in the twenty-year inter-war period, the "Prometheus Movement," inspired by Piłsudski, whose purpose was to coordinate the struggles of nations dominated by Soviet Russia, was linked to this very picture made in prison.

Units of the Riflemen's Society were also established in France, Belgium, and Switzerland. Piłsudski went abroad twice to inspect them. During these trips, he gave lectures and presentations to the emigrant communities. In Switzerland, he visited the Polish Museum in Rappersville and met with Zygmunt Miłkowski (T. T. Jeż). In Zurich, he gave a lecture on armed insurrections.

Insurrections and armed movements were part of every generation since Poland was partitioned. This must again happen now, when the moment of trial is near. Every generation of Poles must pass this test. Now it is our turn.

Later, Adam Pragier commented: *Piłsudski spoke without any oratorical effects, he was restrained and composed. His voice was weak, his clothes shabby, his appearance worn and stooped. But he was able to project his deep conviction, which emanated from the whole of his persona.*

Because of this vision of the course of the future war, the lecture given by Piłsudski in Paris on 21 February 1914 deserves particular attention.

We have come to take notice that typical Polish characteristics are enthusiasm, thoughtlessness, and the failure to appreciate strength, or rather the preference given to the emotions (the heart) over reason (the brain). This is what drove Poles to insurrection. This always ended in failure. But after 1863, there was a change. Reason came to the forefront. This new fascination so permeates Poles that if in the former ethos they might say, "The vulture eats not our hearts but our brains," now with a greater dose of truth they can say that the vulture eats out their hearts, leaving the brain, the tiny brain, in peace. Reason is sapping the will and energy of the Poles. Their god is moderation. The eventuality of a war between Russia and Austria poses the question, what to do? In the event of war, six hundred thousand Poles will find themselves in the Russian ranks, two hundred thousand in the German, and three hundred thousand in the Austrian. Over a million Poles will be fated to fight one another, in opposition to their will and their own interests.

A detailed description of the vision that Piłsudski had on the course of the future war was compiled thanks to the work of Wiktor Czernow, a Russian social-revolutionary activist. Summarizing Piłsudski's Paris lecture from February 1914, he wrote in his book:

He anticipated that in the near future, a Russo-Austrian war will break out over the Balkans. He had no doubt that Austria will have, now actually already has, the support of Germany. France will not be able to remain a passive witness to this conflict. Germany will openly support Austria, and this will cause France to be involved on Russia's side. England will not leave France to the whims of fate. If the power of England and France combined proves to be inadequate, then sooner or later, America will be dragged into the conflict. Analyzing the war making potential of these countries, Piłsudski posed a clear question: *What will be the course of the war and whose victory will end it?* His answer: *The victory will move from west to east. Russia will be defeated by Austria and Germany, which then in turn will be beaten by the Anglo-French or the Anglo-American-French alliance. Eastern Europe will be conquered by Central Europe, and Central Europe by the European West. This points the direction of how the Poles should act.*

After returning to Poland, during ceremonies commemorating the 120th anniversary of the Battle of Racławice, Piłsudski gave a speech in Lwów which caused a great impression on his listeners and was noted in the press of Galicia.

In the last decades, Poles made great sacrifices fighting in the armies of their oppressors, for foreign interests at: Solferino. Magenta, Sad-

owa, Sevastopol, Kaukaz, the Russo-Japanese War, and the Franco-Prussian War where our "Victorious Barteks"[33] made such great fame for themselves. In the war which Europe is now facing, if we must fight and die, then let us die for our own homeland and the freedom of our own nation.

The beginning of the war was but months away, but the tension seemed to ease. Preparations made by the Poles were far from adequate. Political difficulties, arguments, and quarrels that evoked "Polish Hell" reached apocalyptic dimensions when the Polish Military Fund received an infusion of contributions from American Polonia.

The Temporary Commission of Confederated Independence Parties, after the congress at the end of 1913, was no longer "temporary," but simply the Commission (KTSSN). Its job, within Piłsudski's concept, was treated as the embryonic future national government. Yet it was not built up, and consumed by internal struggles, instead losing most of its authority and ability to do anything constructive.

On 24 June 1914, speaking at the funeral of Józef Strzemieńczyk-Janowski, member of the National Government of 1863, Piłsudski said: *Only our own government, respected and demanding obedience, is worthy of the nation. They, our progenitors, whom our dear departed led, had such a government. We stand before the National Government, boys. Let us bid it farewell in a soldierly fashion – attention!*

In the first days of July 1914, in Tyniec near Kraków, the last maneuvers of the Riflemen before the Great War took place. After the exercise was completed and the assembly formed, their Commandant spoke. *We will also use next year to increase our military knowledge. This will be needed in the time of the future war.*

Famous Activists of the Fighting Oranization of the PPS

(Left) Stefan Okrzeja (1886 – 1905), one of the lost fighters.
(Right) Józef Montwiłł-Mirecki (1879 – 1908), who carried out many successful actions (Opatów, Pruszków, Rogów, Łapy). Arrested in 1907, executed on the site of the Citadel.

(Left) Jan Jur-Gorzechowski (1874-1948), famous for directing the escape of ten prisoners from Pawiak Prison. (Right) ALesandra Szczerbińska – Ola (1882 – 1962), the second wife of the Marshal and the mother of his daughters: Wanda and Jadwiga. She took part in many actions.

Participants in the Bezdany Raid Who Became Prime Ministers in the Second Polish Republic

(Left) Józef Piłsudski.
(Right) Tomasz Arciszewski (1877 – 1955), the last Premier of of the government of the Polish Republic in International Affairs, who by July 1945, had an international reputation.

(Left) Aleksander Prystor (1874 – 1941) murdered in the USSR.
(Right) Walery Sławek (1879 – 1939) was part of a small group of those whom the Marshal called, "On You".

Chapter 7
After the Outbreak of the World War – At the Head of the Riflemen

Events at the end of July 1914 were surprising, even for such a far-sighted visionary as Józef Piłsudski. The successor to the Austro-Hungarian throne, Archduke Franz Ferdinand, was killed by an assassin in Sarajevo on 28 June. The initial restrained reaction coming from Vienna gave reason to believe that this time the effects would be limited to diplomatic protests, but over the next few weeks, the situation grew worse. On 28 July, Austria-Hungary declared war on Serbia. On 30 July, Russia announced a general mobilization, and Germany issued an ultimatum demanding the mobilization to stop; but when their note was rejected, they declared war on Russia on 1 August. Two days later, Germany announced that they were in a state of war with France. The die had been cast.

On 29 and 30 July, Piłsudski issued orders to mobilize all the riflemen's groups, but the unfolding events and Polish impotence threw him into despair. His representatives went into the Russian zone of partition in order to impede the Russian mobilization. They returned with unverified news that support for the Russians was holding, that the mobilization was going ahead without interruption, and that news of the formation of a Polish military force in Galicia were being received with apathy or even with hostility.

As commandant in chief of all the military organizations united in the Confederated Commission of Independence Parties, Piłsudski had thirty-six thousand crowns and a small supply of arms at his disposal. The only fully mobilized unit turned out to be the participants of the summer military school, gathered at the so-called "Oleanders" (next to Jordan Park) in Kraków.

The administration of the Polish Military Fund issued an appeal. *On Polish lands, powerful armies are beginning lethal battles which must change the map of Europe and decide the fate of our nation. The Polish riflemen's groups will do their duty when they receive the order to go into action. They will go to fight against the Tsar, giving their blood and lives in sacrifice for the freedom of our nation. Let us do our duty. Let us go to help the fighters supplying them with arms, clothing, and food. May our sacrifice be in appropriate measure to the seriousness of the current situation.*

Piłsudski was counting on getting assistance from the Austrian government, which was, after all, interested in getting Polish assistance. But the government showed typical bureaucratic slowness and inefficiency. Piłsudski's suggested that Polish units move into Zagłębie Dąbrowskie, since there would be the greatest social support for this action, but it turned out to be impossible to execute because the area was occupied by Germany on 1 August.

On 2 August the Austrian authorities gave formal permission for a separate mobilization of the riflemen's units. It was then decided that the Polish units could cross the frontier before the Austrian army, not in the Zagłębie area, but on the Miechów-Jędrzejów-Kielce line.

On the night of 2-3 August, a patrol consisting of seven uhlans, commanded by Władysław Belina-Prażmowski, moved into the Russian area to conduct a reconnaissance. At this point in the war, the uhlans did not have horses, so their mission used two carriages. The patrol was a good start because, on getting news that a force of some kind was approaching, the Russians closed down the recruitment office in Jędrzejów and fled. The Polish cavalry now had horses.

The "Stubborn Lithuanian" as some called Piłsudski, showed inexhaustible energy and hardiness of spirit during those days. In his apartment at Szlak Street in Kraków, he coordinated the mobilization. Everyone waited for Austria to declare war on Russia with impatience.

On 3 August, Piłsudski addressed the First Cadre Company (one hundred and seventy-two soldiers from the "Strzelec" and Riflemen Groups), giving one of his most important speeches.

> *Soldiers. You have the great privilege of being the first to go into the Polish Kingdom crossing the armed frontier of the Russian zone of partition, as the spearhead of the Polish Army, going on to liberate the Homeland. All of you are equal to the sacrifices which you are obliged to make. All of you are soldiers. I will not appoint your leaders but ask that the more experienced ones take the place of officers. You will receive your rank in battle. Each one of you can become an officer and then return the ranks, but I would not want this. I look upon you as the cadres from which should develop the future Polish Army and greet you as the First Cadre Company.*

But the departure did not commence on the 4th or the 5th of August. The Austrians were delaying, but momentous events could not be held back. War was declared on 6 August, and on that night, Piłsudski received the following order: *Your company is to gather at the place of assembly and march out at 3 am. The assembly is to be conducted quietly and without publicity.* After fifteen minutes, they were ready. The adjutant called the officers together. Soon they returned jubilant. Their Commandant was there. He took the last report and walked down the ranks repeating one word, "Congratulations!"

The first company was led by Tadeusz Kasprzycki. They proceeded through Prądnik, Łobozów and Babie toward the frontier of the Russian zone of occupation. In the ranks of the First Cadre Company there were eight future generals, several colonels, many future ministers and voievodes, town mayors, and other outstanding co-creators of the Second Polish Republic. At 9:45 AM, the company reached the border markers near Michałowice and continued on to Miechów.

On the day after the departure of the 'First Cadre,' there was a meeting of the KSSN where Piłsudski proposed to issue the following statement. *Poles! A National Government has been formed in Warsaw. The duty of every Pole is to be in solidarity and accept its authority. The command of the Polish military forces had been given to Józef Piłsudski, whose orders should be obeyed by all.* At this point, the government was only a dream, but as Piłsudski wrote in his *Corrections to History*, he preferred a secret and far-away fiction over nothing. *From that time started my long loneliness which has been so significant in my life.*

Not resting a moment, on the afternoon of 6 August, he went to Krzeszów with Sosnkowski, where a gathering point for the campaign was situated. After the First Cadre Company, other units were getting on their way. On 9 August there were already four rifle companies (about eight hundred and forty men). Under Piłsudski's personal command, they moved from Jedrzejów toward Kielce taking it on 12 August. According to Austrian orders, the Polish units were to only go as far as Jędrzejów. It was thought that this hundred-kilometer march, conducted under the threat of meeting the enemy, was beyond the capabilities of the poorly armed and ill-equipped Poles. Kielce was the nearest town designated as a possible contact point between Russian and German forces. Taking Kielce had significance beyond the military. It was the capital of the bishopric and of the province.

Piłsudski's ambition and contrariness did not let him remain in Jedrzejów but drove him on to Kielce to get there before the Austrians. This made political sense. Arriving at Kielce first, he could take over the Russian governor's palace as his headquarters. *They would not dare to remove me from the palace. ... The Austrians and Germans came to me with humility, probably believing that since I was in the palace that I held a higher rank*, remembered Piłsudski. Thus, Polish dreams were realized. The universal war, for which Mickiewicz prayed in his, *A Pilgrim's Litany (Litania Pielgrzymska)*, and which was awaited by generations, was a fact. The riflemen felt themselves to be the true successors of Puławski,[34] Kościuszko,[35] Dąbrowski,[36] Poniatowski,[37] Dwernicki,[38] Sowiński,[39] Sierakowski,[40] Tragutt[41] and many, many others. With high hopes, they started the next round in the Polish struggle for independence of the Homeland, still fooling themselves that they would ignite an insurrection – but one that would be victorious.

During the march to Kielce, a song was written and sung to an old Warsaw tune, "the heart is glad, the soul is joyous." One of the song's stanzas said, "when the uprising ends in victory, then the first cadres will become a guard."

How were these actions interpreted by Polish society? Piłsudski's initiatives had the support of the Polish Socialist Party and the Polish Peasant Party. In coordination with them, the commandant put out two appeals. One was in the name of the National Government, the other in his own name. In the second one, he wrote:

The hour of decision has struck. Poland has stopped being a slave and wants to build her own future, throwing its own armed force into the fray. Cadres of the Polish Army have crossed into the Polish Kingdom, taking the land into the possession for the only actual, only and proper owner – the Polish people – who had fertilized and enriched it with their own blood. We aim to break the shackles binding the nation and give its various states the conditions for normal development. Today, the entire nation should gather into a single camp, under the direction of the National Government.

By putting distance between himself and specific parties and political groups, Piłsudski sought that in gaining independence, all the nation's strength should be united. The awareness of the people was not what was demanded by the situation. The soul of the nation was still in the grip of fear and lack of faith in its own strength. There was a universal fear of the reprisals Russians may exact if they returned. The fighting power of the riflemen was regarded as weak, and not without cause, while Russia was considered a power that was impossible to defeat.

A team of rifleman on exercises in Zakopane. In the lead are Józef Piłsudski and Kazimierz Sosnkowski.

The staff of the riflemen after taking Kielce, in front of the Governor's Palace. 12 August 1914. In the first row standing from the left: Ignacy Boerner, Aleksander Litwinowicz, Michał Sokolnicki, Kazimierz Sosnkowski, Józef Piłsudski, Władysław Belina-Prażmowski, "Ryszard" Trojanowski, Walery Sławek, and Gustaw Daniłowski.

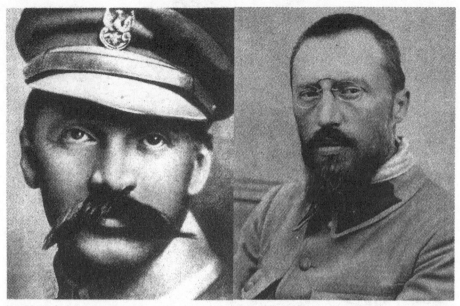

(Left) "I did not want to let the new frontiers of the countries and nations of the Poles themselves be lacking in the time when the body of my country was wielding swords!" A photograph made in the first month of World War I.

(Right) Jerzy Żuławski (1874 – 1915), an outstanding poet, dramatist, novelist and essayist. He served in the ranks of the riflemen, then co-organized the Legion's newsletter, *Do Broni (To Arms)*. He died of typhus at a military hospital.

(Left) Komendant Józef Piłsudski and Prince Bishop Władysław Bandurski (1865 – 1932).

(Right) Two 2nd Lieutenants of the Legion: Stefan Rowecki (1895 – 1944) and Wacław Styk-Stachiewicz (1894 – 1973).

Chapter 8
The Legions

The entry of the riflemen's units into the Russian zone of partition did not cause an uprising, but it is not true that it did not have some of the effects on which Piłsudski was counting. At that moment, the effects were intangible, while the Austrians were irritated by the fact that plans for snatching away the Polish recruits from the Russians did not work out. Every day this continued to spoil Piłsudski's chances and negated his value in the political game.

Not getting the advantages they expected, on 12 August 1914, the Austrians demanded that Piłsudski dissolve the riflemen's units or incorporate them into the "Landsturm." The situation looked hopeless, but the people engaged in Polish politics, inspired and satisfied with what was accomplished, and managed to operate with great dedication and solidarity necessary under these difficult circumstances.

Meanwhile, on 13 August e riflemen had to leave Kielce and undertake a rear-guard action at Brzegi along the Nida River. Despite this reverse, the riflemen's units were reinforced by volunteers and deserters from the Russian ranks. Fortunately, Piłsudski had the good fortune of enlisting Gustaw Orlicz-Dreszer,[42] who later became a famous general. The father of future saint, Maximilian Kolbe, had less luck as he was captured by the Russians and later executed on the scaffold.

After making the necessary arrangements and completing "diplomatic" procedures, a meeting of the Polish deputies from the Vienna Parliament, delegates of the Commission of Confederated Independence Parties, and representatives of Galician organizations gathered into a Central National Committee, took place in Kraków on 16 August.

All these groups and political orientations supported the creation of a Committee of National Leadership – NKN – as the top civil authority, and the Polish Legions as the national armed force. In one of the discussions (August 20), when they were considering what kind of guarantees they should ask of the Austrians for Poland, Piłsudski impatiently murmured under his nose, "And why the hell should we ask them for guarantees when they will lose the war."

Organization of the Legions began, based on the existing and fighting riflemen's units. In accordance with the agreement reached with the Austrian authorities, the Legionaries received the weapons and equipment also issued to the regular army.

The new situation was explained by Piłsudski in a special order issued on 22 August 1914.

Soldiers! Because of the universal passivity within our society, the current historical events have surprised the Polish people, leaving them without a specific viewpoint, without the possibility of a united and forceful expression. It would be necessary that the bravest and most energetic among them would take upon their shoulders the responsibility and the initiative for putting the spark to gunpowder. You have ignited the spark, giving example to others as the leaders of the Polish nation in its fight for the independence of the Homeland. We, a mere handful, went into action. In Kielce and at Brzegi we have halted the overwhelming might of an ancient enemy, protecting with our bodies that which was free from the encroacher's grasp. Now the nation is awakening and does not want to leave us alone as we were to date. In Kraków, the leading National Committee, consisting of all the Polish political parties, has been established. It, with the consent of the Austro-Hungarian government, is to prepare the Polish Legions to do battle with Russia. After reaching a secret understanding with the National Government in Warsaw, I have declared in my own and Your name our membership in this larger organization. Our units are to become the cadres for the Legions now being formed.

At the head of the Legions, the Austrians placed the retired general Rajmund Baczyński, a man devoid of Polish patriotism, and a typical representative of the military bureaucracy. Włodzimierz Zagórski (1882-1927), a member of the Austrian security service, totally loyal to Austria, became the chief of staff for the Legions. Piłsudski tried to maintain the autonomy of the Legions, so that between him and the Command there were continuing controversies and quarrels.

Piłsudski would write the following about this period:

I had to protect myself from constant intrigues and plots. At the same time, I had to use my authority to reduce internal friction that resulted from the quick induction of incoming volunteers. I felt that the work was moving ahead, but I had to admit that it was difficult. What made it harder was the fact that from the start, everything was happening in the field, during skirmishes with the enemy, often in battle or awaiting battle. Sometimes, before the war, I dreamed of such work as an experiment that negated the routine thinking in the armed forces. This experiment did not accept any official or non-official doctrine. It seemed to me that Poland was condemned to quickly improvise an armed force, if it would want one. Everything that was theory, everything that was considered doctrine, all that was per-

manent and universally repeated by all the parrots, stated: "Lasciate ogni speranza!" [Abandon all hope!] - it is idiotic, it is impossible. Now I had in my hands the possibility of improvising an armed force and suddenly so many intrigues and plots, and so much ... incredible, cowardly stupidity.

The first battles of the legions, personally led by Piłsudski, took place in the second part of September 1914 on the left bank of the Vistula in the region of Now Korczyn-Opatowice. Felicjan Sławoj-Składkowski wrote that, *The Commandant was everywhere, where he felt the boys needed encouragement. He was in the trenches, at the first-aid stations, and with the reserves.*

One of the greatest battles of that period took place at Laski (23 – 26 October 1914), where Michał Karaszewicz-Tokarzewski[43] was severly wounded. Piłsudski, together with Doctor Skladowski, tried to save his life. During the bloody course of the battle, a fragment of shrapnel struck Piłsudski's head, but the contusion was not serious.

The Austro-German offensive against the Russians failed and a retreat began. Orders that Piłsudski received expected a retreat to the west, beyond the territories inhabited by Poles. This was contrary to Piłsudski's political agenda, which held that it was imperative to keep and develop the embryonic Polish Army among their own people.

It was possible to disregard the Austrian strategy because orders had been given that the Legions conduct reconnaissance of Russian strength in the Żarowiec-Michów sector. In executing this order, Piłsudski took the risk and maneuvered between the Austrian and Russian armies in order to reach Kraków. It was an extremely dangerous march through Ulina Mała.

Taking such dramatic risks could have turned into a tragic end to "The Act of August 6" which, according to Piłsudski's plan, was to awaken the fighting spirit in an "unchivalorous, servile nation." It is obvious that in such circumstances, he must have considered the possibility of his own death but had the satisfaction of knowing that even death could have a great significance to the Polish cause, if it occurred in the proper place and at a high enough price. As a leader, he knew well that history does not respect insignificant sacrifices. In his memoirs about Ulina Mała, he wrote:

To Kraków? After all it is a fortress, it will not fall at any moment, in a day. If one has to die, then it should be there, the sacrificial offering must leave a trace. This will not be on the Elstera, but on the Vistula. To Kraków, or better yet to Nowy Targ. If indeed the Austrians feel so defeated, that they are making such a speedy retreat as if in a few days they had to defend Moravia and Czechia, then the enemy must bypass Galicia. In the difficult to reach mountain regions, one can hold on for a longer time than elsewhere. The Mountain Men (Górale) will probably help. ... And when the sacrificial offering is made, then in the mountains it will be of a greater historical value, because it was made by ourselves alone, on a scenic background.

Giving the orders to march, Piłsudski said to Sosnkowski: *We will defend Kraków, or we will go to Podhale.* There was a great amount of trust in this statement, for without artillery and machine guns, the march could have ended in a total disaster. The maneuver was successful, and on 11 November 1914, to the great joy of Poles and extreme dissatisfaction of the Austrians, Piłsudski arrived in Kraków at the head of the Legions. He remembered this escapade with a mixture of pride and joy. *Only after Ulina did I start to trust myself and believe in my own strength.* This he wrote when interned at Magdeburg in the summer of 1918.

But it was still the year 1914. The first regiment of the Legions which Piłsudski commanded developed into the First Brigade. The diversity among the uniforms disappeared. The entire First Brigade wore shooting jackets and the famous "maciejówki" caps.[44] Very significant was the age of the officers appointed by Piłsudski, as most of them were under thirty. The Chief of Staff and Piłsudski's deputy was Kazimierz Sosnkowski. The battalion commanders were as follows: Marian Żegota-Januszajtis, Mieczysław Neugebauer-Norwid, Edward Śmigły-Rydz, Tadeusz Wyrwa-Furgalski, and Michał Karaszewicz-Tokarzewski.

In addition to the infantry, the First Brigade included a division of cavalry commanded by Captain of Horse Władysław Belina-Prażmowski, and two batteries of rapid firing field artillery.

After a bloody battle on the hills near Łowczowek (22 November – 5 December 1914), the First Brigade was withdrawn to the Zakliczyn region (Lipnica Murowana) and then to the Kęty region. The well-deserved rest lasted until the end of February. At the beginning of March, the First Brigade was placed on a segment of the front along the Nida River. The Russian positions stretched along the hills near Pińchow. The First Brigade spent March, April, and half of May in these positions. The Central Powers were not able to resolve the war to their advantage on the Western Front, so they decided to push back the Russian front to a maximum point, and then in consequence they could concentrate their full effort toward the west.

After the Russians fell back on 11 May 1915, the First Brigade crossed the Nida River and started marching east. The Russian High

Command ordered a total retreat, and through this, avoided encircle-ment from the north and south. The new line of resistance was to be the Bug, Stochód, and Styr Rivers. Before this new line was organized, there were many weeks of battling for position. The largest battles took place at Konary and Otorowo where, for the first time, the Legionaries saw the burned-out ruins methodically left behind by the Russian army.

Piłsudski would later write about those days.

The Muscovites burned Poland as they moved toward the east. My patrols reported that the town of Ożarów was totally burned, and that the people were chased to the east. The church would not burn, so they doused it with kerosene three times to destroy it. Our line halted at Ożarów, where in the ruins of the town are outposts of the Russian army. In Bidziny at evening, life stops. My staff is housed in a cellar, and our hosts have discreetly left me alone. In the park and orchard, something is quietly murmuring; there are no shots heard from the front, instead there is the usual barking of dogs. One could think that one is somewhere visiting neighbors, with cake on a plate – the war, for the moment, seems not to exist, for there is nothing to call it into one's awareness.

There's confusion in my head, I cannot comprehend this quiet when my brain is tortured with the question – what is the mean-ing of these fires, this burning of Poland? I cannot find an answer to this question and it bothers and worries me. The most likely hy-pothesis seems to be that this is the harebrained idea of some Rus-sian staff-officer, in St. Petersburg or in the headquarters of the Great Prince Nicholas, whose memory reached back to the "defensive war" of 1812. I know that this war was considered an example of Russian patriotism and military logic. How many poets, even the great ones, praised it. After all I was taught Lermontov's verse in school:

*We will not give it up,
Moscow will rather be burned
than given to the French.*

Somewhere, history and documents tell a different story, that the buffoon Roztopczyn considered the fires to be his doing even though they were set by common robbers and looters. The legend made of this is not only a great legend, but a deed of great sagacity which drove Napoleon out of Moscow. A horse would have a laugh at such wisdom! So now another fool from the Russian staff, in his Polo-Rus-sian patriotism sang:

We will not give it up,
Poland burned to the ground,
We'll give to the Germans.

With that lack of concern, orders were given - burn, chase out the people, leave only a desert. Bravo! A desert, a beautiful desert! As far as the eye can see there are field and fields full of grain await-ing the harvester, each stalk heavy with ripe grain. The scythe man will come, who sowed it, or be they left to a new master who would not have chased the peasants away. Is there a shortage of houses to live in? This is nothing to the army! ... Because it's impossible to burn completely even if they imported trainloads of kerosene from the Caucasus. There is no reasonable sense or sufficient means to do this but burn it must to our awful impotence. They chase the boys and women with their whips, let loose the conflagration, and then let all go to blazes. It's the destructive nature of the east.

On 3 August 1915, the legions entered Lublin. On the occasion of the first anniversary of the cadres marching out to war, Piłsudski de-scribed the essence of the Legionaries' accomplishment.

I could not allow it that at a time, when on the living body of our Homeland, new borders of countries were drawn with swords, that Poles would not take part in this enterprise. I could not allow, as swords were put onto the scales, there be no Polish saber among them. Soldiers. Today, after a year of war and work, I am sorry that I cannot congratulate you on great triumphs. But I am proud that now a year later I can call out you with greater calmness: Forward, Boys! For life or for death, for victory or defeat, may you with your warlike stance awaken Poland to rise again.

At this time, there were three active brigades in the Legions, but Piłsudski remained commandant of only the First. The main command of the legions and the Military Department of the NKN directed by General Władysław Sikorski, did not wish to take into account either the personal status of Piłsudski, who was the charismatic leader of all the legions, or the political concepts he represented.

The First Brigade stressed its drive for Polish independence at every turn and opposed any concessions toward Austria or Germany. Pił-sudski later remembered:

My brigade stood totally apart, both politically and spiritually, from the Central Powers. I personally gave it the political orientation ... My officers and soldiers decided in silence that everything that had to do with politics was on my head. Knowing that we needed funds, they decided to take only one hundred crowns from their salary per month, leaving the rest for our common needs.

His Austrian Imperial Majesty's command of the Legions was commonly called the "CK-mand." The disdain was obvious from both sides. Evidence of this may be found in the recommendation that was written in the request for a decoration for Piłsudski.

The officer of the legions of the VI rank, Brigadier Józef Piłsudski, has some military skills and accomplishments which would normally be enough for him to be awarded the highest decoration, but at the present time, I must disapprove this application. Piłsudski leads the First Brigade of the Legions formed by him, but which differs totally from Brigades II and III, created by His Majesty's Legion Command, as far as spirit and attitude is concerned. He and his Brigade represent that element, which seeks to establish a free and independent Poland, and considers cooperation with the Austrian Army as only a means to an end, ready to change orientation at any time. ... From the beginning of the war, he has set himself a goal – to take over full command of all the Polish Legions in the hopes that, at a given moment, he would be able to make demands... Understanding the fact that Piłsudski's fantastic ideas are without any realistic basis, and are even counter to the Austrian raison d'etat, the Legion Command has, since the beginning of the war, worked to suppress his influence.

In September 1915, at a meeting of independence activists in Warsaw, Piłsudski presented his assessments and the most important tasks. In his opinion, the Legions had already fulfilled their mission. The captured Polish lands in the Russian zone of partitions cannot be treated as part of Galicia. A National Council of the former Congress Kingdom must be created. This Council must then declare that it will give no more soldiers to the Legions but go on to form a separate Polish army. The most important current task for the independence activists is to support the conspiratorial Polish Military Organization.

In autumn of 1915, all the brigades in the Legions were in Wolyń. It was a time of bitter battles and an opportunity to reveal leadership talents and stances. Piłsudski was among his soldiers and lived their life.

The same black unsweetened coffee and the meager food, and, well ... the same lice in the sweaters and uniforms, with which the commandant had to fight like any of us.

The above quote comes from Ignacy Daszyński, one of the officers in the Legion, who supplemented it with a description of the dugout in which the commandant lived and worked. *A hole dug into the earth lined with birch logs. A few square meters allotted for place for a bed and chair. Dampness in this hole had a bad effect on Piłsudski's organism, which all his life fought diseases and lived despite doctors' opinions to the contrary.*

In this miserable dugout, Piłsudski learned that Aleksandra Szczerbińska was arrested by the Germans. She had directed the courier service for the Legions and was accused of subversive activities. Her place of imprisonment was later in Lubań Śląski.[45]

The daily battles of the Legions on the Wołyń front, among the difficulties and dangers, allowed all the formations in the legions to grow closer together spiritually. The factor that integrated them was mainly Piłsudski's presence, but a major role was played by the already formed First Brigade and the political consciousness of its officers and men. A great role in forming this consciousness was such men as Bishop Władysław Bandurski,[46] a friend to Piłsudski, and the chaplains. The most famous of them were Capucins: Fr. Kosma Lenczowski (1881-1959), the first chaplain of the riflemen's units, then of the First Brigade, and Fr. Franciszek Wojnar (1896-1966). Both had the courage to publicly speak Piłsudski's name even during the time of Stalinist terror, and always with great respect for his achievements.

There were more disagreements with the "CK-menda" and even open conflict. One of these concerned badges. It would happen that officers and sub-officers in many units would, of their own volition, change their badges to those as were used by the First Brigade. An investigation started, and arrests were threatened, but the matter was withdrawn because a mass mutiny was feared. In a letter to Ignacy Daszyński, Piłsudski described the situation. *Relations became very sharp, threatening at any time to break out in scandal... The men would eat at separate tables, the Austrian officers by themselves, the legionaries by themselves.*

Because of their relative closeness, there were possible frequent meetings among colonels in the Legion for political-military discussions. These meetings quickly led to the creation of an unofficial Council of Colonels. This council functioned from 14 February 1916 and became an additional means for Piłsudski to influence the Legions, but also another reason for the worsening conflict with the Legion Command and the

Military Department NKN.

The stance of the Legion soldiers on the Russian front drew admiration from the Germans and suggested solutions from which they wanted to draw advantage for themselves. An expression of this is a letter written by General Ludendorff on 17 July 1916. *The Austrian forces are not reliable. My attention rests on the Poles. The Pole is a good soldier. If Austria fails to supply additional forces, then we can form the Great Polish Kingdom of Warsaw and Lublin and have a Polish army under German command.*

Piłsudski had the correct measure of German intent and thought, that in a properly conducted political game, Polish demands for independence could be intensified, if on the grounds of the former Congress Kingdom there would arise a national government to represent the people. The Polish army would then subordinate itself to it.

Chapter 9
The Polish Military Organization

In the game to recover Polish independence, Piłsudski was an exceptional player and did not limit himself to the "chessboard." Already on 19 August, in the course of transforming the riflemen's societies into the Polish Legions, the Polish Military Organization (POW) was formed in Warsaw in order to create an intelligence service and conduct diversionary activities behind the Russian lines. Piłsudski's adjutant, Tadeusz Żuliński (1889-1915), was appointed commandant of the POW. He was the creator of the name POW and its initial structures. He fell at Kamieniucha.

The situation was fundamentally changed after German and Austrian forces occupied the Congress Kingdom. Specifically, the Germans and Austrians were against anything that favored the independence aspirations of the Poles.

The political authority in the areas occupied by the Germans were to be administered by the Polish National Organization (PON). The leaders of PON were: Jodko, Sokolnicki[47] and Ryś-Trojanowski.[48] In 1915, the units operated by the PON were exposed and lost significance. After these resources, which connected the PON to the legions, were exhausted, Piłsudski decided to further develop the POW. As the political base for this organization, the Central National Committee was created. It was a coalition of the PPS, the National Workers' Union, the Independence Union, the Patriots' Union, and the Polish Peasant Party.

Creating a united and independent Poland could only be accomplished through an effort of international proportions. Under no circumstances could they agree to offer up Polish soldiers to a foreign cause. Russia was on a course heading for disaster. This placed new challenges in front of the independence camp - that is how Piłsudski, taking the matter in general, recounted his position in mid-1916.

Meanwhile, on 4 July, the largest and bloodiest battle at Kostiochnówka began. It lasted three days, and all three brigades participated in it. Piłsudski directed operations giving orders under withering fire. Losses for the First Brigade (thirty officers and five hundred men) and the reluctant position of the Austrian authorities, who wanted to continue treating the Legionaries as "private" volunteers fighting against Russia, accelerated the decisions which Piłsudski was contemplating for some time.

In writing on 29 July 1916, he requested to be released from his responsibilities connected with commanding the First Brigade of the Polish Legions. News of this resignation quickly spread among the legionaries and caused an avalanche of requests from officers, also asking to be released from the Legions.

On 6 August, Piłsudski gave his second anniversary order, connected to the march-out of the cadres.

Soldiers. Two years have passed from the date that we will keep in our hearts – August 6, 1914, when on Polish soil we lifted with our hands the long-forgotten banner of the Polish Army going into battle in defense of the Homeland. When I went into the field at the head of your ranks, I was clearly aware of the enormous hurdles which were standing in our way. When I led you out of Kraków's city walls, where none trusted in your might, when I led you through the towns and villages of the Polish Kingdom, I always saw before me a terrible phantom – coming from the graves of our fathers and grandfathers – the phantom of the soldier without a homeland. Is this how we will remain in history, will our only legacy be "the abbreviated weeping of women and, among our countrymen, long discussions that go into the night"? The future will have to decide. Two years have passed. The fate of our Homeland is still in the balance. May I be allowed to wish for myself and for You, that my next order given on this our anniversary, would be read to free Polish soldiers, in a free Polish land.

On 30 August, the Council of Colonels sent an incisive memorandum, signed by, among others, Piłsudski, Sosnkowski, Haller, and Roja. [49]It was a declaration to the Austrian government that the Legions are a Polish army which "fight and die for Polish independence" and a demand to come to terms with a delegation of the Parties in Warsaw in order to form a Polish government.

The Austro-German authorities did not conduct any political discussions with Piłsudski on 29 September 1916. He was only informed that his resignation was accepted. Witnesses noted that the Commandant was calm but sad. He did not conceal the fact that, for the moment, his plans did not pan out; but the thought of staying with the Legions any longer, only to feed the Austro-German war machine, without any concessions on their part, would be contrary to honor and the dignity of the nation – "a deed contrary to the interests of Poles." An expression of support to Piłsudski's stance was a great demonstration organized in his honor in Kraków. As an act of appreciation toward the Commandant of the Legions, he was handed an address signed by fifty thousand persons and a gold medal to mark the occasion.

Even Piłsudski's political adversaries could not question the great role he played. Władysław Leopold Jaworski noted the following opinion in connection with this event. *Something moved, like the spirit of greatness on a narrow street, and I felt its breeze. It seemed to me that it would be better for Poland if we all take part in paying respects to this daredevil.*

On Piłsudski's recommendation, all attempts by the Austrians and Germans to recruit soldiers were boycotted. Instead, all efforts were concentrated in building up the Polish Military Organization. This action, combined with mass desertions of Poles, turned out to be very effective, and by October it was clear that the Germans and Austrians would have to make concessions. The Polish delegation was received by the German Chancellor and the Austrian Foreign Minister. On 5 November 1916, a declaration was issued by both Emperors (Franz Joseph I and Wilhelm II) that created a Polish Kingdom.

This was, regardless of Austro-German intentions, a great success for the Polish cause. In light of this new position, Piłsudski sent his orders to Śmigły-Rydz: *You must now exercise justified patience and trust that the Polish soldier will win back his Homeland from this World War ... You should now withdraw your resignations.*

After appraising the new situation, the most accurate and most believable is what Piłsudski said in a conversation with Władysław Baranowski.

You are correct that we are finished with Austria. Even more, we are done with the gentlemen from the NKN. In this negative auction conducted behind my back and against me was the readiness to sell something cheaply which we cannot morally give without asking for the consent and opinion of the nation, which is frightened by the threat of martial law. This I can no longer stand. This attempt to obtain favor from foreigners by diminishing and devaluing the Polish cause, this cannot be repeated, as long as my persona is taken in some consideration or combination.

Now we will talk in Warsaw, and we will talk only under new conditions with the Germans. We can still win them over if they see their own interest in the creation of a Polish Army on the Russian front. Today, the Germans must impress on the Austrians the necessity to normalize the socio-political status of the Legions and establish them quickly as the basic formations of our forces. It is also necessary to normalize the POW's (Polska Organizacja Wojskowa) status, which awaits only my order to subject itself to a Polish government which it could be in this moment with the TRS. Only under this condition and to normalize these two most important matters am I ready to join the Council of State, from which activities – sensing it by smell and I hope to be wrong – I unfortunately do not expect much.

Piłsudski's personal joy was due to freeing Aleksandra Szczerbińska from imprisonment for her activities in the POW. In a good mood, he wrote to her in Kraków.

In general, women are the most devoted propagators of my name and influence, and I am extremely grateful to them for they have done much good through their nationalistic instinct. The children seem to demonstrate the most, as in Kraków they have mobbed me with their delight and affection in the streets. Some of these children are quite amusing. And I, not used to such exhibitions of the national pride and contented myself to be the unostentatious Lithuanian, whose sensitive nature rebels within in protest to becoming the object of public theater for the sake of an audience.

Piłsudski was also enthusiastically greeted in Warsaw. The authorities, considering his great prestige, proposed that he become a member of the so-called Temporary Council of State and take over the function of Director, Military Department. Piłsudski accepted this proposal. His thoughts, including arguments "for and against," are best summarized in his own declaration.

The Germans need the Polish Army as much as we do. Yet, the only fact necessary to know is that we ourselves need it ... I would like to state a principle, that was voiced by one of the greatest men of this world, Napoleon: "The art of overcoming obstacles, is the art of not considering this or that to be an obstacle." First of all, we must remove the mental obstacles, and then do what is most appropriate.

In order to encourage the Council of State to take a more decisive stance toward the Germans, Piłsudski decided to reveal the Polish Military Organization. It was quite a force. In Warsaw alone, there were eight trained battalions of the POW. Piłsudski had no intention of turning them over to the Germans until his political conditions were met. These conditions were stated in three points.

1. The Council of State was to be recognized by the Austrians and Germans as the de-facto Polish government.
2. The Legions were to be turned over to the Council of State as part of the Polish Army.
3. The Austrians and Germans were to agree to the creation of a recruitment organization for the Polish Army, working under the Council of State.

The German General Beseler[50] tried without success to persuade Piłsudski to be "flexible," trying to paint a rosy picture. *Before you the road to fame and honors is open, one you cannot even imagine.* But Piłsudski would not go back on any of the stated conditions. In reply to Beseler's tempting offers, he answered plainly and to the point. *You are wrong. You might gain one Pole, but I would lose my entire nation.*

What is interesting and meaningful is the way Piłsudski is characterized in the report issued by Beseler, dated 20 December 1916.

> *POW, the secret military organization, has unconditionally turned itself over to the command of the well known "Brigadier" Józef Piłsudski, whom they all consider to be their "commander-in-chief." This man is not without ability, undoubtedly is brave himself, but is undisciplined and has little actual knowledge, is a military dilettante and demagogue, having a nearly hypnotic influence on those surrounding him and their organizations. This creator of the Legions is admired and venerated like a national saint. Only he can organize an army and lead it. Seeing the blind obedience of his supporters, it would be proper to make an ally of him, but I have doubts about the result. Piłsudski believes, or has convinced himself, that he is the savior of his nation, and especially that he is the proper commander for the army. He considers as inappropriate what others do and forbids his subordinates to follow the advice of others, that is, us. Because here and now we are undoubtedly the lawful authorities, this stance, to be brief, is traitorous.*

On 19 February 1917, the first congress of the Auxiliary Military Committees took place in Warsaw, with five hundred representatives from all the provinces of the Polish Kingdom, who were the political representatives of the POW. In a speech given by Piłsudski, he emphasized that "this must be a national army, it must have close ties to the people, so that a demarcation line cannot be drawn between it and the nation."

The political situation of the Legions was getting worse. Austria, which was stubbornly supported by the NKN, was showing even greater weakness, while the Germans wanted to treat the Polish Army as "cannon fodder." Piłsudski had a firm grasp on the situation and insisted on the expansion of the Polish Military Organization – POW, encompassing not only the Kingdom, but also Lithuania and Ukraine, as well as Upper Silesia and Greater Poland in its activities.

The German successes on the eastern front, the February Revolution in Russia, the abdication of the Tsar, and the recognition of the Temporary Government of Poland's right to independence changed the situation radically. The Germans were now less willing to treat the Temporary Council of State seriously. Meanwhile, Piłsudski was more and more aware of the necessity for making another move in the Polish politics for independence. In April 1917, he proposed the concept of announcing resignations in the TRS, and he sharpened the tone of his demands. A direct cause of the ensuing crisis was the loyalty oath. The Germans demanded that the Legionaries take an oath confirming, t*hat on land and sea, in every place, they will serve loyally and faithfully; and that in the present war they will be faithful to the brotherhood in arms with the armies of Germany and Austria, and their allies.*

The Temporary Council of State, despite Piłsudski's categorical objections, accepted the wording of this oath on 2 July 1917. This became the direct cause of his resigning from the TRS. Speaking to the Legion officers, he explained his stance and gave an assessment of the situation.

Our combined travel with the Germans has ended. Russia, our foe, has stopped being our common enemy. We no longer have a collective interest. All our interests are now in opposition to those of Germany. It is to the Germans' advantage that they overcome the Allies, it is in ours, that the Allies defeat the Germans.

Piłsudski forbade all his officers and legionaries from taking the oath of declaring brotherhood-in-arms to the German and Austro-Hungarian armies. He was sure that soon the fate of the war would be decided in favor of France, England, and the United States. The legionaries who did not take the oath were interned in special camps in Benjaminów near Warsaw and Szczypiorne near Kalisz.

Part of the Legions decided not to lay down their arms and allow themselves to be locked up. Piłsudski was in a quandary.

I had nothing to achieve then, only my own demise. For a while, I vacillated whether to make a stand with weapon in hand. But I decided that the time was not yet ripe for this, that any resistance offered would be futile. Then I thought that perhaps such an action might be taken on terrain occupied by the Austrians. That with armed force we could take Dęblin and hold it until new terms could be obtained. The absence of my most appropriate units from the Dęblin area caused me to reject this plan. I also had the option of going to Russia and even prepared for the trip, but my honor as a commander stopped me. Then I wrote a letter to Beseler that I wished to be interned with my men.

Piłsudski appealed to his soldiers.

This is not the time. It is not the right moment. A nation that is plagued by seizures, starved, frightened by repression, will not rise-up, it will not support us. ... I cannot give my permission, instead I insist that you not resist with arms. I am a soldier. I understand you and it is difficult to give you this order, but you have gone onto the field of battle to fight for the Homeland, now you must go into prison for it.

The Germans did not limit their repression to interning the Legionaries. By mid-July, they started a massive arrest of POW activists. Walery Sławek, Wacław Jędrzejewicz, Piotr Górecki, Stefan Pomarański, and many others were sent to prison. On 22 July 1917 around 5 am, police and army units surrounded a house on Służewska Street, number 5, in Warsaw. This time, the dangerous individual arrested was Józef Piłsudski. His first month of imprisonment was spent with Sosnkowski, in transport and in gloomy cells located in Gdańsk, Berlin, and Wesel.

To sway public opinion, his captors tried to suggest that he had used falsified documents, but any attempt at conducting of a criminal investigation was quickly dropped. Instead, they tried to show that the "political game conducted by the former Brigadier of the Legions" was undisciplined and irrational and did not deserve any consideration. By putting out Polish flags and insignias at every opportunity, the Germans tried to create the impression that now, after the troublemakers were arrested, there were real chances of restoring a Polish state. The highest authority in the Polish Kingdom was given into the hands of a three-person Regency Council. Its members were: Primate Aleksander Kakowski, Zdzisław Lubomirski,[51] and Józef Ostrowski.[52] A government was organized with Jan Kucharzewski[53] as prime minister.

This posturing did not fool the Poles. The internment of Piłsudski caused widespread indignation and disgust. The Polish Military Organization went further underground and started conspiratorial activities. Its head, according to an earlier-made plan and with the Commandant's approval, was Śmigły-Rydz. Meanwhile, on 22 August, Piłsudski was taken to the Magdeburg citadel. The Commandant was scrupulously isolated but was treated with some tolerance, as his guards did not intrude.

It seems that I was born to a life in prison, he wrote. I am not overly troubled by the loneliness, not being as sensitive to it as some others. On 12 December 1917, in a letter to Ola Szczerbińska, he described a typical day's routine.

I rise at 7:30, breakfast at 8am. Then a walk for two and a half hours. I read the only available newspaper, the Magdeburgische Zeitung. *At 12:30, dinner. Then the nicest moment, tea which I make myself. In the afternoon I read and write and study chess. At 18:30, a fairly decent supper. In the evening, to save my eyes, the light being dim, I play solitaire and walk around the room. In bed at 22:00.*

Weeks and months passed. Only in mid-March 1918 Piłsudski learned that Ola Szczerbińska gave birth (on 7 February) to her first daughter. In a letter to her, dated on 18 March, he wrote the following:

It is rather amusing that on the night of 7-8 March, I dreamed of you. You said to me that I must lie down, while in a neighboring room a child was crying ... I am very sorry that I am not with you now. It must be strange, to see how a baby is born. To date, I had nothing to do with something like that. ... Tomorrow is my name day. If you want to send me a present, send me two decks of cards for solitaire. The ones I have are very worn. I read more now, including some French books. ... The packages come through, but I don't know from whom, so I don't know who to thank.

Of the many letters Piłsudski sent to Alesandra Szczerbińska, only a few got to her.

I am very grateful even for the smallest bits of information about the child. ... For example, in the last page from March 27 is a detail over which I have pondered for two evenings. God has given me a great deal of imagination, but it is beyond me to figure out how this poor girl "does gymnastics" and, so you write, smiles about it. Does she laugh already? As you know my mind is conservative-reactionary, so I am filled with fear that during these experiments you may twist the child's arm or leg.

Later on, he wrote that he received neither the holiday cake nor the pictures of little Wandzia (deminuative of Wanda) that were with them. He also stated that he smoked little; his health was fair, though he thought that he must undertake a cure before being able to do solid work. In May, he dreamed about his brother Bronisław, who was drowning in dark water. Only a few months later, he learned that on 17 May his brother really had drowned in the Seine (for a few years Bronisław had lived in Paris and worked in the office of the Polish National Committee).

During his long walks in the garden of the Magdeburg fortress, or in his room in the evenings, Piłsudski analyzed his experience as a leader.

For ten years I tried to penetrate the depths of leadership, into the nature of danger, as Clausewitz says, into the environment of uncertainty, and that of, as I describe it, eternal contradictions not to be resolved, that can only be cut with a sword like the Gordian knot, with the sword of command.

Thinking long and deeply on these problems, Piłsudski decided to write down his experiences during the difficult moments when the legions were involved in fighting. In the spring and summer of 1918, he had written his first two works: *Ulina Mała* and *Limanowa - Marcinkowice*. A third theme, concerning the most difficult battle among the forests and swamps of Polesie Wołynskie, he decided to leave for later. Instead, he wrote about the battles along the Vistula, Nida, and Dunajec Rivers, titled: *Nowy Korczyn – Opatowiec*. All three works were published in a book: *Moje Pierwsze Boje (My First Battles)*.

Piłsudski's isolation in Magdeburg ended in August 1918 when the German authorities brought Colonel Sosnkowski to the fortress. On 3 September Piłsudski wrote to Ola Szczerbińska, *First of all I would like to tell you that for a week now I am not alone. I have been given Sosnkowski as a companion, who helps me to while away the time. We have already been able to play out several games of chess.*

Sosnkowski described a typical day as follows.

In the morning at breakfast, we diligently study reports from the field of battle. On the walls I have hung maps, in a way becoming a chief of staff once again, where I mark the progress of the Allied Armies. After breakfast, we spend a few hours in the garden. We have spent hours walking while having a lively discussion on a wide range of topics. Speaking of the near future, the Commandant became very animated and started thinking out loud, making penetrating statements, that speculated on the future progress of an independent Poland into a world power. Engaged among nations, passing through deep wartime crises, she will start in a race to a new level of achievement, having before her several years graced by historical advantages. ... The Polish state will have every chance of becoming a bastion of strength and order in Eastern Europe.

On 4 October 1918, the Germans approached to the Western Allies in order to establish peace on the basis of the Fourteen Points formulated by United States President Woodrow Wilson. The thirteenth point addressed the necessity for rebuilding an independent Polish state, with access to the sea. The situation of Germany and Austro-Hungary was becoming catastrophic. During the attempt to find some stable solution in the Polish Kingdom, they remembered the Polish leaders imprisoned at Magdeburg.

According to Sosnkowski, in the first days of November 1918, a guard ran up to the prisoners during their daily walk. He showed them a copy of the weekly *Die Woche*. In it was a large photograph of the Commandant, with the caption, General Piłsudski. From the accompanying article, it appeared that Piłsudski was the new commander-in-chief of the Polish Amy.

On the next day, Count Harry Kessler,[54] communications officer of the German general staff, arrived at the Magdeburg fortress. The Commandant made his acquaintance during the battles in Wołyń. He brought an offer where the prisoners would be freed on condition that they promise cooperation with the German authorities. *Non possumus,* said Piłsudski. *Keep me in prison, but in this situation, I will make no promises.*

During the night of 7-8 November 1918, the council of ministers in Berlin decided to free Piłsudski and Sosnkowski unconditionally. The representative of the German government (Kessler) came to Magdeburg on the morning of 8 November and informed the prisoners that they are to accompany him to Berlin. He wrote in his report, *Piłsudski walked beside me in his old worn soldier's coat, with a blanket over his shoulder, slightly stooped, serious, and deep in thought.*

After arriving in Berlin and some initial conversations, Piłsudski and Sosnkowski were invited to breakfast at an elegant restaurant on the Unter den Linden.[55] The Polish situation, from the German point of view, was presented by Prince Hatzfeld. The atmosphere during breakfast was awkward or simply false. Talks were interrupted when Prince Hatzfeld was repeatedly called to the telephone. After several such calls, he explained that a revolution had broken out in Berlin and that Piłsudski and Sosnkowski should immediately leave for Warsaw.

At some little station, already on Polish territory, Piłsudski spotted a fiddler surrounded by a group of listeners. Later he said:

And imagine, he was playing his fiddle and singing our "First Brigade" song. The words of this proud Polish song gave me strength and unusual encouragement. I thought that apparently my work had survived and lives, since it became part of the repertoire of a travelling fiddler.

A recruiting poster for the Legion

Józef Piłsudski at breakfast in the company of J. Stachiewicz, T. Kasprzycki, Downarowicz, Sławek, and Wieniawy-Długoszowski

Józek Piłsudski during the war – (left) taken November 20, 1916 and (right) in 1917

The Supreme Command of the POW in the field before Warsaw in 1917. Standing on the left: Karol Krzewski, Tadeusz Kasprzycki, Bogusław Miedziński, Janusz Gąsiorowski, Józef Piłsudski, Jan Wojsznar-Opieliński, Henryk Paszkowski, Wacław Denhof-Czarnocki, Wacław Jędrzejewicz, Sambor-Trojanowski, and Stefan Pomarański.

Chapter 10
11 November 1918 – the Day Has Arrived!

Over the doorway portal at the Hotel Lambert in Paris, which for generations was the center for the Polish émigré government, there are carved words which no Frenchman and not even many Poles could understand. "Ten Dzień Nadejdzie!" [The Day Will Come!]. It referred, of course, to *The Day* when Poland would recover its independence.

Historians and writers together emphasize, and not without basis, that the day of 11 November is more than a great date, it is a symbolic day – *that day*, which was expected and finally arrived. It should be mentioned here, that it was only in 1937 that 11 November was officially recognized as a state holiday – as Poland's Independence Day. This does not mean that the day was not celebrated earlier, nor was it forgotten as the day when Piłsudski took over as Commander-in-Chief of the Polish Army and the formal end of hostilities in the Great War of 1914-1918 took place. War continued on Polish territory for another two years, but this was a different matter. In this extended warfare, Poles participated not as subjects of occupying powers or "romantic irredentists," but as citizens of the Second Polish Republic, resurrected to independence after One hundred and twenty-three years of servitude.

Having taken note of the epic significance of the fact that Poland recovered its independence in 1918 and the enormous role played in this matter by Józef Piłsudski, one should carefully examine the events which decided the fact that 11 November achieved such importance in our history.

Countrary to what the legend tells us, Piłsudski returned to Warsaw on 10 November, not on the 11th. He was not greeted by enthusiastic crowds and no photographs were taken. The train taking Piłsudski and Sosnkowski reached the Vienna Station in Warsaw at 7am. It was fifteen minutes before the sun rose. In addition to Prince Lubomirski of the Regency Council, who was officially informed from Berlin, waiting at the station were representatives of the POW, who received this news via their intelligence service.

The POW Commander in Warsaw was Adam Koc, and here is listed a fragment of his reminiscences.

At 6:30, a car arrived with Prince Lubomirski of the Regency Council and his adjutant Captain of Horse Rostworowski. The guards let them through, and with Major Krzaczyński, I took advantage, join-

ing their company to the surprise of the regent and his adjutant. On the station platform, we introduced ourselves, and I communicated that I was the Chief Commander of POW. Prince Lubomirski was very excited and perturbed, repeating, "At last he is coming, this is good!"

It was important to me that I should be the first to greet the Commandant after he came out of the rail car. At last, the train pulled in. The Commandant came out accompanied by Colonel Sosnkowski. He was pale and worn from his imprisonment. But it was apparent that his inner strength had not left him. I went to him and said, "Citizen Commandant, in the name of the Polish Military Organization, I greet Citizen Commandant in the capital." The Commandant saluted me. Prince Lubomirski led him to his car. I also boarded that car. The regent repeated several times, "At last Commandant, you have arrived, such things have been happening here, such things have been happening here!"

To fully understand the providential role that Piłsudski played at this time, one must understand the drama conveyed by Lubomirski's words, *Such things have been happening here!* The authority of the Council of Regents was purely fictional. In rebellion against it was a government organized by Józef Świerzyński. In opposition to that government stood the entire left, which on 7 November created a "Provisional Government of the Polish Republic." The prime minister of this government was Ignacy Daszyński. Military matters (in the absence of Piłsudski, so in a sense based on his authority) were placed into the hands of Śmigły-Rydz.

A separate center of Polish administration was the Polish Liquidation Commission (organized on 28 October 1918 in Kraków). The German occupation administration which had over three hundred thousand Wehrmacht soldiers in the territories of the "Ober Ost" was also of importance. In fact, all of these groups were, to some extent, in revolt; but due to improper actions by the Polish authorities, the results could have led to a dangerous and unnecessary spilling of blood.

Piłsudski's part in this situation – to state it once again – turned out to be providential and impossible to overvalue. After a breakfast with Prince Lubomirski at the "Frascati," Piłsudski went to the apartment on Moniuszko Street, which had been rented for him. There was no time for rest; in front of the building, a large crowd started to gather awaiting a pronouncement by the "Commandant." Piłsudski went out onto the balcony and gave his first official speech.

Citizens! Warsaw greets me for the third time. I believe we will see each other many times and under happier circumstances. I have always served and will serve with my life and blood for the Homeland and for the Polish people. My greeting is short, for I am stricken with a cold.

About noon, an important conference took place among the leaders of the POW. One of them was Józef Jęczkowiak – known as "Poznaniak." In the Warsaw Wehrmacht garrison, he had organized several groups of ready and determined men. On Piłsudski's orders, Jędczkowiak had these POW men gain control of the barracks on Ludna Street and in Mokotów and take over the command center at the train station. An appeal to the German soldiers was printed, with specific attention paid to Polish soldiers from Greater Poland, Silesia, and Prussia.

Immediately after the POW conference, Piłsudski met with the remaining two members of the Regency Council: Archbishop Aleksander Kakowski and Józef Ostrowski.

It was not until the afternoon that Piłsudski was able to go to Praga and see Aleksandra Szczerbińska and his daughter Wanda. Before the house at 25 Mińska Street, where they lived, a crowd began to form, which cheered the Commandant.

In Piłsudski's close circle, it was considered important that he visit Lublin, and then Kraków, where the largest Legion forces were stationed. The Commandant did not share this view. Warsaw was the nation's capital, and from there, one must make decisions.

Near midnight, a delegation from the German Soldiers' Council (Soldatenrat) came to see Piłsudski. They declared that the Soldatenrat is in command over the German forces in Warsaw and asked Piłsudski, as the commander-in-chief of the Polish Army, to guarantee their safe passage to Germany. Piłsudski answered that this will be possible on condition that they surrender their arms. The negotiations with the soldiers did not end that night.

Next morning, the streets were white with snow, and the morning sunrise seemed to be brighter than ever before. Soon, news reached them that all the warring powers have decided to suspend hostilities on 11 November. German soldiers appearing on the streets were immediately disarmed by members of the POW. The PPS organized a great demonstration during which many slogans were shouted, but most frequently the name of Piłsudski was chanted. The demonstration moved toward Moniuszko Street, where the Commandant was staying.

A delegation which he received in the apartment, declared support. Tadeusz Szturm de Sztrem,[56] pointing to the red banner that he was

101

carrying, said: *In the action of being the fighting arm of the PPS, we continue the fighting tradition. Take this banner and stand with it at the head of the Polish nation.* But Piłsudski answered: *I cannot carry the symbol of one party, my duty is to act in the name of the entire nation.* The momentary embarrassment was dispelled by the same Tadeusz, who then asked Piłsudski to step out on the balcony and greet the workers of Warsaw. Piłsudski did not refuse this request. Everyone went out onto the balcony. The red banner waved over Piłsudski's head, and though he did not take it into his hands, it testified that former comrade Wiktor had not broken his ideological connection with the socialists.

"Long live Piłsudski, Piłsudski, Piłsudski!" cheered the crowd. The echoes of this event no doubt reached the Regency Council, which after 5 pm, following a lengthy debate, decided to give Piłsudski command of the armed forces and make him commander-in-chief. He was entrusted with the mission of forming a national government. On that same historic day of 11 November, the Commandant gave his first order to the entire Polish Army, over which he now took command. Calling attention to the harmful heterogeneous composition of the Polish Army, he asked the soldiers and officers to eliminate any differences, frictions, cliques, and intolerances.

An important matter was to avoid any armed conflict with the German armed forces that were stationed in Poland. There were about eigthy thousand troops, with over thirty thousand in Warsaw itself. In this matter, he issued a proclamation, in which he announced that he had taken over as commander-in-chief over the Polish armed forces, and that the occupation of Poland was now ended. The German soldiers were to leave Poland and their departure was to take place in total order, with Polish society maintaining composure, reason, and peace.

On 12 November, the chief representatives of the Lublin based Provisional Government arrived in Warsaw, together with members from parties that formed its body. At a meeting that took place on Szpitalna Street, Piłsudski explained his assessment of the situation. In public, he did not repeat his critiques, which he had earlier voiced to Śmigły-Rydz, speaking bluntly that: *you should rather watch chickens, than create policy*, but he mockingly characterized the significance and function of the Lublin government, casting doubts on the power and significance of the parties supporting that government, as well as the professionalism of its ministers. *Outside the parties, there is the greater part of the nation, and a minister of the post office has to have a greater knowledge of its function beyond the experience of having glued on a few stamps.* The meeting did not resolve anything, and it became a reason for the leftist politicians to organize a strike in support of their government and demonstrate on the streets of Warsaw.

"Long live Daszyński! Long Live Piłsudski! Long live the people's government!" were the slogans shouted by the demonstrators as they marched from Saski Square to Krakowskie Przedmiescie, reaching the Royal Palace. In the great enthusiasm of the crowd, a red banner was waved, perhaps the same one which Piłsudski would not accept. The workers' demonstrations could not save the Lublin government, but without doubt contributed to the progression of events and placed pressure on the Regency Council. In effect, among much consternation, the Council dissolved itself on 14 November, with a final decree that read: *We place our responsibilities and duty toward the Polish nation into the hands of Józef Piłsudski.*

Having full authority and the confidence of the Polish people, Piłsudski issued a statement, entrusting the mission of forming a government to Ignacy Daszyński. He added the assurance that the government must be composed of professionals who have the nation's confidence, that elections for the Legislative Assembly will be organized as quickly as possible, and social reforms will be enacted. It is undoubtedly characteristic that in his statement, Piłsudski did not mention the decree of the Regency Council but relied on actual circumstances, which obligated him to make decisions about the most important matters concerning the re-establishment of the Polish state.

Recognizing the necessity of Poland taking part in international relations, Piłsudski sent the following letter to all the powers that took part in the Great War, as well as to the neutral countries.

As the Commander-in-Chief of the Polish Army, I wish to notify the warring and neutral governments and nations that an independent Polish State has come into being, uniting all the areas of Poland. The political situation in Poland and the burden of occupation did not allow the Polish nation to freely have a say about its fate. Thanks to changes which have occurred thanks to the victories of the Allied forces, the independence and sovereignty of Poland are an accomplished fact. The Polish state arises from the will of its people and bases itself on democratic principles. The Polish government will replace the force that for one-hundred-forty years decided the fate of Poland. Depending on the Polish Army under my command, I trust that no other army will cross into Poland, unless we formally permit it to do so. I am convinced that the great democracies of the West will lend their brotherly assistance and support the Polish Commonwealth that has been reborn as an independent country.

Polish independence, whose recovery is linked to the date of 11 November 1918, was not given by the act of a foreign power but was born of the struggles and efforts over many generations. The providential role and greatness of Józef Piłsudski was based in the fact that he turned out to be the only leading Polish politician who had prestige among both the left and the right. Poles were united around Piłsudski and the Council of Ministers, together with the mood of public opinion – on city streets as well as under the thatched roofs of village homes.

Chapter 11
Creation of a Government, Borders, but Mainly an Armed Force

The mission of creating a coalition government, entrusted to Ignacy Daszyński, was not successful, because personal matters created too much controversy. As a compromise, a government was created under the leadership of Jędrzej Moraczewski.[57] The first official act of this government was a decree dated 22 November 1918, which made Józef Piłsudski the Provisional Head of State, the highest office of the Polish Republic.

On his second day in office, Piłsudski introduced a law creating an eight-hour day, and a forty-six-hour week. This was a law precursory to that which would become normal in contemporary Europe. Setting a goal of having the Sejm (Parliament)[58] meet as quickly as possible, Piłsudski signed a decree on 26 November, concerning the election rules and the date when voting would take place. This was set for 26 January 1919.

In this incredibly short time, conditions for shaping a democratically elected government were created. During this period, Piłsudski showed extraordinary energy, strength of will, and great political dexterity. With his prestige, he held in check the liberated passions of the various political parties in the name of the greater good, which was the newly regained independence. Though he had dictatorial powers, he did not use them. He would hear everyone out with a great deal of patience. Later he said, "I spoke with hundreds of persons, with representatives of various territories, organizations, societies, interests, ... Each said that they represented the entire nation, everyone wanted to have their own government, everyone threatened that they would obey no other."

Between 5 - 10 December 1918, Piłsudski conducted a series of negotiations with Stanisław Grabski[59] of the Polish National Committee. For over a year, this committee was active in Paris and had the recognition of the Allied Nations. A large part of this committee thought that on this basis, they could usurp the power to represent all Poles. Stanisław Grabski would later complain of Piłsudski "that the mainly one-party oriented nature of Moraczewski's government worked against national unity." Piłsudski was to have replied that he considered this government "a protective inoculation of Poland," which was necessary in the face of the "revolutionary ferment" which was rasing its ugly head nearby, especially in Russia and Germany.

Despite numerous differences in views on the forms and methods of restoring Polish statehood, a consensus was reached as to the possibility and necessity of cooperation between all the political parties. Piłsudski expressed readiness to recognize the Committee as the official body that would represent Poland in negotiations with the Allied Powers, in return for giving recognition to the government that was installed in Warsaw. A letter which he wrote to Dmowski on 21 December 1918, in Przemyśl started with the words: "Dear Roman," and contained the following formulations.

I would like to ask you that you do everything to make the negotiations easier. Please believe me, that above all I wish to avoid having a duplication in Poland's representation with the Allies ... Based on our old acquaintanceship, I hope that in this instance and at such a pivotal moment at least a few people – if not all of Poland – can rise above the interest of parties, cliques, and groups. I would like to see you, dear Sir, among those people.

Overworked and absorbed in organizing the military, Piłsudski moved steadily forward, ready to make concessions and unbending only when it came to matters of the highest import to the rebirth of the state. As a result of his efforts, which found recognition in France, at the end of 1918, Ignacy Paderewski[60] arrived in Poland as the official representative of the Paris Committee. A common concern for the future of Poland and the dislike that both leaders had for party factionalism led to a compromise solution. On 16 January 1919, the Head of State dissolved Moraczewski's cabinet and entrusted the mission of forming a government to Ignacy Paderewski.

Elections to the Sejm went according to the plan, and on 26 January 1919, two hundred and ninety-six deputies were elected. The largest group of votes was received by the right, which had forty percent of the representatives. After a supplementary election, which could take place in Greater Poland only on 1 June 1919, the representatives of the right were further augmented. At that time, Piłsudski's persona was identified with the left, but his eventual conflict with the right appeared to be inevitable. Before the elections, the authority of the Provisional Head of State was generally unquestioned.

On 10 February at 11:15 AM, the newly elected Sejm started its first gathering. Opening the session, Piłsudski stated:

During the great upheaval when millions of people are resolving disputes only with force and violence, I want to create a situation that in our Homeland those necessary and unavoidable social disputes should be resolved by democratic means with the help of laws legis-

lated by representatives chosen from the nation. This main task of my administration was not easy to complete. It is not easy to keep order among a raging storm, among the general insecurity and shakiness of institutions created by men. It was not easy to maintain a balance while governing without sufficient material and technical resources – governing during a war that erupted on all of our borders. There- fore, I consider this a pleasant duty to praise with gratitude the work of those who have made this difficult task easier and assisted me in completing it with success.

On 20 February 1919, at the third session of the Sejm, Piłsuds- ki read a declaration in which he resigned from the post of Provisional Head of State. At that same session, the Speaker of the Sejm, Wojciech Trąmpczyński, announced that he received a resolution from the depu- ties: Daszyński, Korfanty,[61] and Witos,[62] along with several hundred sig- natures from other deputies representing all societies and parties. The first article of this resolution accepted the declaration and expressed thanks to Piłsudski. The second article granted him continuance in per- forming the office of Head of State and described the principles on which he should base his administration. These principles were ratified by the Sejm and called the "Little Constitution." They were as follows:

1. Sovereign and legislative power in the Polish State is based in the Sejm. Resolutions are proclaimed by the Speaker of the Sejm with countersignature of the President of the Ministers, and that of the appropriate corresponding minister.
2. The Head of State is the representative of the State and its highest executive for resolutions of the Sejm in civil and military matters.
3. The Head of State establishes the government in its full assembly, on the basis of agreement with the Sejm.
4. The Head of State and the government are responsible before the Sejm for exercising their offices.
5. Each act of the government made by the Head of State requires the signature of the appropriate minister.

The above listed principles of the "Little Constitution" limited, in a basic way, the authority of Piłsudski. His fate and the fate of the Pol- ish State now depended to a great extent on the Sejm. But the Sejm was fragmented and quarrelsome, containing a large number of competing factions and political parties, all of which was not conducive to fruitful cooperation.

Piłsudski expressed his doubts and worries, which concerned also his own personal qualities, after accepting the resolution concerning his continuance in the post of Head of State.

Deeply moved, I thank you gentlemen for this honor and this resolution, through which you have again entrusted this authority to me, just after I had returned it into your hands. I consider this a great reward for my hard, sometimes very hard, work of my entire life ... However, I cannot hide the fact that this resolution stands in direct opposition with my most heartfelt plans and intentions. I believe that with my active nature, I will admit openly to my faults, one of which is stubbornness – my Lithuanian stubbornness, and my comparatively small willingness to make concessions in complicated, difficult, and especially irritating political matters. Therefore, I am ill-fitted to execute this office, which is primarily of political character. I had intended to devote all my power and full energy into military matters only. As a soldier, I stand in obedience in face of your resolution, in which you represent the entire Homeland. I accept this office, which you have decided to bequeath to me. I am counting in your confidence to help me in lifting this great load, which you have placed upon my shoulders. I want to believe – my dear sirs – that together with the Sejm, I will finish to execute this testament, that our forbearers groaning under oppression, have bestowed to us. We have created an independent and free Poland. Poland longs to see the final word in this testament fulfilled – that Poland truly be united. I want to believe that with the assistance of the Sejm, we will be able to complete this matter with triumph and glory for Poland.

The Commander-in-Chief surrounded by members of the first government of the Polish Republic in Warsaw 21 December 1918. Seated from the left: Leon Wasilewski, Leon Supiński, Józef Piłsudski, Ksawery Prauss, premier Jędrzej Moraczewski, Stanisław Thugutt. Standing from the left: Tomasz Nocznicki, Stanisław Stączek, Jerzy Iwanowski, Franciszek Woyda, Błażej Stolarski, Jan Wroczyński, Antoni Minkiewicz, Franciszek Wójcik, Medard Downarowicz, Marian Malinowski, Tomasz Arciszewski, Bronisław Ziemięcki.

Józef Piłsudski reviewing new recruits, 1919

Head of State with the President of the Council of Ministers – Ignacy Paderewski, 10 July 1919.

The Head of State with the Primate, Cardinal Krakowski, and the then Papal Nuncio in Poland, Achille Ratti (later Pope Pius XI), 1919.

Chapter 12
Federation or Incorporation?

In the camps that tried to create a program for the Polish state, two opposing concepts were vying for primacy: incorporation, backed by the National Democrats, and federation, promoted by Piłsudski and his supporters.

The concept of incorporation consisted of including within Polish territory the greatest amount of land from the former Polish Commonwealth, assuming that the people living there who might have been Germanized, Russified, or denaturalized, would undergo gradual Polonization within the restored state. The problem of nationalities on the territory of the former Polish Commonwealth were complicated not only by Germanization and Russification that took place during the one hundred and twenty-three years that Poland had been partitioned. During the nineteenth century, the modern national awareness of the Lithuanians, Ukrainians, and Byelorussians started to mature. In the eastern reaches of the Commonwealth, a large percentage of the population was composed of Jews, who as a part of the Russian anti-Jewish campaign of pogroms, were resettled into those territories from all over Tsarist Russia.

Dmowski, the main ideologue of the National Democrats, stated in his debate with Piłsudski that: "If we are to talk about a strong state, then we cannot utter the word 'federation.' Federation means weakness, it is not strength, especially when there is no one with whom to federate."

The federal programs appeared in several versions and were deeply rooted in the Polish tradition of the post-partition period. Piłsudski's federalism was closely and directly linked to his attitude toward Russia. "Russia must be cut apart along the national seams; the Russian Empire must be split apart into its constituent parts, and the nations that have been forcibly incorporated into it must become autonomous."

The question "federation or incorporation" was not merely a theoretical inquiry. The final answer was eventually reached not only at the negotiating tables and as part of plebiscites, but also through armed confrontations. In Eastern Galicia, the Poles were fighting a Ukrainian faction who tried to occupy Lwów. The Czechs suddenly made a foray into Cieszyn-Silesia. At the end of December 1918, the Greater Poland[63] Uprising had started.

On 28 June 1919, the victorious Allies ended the Great War when defeated Germany signed the Versailles Treaty. The treaty obligated Germany to return the occupied territories of Greater Poland and Gdańsk Pomerania to Poland; while the dispositions of Upper Silesia, Warmia, Masuria, Cieszyn-Silesia, Spisz, and Orawa were to be decided through plebiscites. The Versailles Treaty totally omitted any mention of Poland's eastern borders. This was the logical consequence of the fact that neither Russia, nor any of the nations that have appeared or tried to arise in that part of Europe, did not participate in the negotiations at Versailles.

Piłsudski thought that in Poland's enlightened self-interest, she should establish her borders to her advantage, maintaing a permanent separation from Russia (actual ethnic Russia) with a band of countries, who because of their proximity to Russia would be Poland's natural allies. Piłsudski's program for establishing Poland's eastern borders was summed up in two statements:

1. Liberate the territories from the force and domination of Russia.
2. Give the local populations a chance to decide on their future and on the form of organization for national existence.

To Piłsudski, there appeared to be a real possibility of recreating, on a new basis, the union that once included Poland, Lithuania, and Byelorussia. If this union were to take place, Piłsudski would not object leaving certain territories to Lithuania that had a Polish population, including Vilnius. *Everyone wants Vilnius*, he said. *I want to make it an object of unity, not of dispute.* There was a general conviction in Poland that without an armed confrontation with Russia, the eastern borders would not be settled. This was a natural consequence of the public opinion about the Bolshevik Revolution. The general distaste for the terror did not blind the Poles, to the extent that they would wish to see to see a reborn Russia which would try to retain its borders from 1914, and thus deny independence to nations that had been in its grasp. The western allies who supported the anti-Bolshevik forces had no intention of supporting this part of Polish policy.

In July 1919, General Tom Briggs, head of the English military mission, arrived in Warsaw. He tried to persuade the Polish military authorities to assist Anton Denikin,[64] who at the time managed to score several victories against the Bolsheviks. In 1900, when Piłsudski, a dangerous individual, was imprisoned in the 10th Pavilion of the Warsaw Citadel, the same Denikin was a staff officer with the rank of captain. His political convictions had not undergone any changes since that time. Piłsudski would not consent to cooperate with Denikin, because in addition to the fact that there was a chance the counterrevolutionaries would win, he considered the imperialism of the Whites to be as dangerous as the internationalism of the Reds.

One forum where there was interchange among Estonia, Finland, Lithuania, Latvia, and Poland was the Warsaw conference in February 1920 where representatives from these countries had a chance to share views. During deliberations, Piłsudski announced that he could not imagine entering into any kind of treaty with Russia before he had reached understandings with the affected nations in this part of Europe.

Poland's negotiations with Soviet Russia (led by Julian Marchlewski) dragged on for many months but brought no results. The Polish side gave evidence of good will by refusing to assist the Whites, but the Bolsheviks would not fulfill even the more general conditions for peace, such as: ceasing propaganda aimed at Polish soldiers, leaving Symon Petliura[65] in peace, and returning Dyneburg to Latvia.

Piłsudski thought that under these conditions, he could not establish a peace with the Bolsheviks, because it would have been a very shaky armistice. He had a low opinion of Leon Trotsky,[66] as a typical doctrinaire communist agitator.

> *The truly dangerous individual is Lenin. In his brand of Marxism, he is flexible and cunning. He can compromise on a temporary basis, and then back up and wait. Apparently, his favorite reading is Clausewitz.[67] Putting Clausewitz and Marx together is dangerous. ... Poland must be ready to slap him on the hands as soon as possible, as long as these hands are still weak. ... Lloyd George[68] himself would bless our march on Moscow, but our road does not lead there. Their sensitive point is Kiev – Ukraine. They would not dare to ignore the threat that an independent Ukraine would present to them and would have to go into full action. Lenin is an extreme opportunist; every compromise, every shady deal, he considers perfectly allowable and even necessary. He will break all the agreements and alignments, when it is convenient for him, and in addition will accuse his partners that they had gone back on their word. The international community does not understand the Russian situation and knows nothing about men such as Lenin.*

In the above quoted opinion, Piłsudski was very penetrating, but also very much alone. This opinion could only be accepted by the Russian social revolutionaries (Boris Savinkov and Nicholas Czajkowski) with great difficulty, even though they came to Warsaw as delegates of the Russian National Committee. They were supplicants not potentates of the Russian autocracy. Poland's Commander-in-Chief declared that he was ready to give military assistance to the anti-Bolsheviks, but Russia would have to constitute a democratic government which would then recognize not only an independent Poland, federated with Lithuania and Byelorussia, but also an independent Ukraine. Piłsudski said: *The will of the nations occupied by us is a dominant factor for me. For nothing on earth would I want to have a Poland in whose possession are territories inhabited by people who consider themselves our enemies.*

Piłsudski considered the creation of an army as one of the most important and necessary tasks for the reconstituted Polish state. On 1 November 1918, when he became commander and head of the military, he had about fifty thousand soldiers in the Polish Military Organization, thirty-five hundred legionaries, a little over seven thousand men in formations in the Austrian zone of partition, and a few thousand soldiers from the army formerly commanded by Dowbor-Muśnicki.[69]

Following the line of least resistance, most politicians, and especially the higher rank officers, thought that the problem of organizing the army should be solved by announcing a general mobilization as quickly as possible. Piłsudski was categorically opposed to such ideas, because he decided that without having uniform cadres, and not having them imbued with the same spirit, the newly mobilized recruits will not be able to create the military force that independent Poland needed. The commander was mindful that the newly organized army should be based on well trained volunteers, on cadres tested in the POW, in the Legions, and other units that were connected to the independence movement.

On 15 November 1918, the commander gave an order to mobilize the POW. During several weeks, nearly sixty thousand persons reported to the ranks – adequately trained and full of patriotic fervor. At the end of November 1918, Poland had an army of one hundred thousand at its disposal. On 15 January 1919, the first voluntary recruitment was announced. In February of 1919, the size of the Polish army exceeded one hundred sixty thousand.

The conditions under which independent Poland's armed forces were formed reflect the orders that Piłsudski personally composed. It is characteristic and worthy of note that no commander-in-chief in the world wrote such orders for his soldiers. The form and content of these orders were devoid of the then universal military routine and resembled more letters written to friends. Here are a few of these orders and the dates when they were issued.

5 December 1918. *The Polish Army is being formed under unusual and difficult conditions. The armies of the three partitioning powers were crushed under the burden of war and defeat. ... We must undertake this work with full understanding of the new conditions and*

the deep changes which society is going through. We cannot take the road of routines and habits that we have inherited from five differing armies. The deep psychic change has outpaced the limited assortment of techniques that we have from those now fallen armies. But we must achieve effectiveness and discipline in an army. ... I require work that is directed toward making each soldier voluntarily give himself over to the direction of his officers. There are no regulations or principles for doing this. Most important is the strong and decisive will in the officer's character. Each officer must be an example and a role model for his soldiers in fulfilling their duties. Only an officer who is first, ahead of the appointed hour, on the training and exercise field; only one who demand more of himself, can inspire and become a true leader.

28 December 1918. *In these breakthrough times, the soldier must absorb an understanding and a deep feeling for unceasing service to the nation. This means that he considers that abandonment of any position is shameful. The lofty feeling of honor, that we have from our sacred traditions, cannot be downgraded.*

1 January 1919. *Soldiers! Fifty-six years ago, our fathers and grandfathers started another action to retrieve the independence of the Homeland. They did not march in shiny uniforms, but shoeless and in rags. They had no advanced weapons, but hunting rifles and scythes, going against cannon and carbines. They conducted this war for a full year, becoming soldiers who established a high ideal in their fervor, willingness to sacrifice, and steadfastness in an uneven battle. They lost the war, and after their defeat, the bitter oppression started to corrode Polish souls. For us, the soldiers of a free Poland, those insurrectionists of 1863 are and will continue to be the soldiers of Fighting Poland and will remain as examples of many soldierly virtues which we will emulate.*

31July 1919. *Today, for the first time in a free and united Homeland, as August 6th approaches, as the oldest soldier of the present generation and the Commander-in-Chief of the Polish Armed Forces, I send to you my greetings. Whether on lonely patrol, or in an entrenched shooting position, or training at a military garrison, on this day we remember all our predecessors who had fallen on the battlefield, died in exile, or in wanderings around the world. Yet at the same time may you feel pride, that you are no longer captives of a foreign power, but free citizens of a free Homeland, called to defend her life against any attacks by enemies. Soldiers! In blood of your forefather's history was written – "She had not yet perished!" You are the fortunate ones; in your blood you write – "She lives and will not be lost!"*

In his effort to standardize the armed forces under his command, Piłsudski ordered that the old Legion units should be recreated within the army. On the basis of three brigades of cadres, it was decided to create three divisions. The restoration of the legionary units greatly increased the number of "legionaries" and at he same time served to erase and differences and animosities which during the years 1914-18 appeared in the individual brigades. The divisions absorbed not only those who remained faithful to the commandant, but those who had "broken faith" by taking the loyalty oath and serving in the Polnische Wehrmacht. In the euphoria of regained independence and in the face of new threats, old offenses were forgotten. Political differences in those units were less than in other formations. An important integrating factor was undoubtedly the great respect shown for Piłsudski as a leader.

The rapid and effective formation of an army as the defensive force for the new independent state was possible because of the engagement evidenced by Polish society, despite any political differences. The only critical voices directed at the armed forces came from the extreme left of the PPS and the communists, but these groups did not have any major influence in Poland.

In general, it can be concluded that one of the greatest historical contributions made by Józef Piłsudski was that in the space of about one year he created an army of a half-million men. This was a great, nearly unimaginable, effort by the entire nation, which was just coming out of captivity and a destructive four-year war. On 19 March 1920, Piłsudski was presented with the highest military rank and office of First Marshal of Poland.

It is worthwhile to devote some attention to the circumstances that preceded the granting of the office of Marshal to Piłsudski, because to a great degree, they characterize the alignment of political power, and also the exceptional, full of personal worth, personality of our hero.

In the summer of 1919, the General Verification Commission presented a resolution to the Sejm, proposing that Józef Piłsudski should be raised to the office of marshal. A gathering of senior members, which consisted mainly of National Democrats, dismissed this resolution as coming "too soon." Such a statement was not only unkind, but also offensive. In this situation, the Commission decided to use another method to accomplish its goal and issued a special document that contained a justification and delivered it directly to the Head of State. On the document that was given to Piłsudski on 19 March 1920, he wrote, *I accept and confirm the Office of the First Marshal*. Later, based on this, Piłsudski was accused of having appointed himself.

There were many reasons why he was not given the marshal's baton with the certificate. The last and least important reason is connected to the Napoleonic anecdote about the shortage of cannon to give the appropriate salute. In this situation, a marshal's baton simply did not exist. One had to be designed, according to old historical patterns, and then crafted. The competition was won by Mieczysław Kotarbiński – a professor of gold-crafting at the Stefan Batory University in Vilnius. This also had a symbolic significance.

Piłsudski was presented with the marshal's baton on 14 November 1920 – the first Sunday after 11 November. The ceremonies included Holy Mass on Plac Zamkowy [Castle Square], a speech by the oldest general - Trzaski-Durski, and a ceremonial presentation of the baton – from the army – by an ordinary soldier, during the cannon salute. An interesting light on the event was shed by the fact that no one from the civil government took part in the ceremony. But Polish history already had a precedent to this, for in 1648, soldiers of the army declared Jarema Wiśniowiecki as their leader and presented him with a baton.

Chapter 13
Announcing Independence and Borders of Poland

When the whirlwind of the Great War was ending, many nations and countries declared their independence. Many did not last through to the spring of 1919. Poland's announcement to the world, issued on 14 November 1918 was as follows:

> *To the President of the United States,*
> *To His Britannic Majesty's Government,*
> *To the Government of the French Republic,*
> *To the Royal Government of Italy,*
> *To the Imperial Court of Japan,*
> *To the Government of the German Reich,*
> *And to all the governing bodies of Warring and Neutral States*

> *As the Commander-in-Chief of the Polish Army, I wish to notify all the governments and nations both warring and neutral about the existence of an independent Polish State, which encompasses all the lands of united Poland.*
> *The political situation in Poland and the yoke of oppression would not allow the Polish nation to freely decide its own future. Thanks to the changes which have occurred through the brilliant victories of the Allied Armies, the renewed independence and sovereignty of Poland is now an accomplished fact.*
> *The Polish State rises as an act of will of the whole nation and is based on democratic principles. The Polish Government, a system of justice and order, will replace the rule of force which had been applied for one hundred forty years and decided the fate of Poland. Relying on the Polish Army under my command, I have hope that no other army will cross the Polish borders, unless we express our formal consent in the matter. I am convinced that the great democracies of the west will give their help and lend fraternal support to the reborn independent Polish Republic.*

> *For the Minister of Foreign Affairs*   *Commander-in-Chief*
> *Filipowicz*   *Piłsudski*

The fundamental difficulty was that the new independent state, which arose through its own efforts, had no stable and recognized borders. To count on the justice of the world powers to guarantee such would have been naïve. On 28 November 1918, Józef Piłsudski, as Head of State, created the Polish Navy.

As with other plans and projects, Piłsudski's ideas had many opponents. When a situation was difficult, in place of physical power, good ideas and political solutions were required. Piłsudski was accused of indifference in the case of Polish representation in the west, of sluggishness in the matter of Lwów, of supporting the Bolsheviks, and simultaneously, of imperialistically grabbing land in the east. But one matter where Piłsudski received the most criticism was his policy on the matter of Poland's borders.

The facts regarding Poland's borders in the Autumn of 1918 were as follows:

On 15 October, Poland's representatives in the Austro-Hungarian Parliament issued a declaration on the matter of national identity that identified them as citizens of an independent Polish State.

On 20 October, a mass demonstration by the inhabitants of Vilnius promoted the notion that Lithuania should join with Poland, in accordance to the ideas of Woodrow Wilson. The German authorities used the armed force which led to a massacre among the protesting crowds.

On 27 October, to a general rally of Silesians in Cieszyn, fifty thousand inhabitants of Silesia turned out and unanimously proclaimed the legalization of a National Council, empowering it to act on behalf of joining Silesia to Poland. Galician Ukrainians, taking advantage of Austrian assistance, proclaimed a West-Ukrainian State.

On 30 October, the Liquidation Commission in Kraków took over administration of Western Małopolska [Little Poland] from Austrian authorities: Count Bening, Colonel Grimm, Colonel Morawski, and Captain Duszanek. At 4:00 pm, they signed a document turning over the city to Poles, and command to Brigadier Roja. On the same day, the National Council in Cieszyn issued a manifesto addressed to the Silesian people, proclaiming the incorporation of the Cieszyn Principality into Poland. The commander of the Ukrainian Rifle Unit, Captain Witowski, set the date for turning over Lwów to the Ukrainians when the Polish Liquidation Committee arrived from Kraków on 1 November.

On the next day (31 October), before the Czechs and Germans could execute their plan, Polish soldiers from the Austrian Army, headed by Matusiak, Bartczak, Skrzypek, and Hellstein disarmed the Austrian garrison in Cieszyn. Full control was taken over by the Poles.

General Bolesław Roja (1876-1940) gave the first military order at the Polish command in Kraków, calling on the senior Polish officers to take over command from the Austrians in Małopolska. Members of the POW and Polish Military Cadres, at a meeting with Major Śniadowski, decided to make armed opposition to the attempt of the Ukrainian National Council to take over Polish Lwów.

It is an absurd accusation leveled at Piłsudski that he was indifferent to the fate of Lwów and did not give the city rapid and effective assistance. On 16 November, Piłsudski sent his order, addressed to Generals Głogowski and Roja in Kraków, describing the conditions for the relief of Lwów. In it he wrote:

> *Attempt to move ahead to the east, securing Przemyśl, so that communications with Lwów may be maintained. Further – spread the rumor that you are but the advance guard, and behind you follows a strong force that will occupy Lwów.*

In connection to the accusations that he did not care about assisting Lwów, Piłsudski gave an interview to the press in which he revealed the base for Polish forces that will act in the defense of Lwów was Western Galicia, and that on 20 November a relief force under General Karaszewicz-Tokarzewski[70] had already reached Lwów and joined the Polish units there, starting its victorious action on 21 November.

The newspapers in Lwów published the following: *The Commander-in-Chief, concerned about the integrity of Polish territory, could not devote all his efforts exclusively to our city. Yet only a month later, on December 21st, 1918, he came to Lwów and inspected the (Zielona Rogatka) rifle pits of the 3rd battalion of the 1st regiment of the Lwów Riflemen. Later, he visited a sector manned by the 5th regiment of the Legions, visiting the most advanced positions.*

Equally unfair, as in the matter of Lwów, were accusations leveled at Piłsudski regarding the Greater Poland Uprising and the Silesian Uprisings. On 22 November, in Warsaw, representatives of the NRL [German Council] concluded their discussions with the Polish Head of State, who for rather obvious reasons, wanted to avoid open conflict with the Germans, but declared unofficially to help the Greater Poland Uprising. The

General Staff recommended forming Greater Poland Regiments in areas which bordered on the former Polish Kingdom.

The successes which the Greater Poland insurrectionists achieved in fighting for their freedom during the final days of December 1918 did not end the Uprising. The toughest battles, which had the support of the Warsaw government and decided the inclusion of Greater Poland into the borders of the Second Polish Republic, took place in the first months of 1919. It was then that Józef Piłsudski turned to the commanders of the Greater Poland Uprising to clarify the situation.

The official document which described the extent of the Uprising was a report written by Major Stanisław Taczka and sent to the General Staff in Warsaw on 6 January. It contained the following: *On Tuesday, January 7, there is to be a meeting of the mixed military commission which will discuss the matters of normalizing relations with the Regency in Bydgoszcz. The Germans have demanded control of the Torun-Bydgoszcz-Piła-Krzyż rail line, basing it on the necessity for demobilizing the army and transporting the soldiers from the former "Oberost." We have established a minimal line of defense on the Notec River and the Bydgoszcz Canal, in the west along the Zbąszyński Lakes.*

On the same day, Piłsudski, as Head of State and Commander-in-Chief, working with the Commissariat of the Main Peoples Council in Poznań, designated General Dowbór-Muśnicki as the military leader of the Greater Poland Uprising. In reality, the general only took over after ten days had passed. It was not without some significance during the entire Greater Poland Uprising that Piłsudski's man, Lt. Colonel Julian Stachiewicz,[71] was the Chief of Staff for the Greater Poland Army from the very beginning.

Piłsudski also took an active part in all three of the Silesian Uprisings: 1919, 1920, and 1921; though this was done without alerting the Germans. The diplomatic, as well as the physical battle for Silesia to be part of Poland, was waged from the first days after the Great War ended. In August of 1919, the Polish population of Silesia reached for arms without prompting. This fight ended without a military success, but it showed the potential of the Poles and their determination.

From February 1920, a Combined Allied Plebiscite Commission was active in Upper Silesia, consisting of representatives from France, England, and Italy.

Taking advantage of Polish setbacks in the war with Bolshevik Russia, the Germans were cooperating with the Polish Communists who were openly preparing a putsch, with the purpose of eliminating all Polish national aspirations in Silesia. The signal for the Germans to intervene was to be news that the Bolsheviks had taken Warsaw. Yet this news was slow in coming, but during 15-16 August 1920, some German fighting gangs appeared in several cities in Upper Silesia to terrorize the Poles. Under these conditions, fighting started and was recorded by history as the Second Silesian Uprising.

Captain Michal Grażyński,[72] an officer closely connected with Piłsudski and the Polish Military Organization, took part in fighting off the German gangs but did not have any leadership function. Only after the Second Silesian Uprising ended, without resolving anything, was Grażyński delegated to work on the staff of the POW which operated under the official sign of the Central Organization for Physical Education. Thanks to his personality and professional expertise in organizing Military structures, Grażyński became a leading figure in this conspiratorial staff.

In January 1921, the Central Organization for Physical Education became the clandestine Command for Defense of the Plebiscite (DOP). Grażyński had the function of the deputy chief of the first department, responsible for organization and mobilization. His cooperated with people like Karol Grzeski, Rudolf Kronke, Adam Kocur, and Jan Wyglenda went well. But a conflict arose between Grażyński and Wojciech Korfanty.

During the night of 2-3 May 1921, the Third Silesian Uprising broke out. As it was well organized as well as being adequately equipped and led, it had some successes. Korfanty treated the uprising only as an element of pressure in the larger diplomatic game. Grażyński was not well disposed toward this type of game, and in a special memorandum, sent to the General Staff of the Polish Army, stressed the lack of a basis for an "understanding on paper." Grażyński was in a group of officers which on 2 June 1921, tried (against Korfanty's desires) to make Karol Grzesik the main commander of the uprising. Piłsudski, despite personal sympathies toward Grażyński, checked his activities and resolved the conflict in favor of Korfanty.

In the windows of a railway car, Ataman Semen Petliura (1879 – 1926) and the Chief of State of the Polish Republic, Józef Piłsudski. Winnica, 17 May 1920.

The Chief of State with the President of the Council of Ministers, Wincenty Witos (1874 – 1945), 1921.

Soviet Banners captured following the Battle of Warsaw in 1920.

The Chief of State with the President of the Polish Republic, Gabriel Narutowicz (1865 – 1922).

Chapter 14
Piłsudski's Eastern Policy

Piłsudski correctly surmised that in the epoch during which he lived, Polish independence was under threat from both the Germans and the Russians. But he also thought that in the case of Poland and all of Western civilization, more could be accomplished in the East. Knowing all the difficulties, he thought that it would be possible to renew the union with Byelorussia and Lithuania, and that an independent Ukraine could be an ally of Poland.

The All-Russia Executive Committee met on 13 November 1918 and canceled the "Brest Peace Treaty" signed with Germany, Austria-Hungary, Bulgaria, and Turkey from 3 March 1918. Simultaneously, the Soviet government called on the working people inhabiting the territory of the old Russian empire to "enter into a brotherly union with the workers and peasants of Russia." Far reaching assistance was announced for establishing a Soviet government in those territories. The resolution cancelling the Brest treaty and the declaration of "aid" in setting up a Soviet government, together with actual operations by the Red Army, all signified a mortal danger directed at Polish independence.

By 18 November 1918, Leon Trotsky, then the Commissar for War (March 1918 - April 1925), was voicing the need to start an offensive that would support the revolutionary movements in Western Europe. This offensive was to progress through Poland.

Trotsky said: *Through Kiev, leads the road to connect with the Austrian and Hungarian revolution, just as through Vilnius and Warsaw leads the way of joining with the German revolution. The offensive must be on all fronts. Offensive on the western front, offensive on the southern front, on all the revolutionary fronts.*

According to this announcement, at the beginning of 1919, Soviet armies started to push into the eastern territories of the old Polish Commonwealth, as well as the independent states (Finland, Estonia, Lithuania, and Latvia) which arose during that time on lands formerly held by Russia. As the German armies, often under the influence of revolutionary Soldiers' Soviets, withdrew from these territories, they mostly favored the Russians.

Józef Piłsudski understood the danger that Soviet Russia presented toward Poland very well:

By 1918, I decided, independently from others, the clear purpose for a war with the Soviets. I decided to expend all possible effort that this happen far away from places where our independent nation was forming its existence, to counteract all attempts and temptations to impose upon us a foreign system, a life that was not designed by ourselves.

After the drawn-out negotiations with the leadership of the German armies, an agreement was signed on 5 February 1919, under which the German armies were to hand over the territories they vacated to Polish forces. By occupying the territories east of Poniewieże, Vilnius, Słonim, Janów, Sarny, Owrucze, Terespol, Brest on the Bug River, Kobryń, and Skidel on the Niemen River, the Poles did not establish borders, but rather the Polish-Bolshevik front line.

On an extremely long and constantly wavering eastern front, Piłsudski established three operational groups:

1. Group North – commanded by Gen. Iwaszkiewicz
2. Group Center – commanded by Gen. Listowski
3. Group South – commanded by Gen. Śmigły-Rydz

Farther to the south, in Eastern Małopolski [Little Poland], operated units under Generals Romer [73] and Rozwadowski.[74] In an order from 14 February 1919, Piłsudski wrote:

The commanders must imbue all grades of their officers, under-officers, and soldiers with a conviction that the good of the Homeland demands their great and combined effort, so that in the span of months they organize a strong army, one which under normal conditions it takes years to create. Every officer and soldier must have the awareness that every well or badly utilized hour may decide the advantage in a future battle. ... The commanders should encourage their charges with the assurance that they are stationed in advanced positions and their low numbers do not indicate the nation's weakness, but this is due to the creation, arming and concentration of forces, ready to strike to secure Poland's borders and cover her soldiers with fame.

At this time, the front ran on the line Mosty-Różana-Berza Kartuska-Kowel-Włódzimierz Wołyński-Rawa Ruska, west of Sambor, and curved in an easterly direction toward Lwów. The first months of fighting on the Russian front were characterized by weakness on both sides. Both Russians and Poles operated with small units spread over a large landscape. The so-called "march to the west" of the Red Army often consisted of foraging for food and other necessary goods which could be liberated from those who still had them.

One of the more serious battles with the Bolsheviks took place in late February and early March of 1919. As a result, Gen. Iwaszkiewicz occupied Słonim, while Gen. Listowski took Drohiczyn, Janów, and Pińsk in Polesie. Poles also prepared to take Grodno, from which the Germans were getting ready to leave.

Piłsudski was well aware that because of the paucity of Polish forces, it was not possible to maintain an offensive along the entire length of the front, and he held back from making some attacks, despite numerous successes at the time. The Polish Army had about one hundred seventy thousand men, but only half of this number could be used on the eastern front. As a defensive line, Piłsudski designated: Niemen-Szczara-Ogiński Canal-Jasiodła-Pińsk.

In the general situation, two main goals for activity were apparent in Polish military operations: 1. In the south – settling the border with Ukraine, and 2. In the north – freeing Vilnius and the Lithuanian-Byelorussian territories from Bolshevik domination. The first goal was undoubtedly easier, but the second one, Piłsudski considered more important and urgent. He set the date for the action on 15 April 1919. The operation was maintained in the strictest secrecy. The forces designated for the Vilnius expedition were concentrated around Skrzybowce-Radziwoniszki. Piłsudski took personal command of this expedition and went to the front on 13 April. Aleksandra Piłsudska noted in her memoirs that this was an important trip, "for the personal items my husband always took with him when he went into the field, that is: a medal with the image of the Blessed Virgin of the Ostrobrama,[75] Sienkiewicz's *Potop [The Deluge]*, and Stryjkowski's *Kronika*,[76] he added a photograph of little Wandzia."

Piłsudski's plan as Commander-in-Chef depended on a simultaneous attack on Brandowicz, Nowogródek, and Lida while a cavalry group and a division of infantry were to operate autonomously and drive the Bolsheviks out of Vilnius.

On 17 April at 5:00 am, the Polish forces took Lida. The cavalry under command of Belina-Prazmowski, over one thousand sabers strong, quickly moved toward Vilnius. Worried that the slower moving infantry division under Śmigły-Rydz would interfere with the crucial factor of surprise, Belina decided to attack Vilnius with the cavalry alone. On 19 April (Holy Saturday), unseen by the enemy, the cavalry entered the city, and in a bold attack, occupied the railroad station. A train was quickly assembled and sent in the direction of Beniaków, where the Polish infantry was located.

The surprised Bolsheviks withdrew in disorder or surrendered to the Polish uhlans. But their numbers were inadequate to take over additional sections of the city. The force of the attack ebbed, while resistance from the Bolsheviks intensified. Fierce fighting went on all day long, and in some instances, it seemed as if the initial boldness of the cavalry might be the cause of their defeat. At approximately 8:00 pm, the infantry arrived, and the balance of battle shifted in favor of the Poles. The defeated Bolshevik forces withdrew in disorder. The battle for Vilnius was over.

On 21 April 1919, among universal joy and jubilation, Piłsudski arrived in Vilnius and was greeted with a great ovation. A "Te Deum" was celebrated at the cathedral. After a ceremonial mass, the victorious army marched in review. On the following day, Piłsudski issued a bulletin to all the inhabitants of the former Grand Duchy of Lithuania. *The Polish army has brought you liberation, it wants to give you a chance to resolve matters of internal organization, nationalities, and religious faiths – as you will decide for yourselves.*

After a ceremonial thanksgiving, before a painting of the Virgin Mary "who illuminates the eastern gate," those present recorded the course of events.

The Commander-in-Chief stood facing the picture, leaning on his saber ... from under his beetling brows, a heavy tear ran down to his moustache. Śmigły-Rydz's face also contorted and tears poured down his cheeks. Meanwhile, Belina bawled like a little boy.

On 28 April in Lida, Piłsudski issued an order that summed up this phase of military operations.

Soldiers! In less than two weeks, thanks to your manly efforts and bravery, you have changed the situation on Poland's eastern frontier. In less than two weeks, you have pushed back the enemy's front line by dozens of kilometers, gaining extremely important military positions such as: Lida, Baranowicze, and Mickiewicz's Nowogródek, and chiefly the country's capital: Vilnius. The enemy, beaten, is retreating in disorder. In the name of the Homeland, which sent you to defend its borderlands, gives you thanks for this work, for your soldierly efforts. You have won the Vilnius campaign, and this will remain always as another fine page in military history. All of you may be proud that you have taken part in it.

I would especially like to thank General Szeptycki, whose energy and unrelenting pressure led to the occupation of Baranowicze and Nowogródek. General Śmigły-Rydz, who despite many technical difficulties brought his division to Vilnius in time and consequently drove the enemy from the capital.

But first, I must address the action of the cavalry units commanded by Lt. Colonel Belina-Prażmowski.[77] His excellently conducted maneuver bypassed the entire enemy position in order to reach the core of the Bolshevik force, then in a bold attack, he took the city and great stores of military supplies, then held his position despite the enemy's numerical advantage until the infantry arrived. This is the most beautiful military operation of the war executed by the Polish cavalry. I thank Lt. Colonel Belina-Prażmowski and his subordinate Major Piskorow.

The Polish offensive continued, and on 28 April, Grodno was occupied. On 16 May, Święciany fell, then 13 June - Wołżyn, 1 July - Wielejka, 4 July - Mołodeczno, 6 August - Słuck, Klec, Nieswież, and Mir, on 8 August, after many hours of battle – Mińsk. Hastening forward, the Polish forces took the line of the Dźwina River, and after crossing the Berezyna, took control of Bobrujsk ad Borysów. The victorious offensive in the north had a positive effect on the remaining segments of the Polish eastern front. On 15 May, General Listowski overcame Stochód, and two days later, Stryj. At the beginning of July, Polish forces occupied Łuniniec, Sarny, Równe, Zdołbunów, Ostróg, Zwiahl, and Płoskirów.

On the Galicia front, a difficult situation played out in the Poles' favor after General Haller's forces arrived from France and went into action. Suffering heavy military losses, the Bolsheviks tired to use propaganda as a weapon. Not sparing any effort and materials, they began a world-wide campaign and used the press of Western Europe to portray themselves as "a peace-loving people" while the Polish state was practicing "degenerate imperialism" and brutally violating the fundamental rights of national sovereignty. Unfortunately, it was true that newspapers, which remained under leftist control, had a large influence over public opinion in Western Europe. They never understood the problems and relations in Eastern Europe, accepting the Soviet propaganda as "honest coin" and had no qualms about accepting hard cash in the form of Tsarist ducats which the Bolsheviks had in plenty. The workers, who through strikes, made deliveries of military supplies to the Polish forces impossible, were not paid in Russian gold, but believed in the press reports and had a well justified revulsion for war.

Piłsudski also disliked war, but outside of this dislike, he had the awareness that unless Russian armies were defeated, there would be no peace in Eastern Europe. He stated this on 12 October 1919, at the reopening of Vilnius University after a nine-year hiatus. *Without freedom, noble souls are bound to a wheel of torture, but the weaker ones are tossed on the waste-heap of debasement.*

It should be stressed that while Piłsudski was a relentless foe of Russian imperialism, he did not think that she should be excluded from the European polity. Russia was dangerous as the "jailor of oppressed nations," but a Russia that would resign its imperialistic habits and ambitions should be supported. It was obvious that in the years 1919-1920, such a Russia did not exist, and this situation could only be achieved by force. The things that Piłsudski proposed were doable, had the Western States decided to understand the situation and give Poland the necessary support and abandon attempts to restore Russia within the borders from 1914.

If one examines the concepts of a federation, advanced by Piłsudski, one must realize that these were all subordinate to the overreaching principle of freedom – freedom for all. The principles of a Federation, if it is not only a ploy used in a political game of pretense and hypocrisy, must include the right to create separate independent states, for this is the irrevocable right of all peoples, in all territories, where they constitute a majority.

Unfortunately, even today, this matter remains unresolved. After the breakup of the USSR, it seemed that the West, especially the United States of America, decided to support the creation of a strong Central-Eastern Europe, with an independent Poland and Ukraine. One may consider that these fears were justified, because after the terror attack on New York on 11 September 2001, faith in reasonable, just, and far seeing plans of Western international policy was seriously damaged. In the difficult war with terrorism, a great temptation, difficult for the USA to overcome, was a new Russia - not one that would be restructured on principles of respect for the rights of all nations to be independent – but one which Vladimir Putin is attempting to rebuild – a Russia that would continue the traditions of White and Red tsarism.

Chapter 15
A Choice Between the White and Red Empires

A problem exists and, as it appears, even at present, has not been consigned to history. At the beginning of the third millennium, as it was after the First and Second World War, one must see the matter with awareness – awareness of the White and Red Russia and awareness of the West. On these matters, Piłsudski was and still remains a master and visionary in these problems, and we can learn much from him.

It is an indisputable fact that the second half of 1919 was a very difficult time for the Bolsheviks - bordering on total disaster. The volunteer army under command of Gen. Anton Denikin[78] took Charków, Carycyn (later Stalingrad-Volgograd), Woroneż, Kursk, and Orzeł, coming within reach of Moscow. In addition to Denikin other counter-revolutionary generals of White Russia were achieving successes, notably Gen. Nikolai Judenicz, who was moving up on Petersburg. The western allies were under the supposition that the Bolshevik revolt would soon be suppressed. There was a common belief that a Greater Russia would return to the family of allied powers and, even without a Tsar, be able to restore its former status and be a solid anti-German partner helping to set the balance of power in Europe.

The generals of the White armies were as optimistic as the western politicians, but even more arrogant on the question of Poland. Denikin demanded that the Poles start an immediate offensive, maintaining a stand for an "undivided Russia within the 1914 borders." *For help in defeating the Bolsheviks*, he wrote in his messages, *we will give up not a handful of Russian soil*. As for Poland, he made an "exception" and generously offered to rebuild an "independent" Poland, strictly allied to Russia, within the borders of the former Congress Kingdom. He also demanded that the territory east of the Bug River, occupied by Polish forces, be administered "in the name of Russia under Russian symbols of state." The inference drawn from this statement was noted by General Marian Kukiel[79] - "Piłsudski would have to return the double-headed eagle to Vilnius and appoint a governor in the name of a future Russia."

Taking into account the weariness and slimness of Polish forces, there was no possibility or sense to widen the offensive action, whose bright beginning was the Vilnius expedition. In August 1919 the entire Polish front line stabilized, encompassing the western part of Podole and Wołyń up to Słucz, with Berezyna and Dźwina at the northern end.

During his stay in Mińsk, September 1919, Piłsudski met with delegations of White-Russian, Polish, and Jewish inhabitants. Among other things he stated:

I am the son of the same land as you, and because of this, I have a better understanding and a feel for your concerns and unhappiness... Every inhabitant of these lands was born into a state of subjugation, with his hands shackled, unable to breathe free... In pushing back the force and violence coming from the east, Poland is not coming with the desire to oppress ... You will be able to speak freely when your state is established.

Piłsudski did not predict, nor did he wish, for a victory by the Tsarist generals. In his discussions with representatives of the western nations, he often sharply expressed his bitterness that Poland was being treated as a Russian subject state. A great difficulty impeding Polish military activities against Red Russia was the propaganda and diplomatic campaigns it launched. As Lenin said: "Whenever the bourgeoisie aims to strike at us, the workers will stay its hand." This statement had a kernel of truth.

Western military aid, mainly from France, reached Poland with great difficulty. To show Europe its "desire for peace," the Soviet government made constant demands for the start of peace negotiations. In an official note to the Polish government, they promised not to cross the existing front line in Byelorussia and Ukraine and forgo making any agreements or treaties with Germany or other nations that would go against Polish interests. The Bolsheviks proclaimed, "there is no issue that cannot be resolved in a peaceful manner with the help of negotiations, mutual compromise, and agreements." Other nations, which in this time tried to liberate themselves from under Russian domination, made the choice to negotiate with the Bolsheviks who seemed agreeable, while the White generals remained intractable.

In October 1919, Finland withdrew from the anti-Bolshevik coalition, putting Gen. Judenicz's forces into internment. At the time, Judenicz held positions in the Pustowskie Hills, just outside St. Petersburg. The Bolsheviks signed a peace treaty with Estonia on 2 February 1920. J. Majski, later ambassador of Soviet Russia in London, called this peace "a Russian window on Europe, opened only twice in history."

The Soviets, without restrictions or conditions, recognized the independence and sovereignty of Poland. In February 1920, the central executive committee of Bolshevik Russia sent a message to the Polish people assuring them of their best peaceful intentions and that "Polish freedom is a necessary condition for Russian freedom." All these official declarations and propaganda activities were intended to put Poland off its guard. The *Biała Księga* [*White Book*] by Sukiennicki and his documented articles published in *Bellona* during 1963-64 confirm in an irrefutable way that already in the autumn of 1919 aggressive plans had been drawn in Moscow against Poland. Their purpose: "to have the revolution march West, mainly to Germany."

Piłsudski did not believe in Russian assurances about their peaceful intentions but tried to counter the propaganda that painted Poland as the "main disruptor of peace in Europe" and agreed to open peace negotiations. He wanted a future peace with Russia to encompass all her neighbors and proposed that the negotiations be expanded into a peace conference that would include all the interested nations. But Russian desire for peace and compromise was only a tactical propaganda ploy in order to create misunderstandings between Poland and her western allies and gain time through delay.

As they started to consolidate their victories over the counter-revolutionary generals (Judenicz was interned, and Denikin was in retreat), the Soviets started to change their stance from apparent willingness to talk into threats that were heretofore unknown in international relations. They insisted that Polish forces withdraw and establish a border on the Bug River. They declared that if this is not done, they would "obliterate the Polish State."

Piłsudski's statement published on February 28, 1920 in the Paris daily, *Le Petit Parisien*, was both significant and informative.

Poland wants peace, because it was always oriented toward peace. Proof of this is the continuance of discussion of the kind of peace that has been proposed to her. Poland does not want to withdraw from the negotiations but – and I will not stop repeating this – we will never be able to consent to talks under whatsoever threat ... We do not want to take advantage of the situation, basing our arguments on the strength of our forces. We do not want a peace that would be imposed by our cannon and bayonets. Unfortunately, what I see among Bolsheviks does not inspire me to believe that we can talk about a peace that has a peaceful basis, but rather – about a peace that will be imposed with threats, as they did to the Estonians. When a pistol is pointed toward me, I do not have good feelings. For I am not a man who cannot be addressed this way. I am sure that all Poland shares my view. We do not want a peace that is imposed by threats. Either we will have real peace, from good will, or we will have war.

Poland had made an unimaginable effort, and by the spring of 1920, already had an army of seven hundred thousand soldiers at its disposal. Of that number, five hundred thousand were stationed on the eastern front, but despite the numbers, they were not large enough to stop the expected Russian offensive. Piłsudski considered the situation even more dire, for toward the Polish border were moving enemy forces that had experienced many victories, could fight with great intensity, and energy and faith in the righteousness of their cause.

The battlefront with Bolshevik Russia stretched for over one thousand kilometers. In case of an intense attack, this front could not be defended from a fixed position. There was no time to fortify a thousand kilometers, nor were there technical resources and personnel available. Piłsudski considered a defense in place to be a bad strategy. The Commander-in-Chief had to make a decision: to stay and wait for the results from defensive warfare or to start an aggressive campaign. The second option had some strategic-tactical advantages (surprising the opposing forces, scattering enemy units while they were concentrating, holding the initiative, conducting war operations beyond the borders of an already wasted country, utilizing the high morale of the troops). All of these factors became the basis for the Polish plan of operations.

The choice for the place of attack was not difficult. Piłsudski knew that the most sensitive point for Russia was Ukraine. In defense of this most sensitive place, already in revolt, the Russians would have to concentrate all of their resources. Piłsudski's reasoning was as follows. *Even if I am unable to create an independent Ukraine, then shattering the main Russian force should assure a true, not an illusionary peace, for Poland.*

Chapter 16
The Kiev Expedition

The mood of the major part of Polish society was much too optimistic. Meanwhile, the Ukrainian nation at that time had neither the awareness nor the willingness to make sacrifices in a fight with Bolshevik Russia for its own freedom and independence and did not turn out to be an ally who would help Poland to achieve a full victory.

The offensive known as the "Kiev Expedition" started on 25 April 1920. Piłsudski's plan, again executed under his personal command, expected that the northern front would be held without changes, while the left flank would make a strong assault from Wołyń on Żytomierz-Koziatyn, and then at Kiev, with the purpose of cutting off the Soviets from crossing the Dniester River. To accomplish these tasks Piłsudski had three armies: The Sixth Army – led by Gen. Iwaszkiewicz on the right flank, the 2nd Army at center on the Słucza River – led by Gen. Listowski, and the 3rd Army – led by Śmigły-Rydz on the left flank north.

The plan of the Commander-in-Chief was being realized with near miraculous effectiveness. On the second day of the offensive, Polish forces already took Żytomierz. On 27 April, they took Berdyczów and Koziatyń; on the 29th, Mochylów on the Dniester, Winnica, and Zmierzyńka; on 2 May, Chwastów; on 6 May, Białocerkiew; and Kiev on 7 May. Within a few days, the divisions of the Red Army massed on this front were shattered or taken prisoners. Among Polish trophies were twenty-one thousand men, one hundred and twenty artillery pieces, four hundred and eighteen machine guns, two armored trains, and more. The famed Sich Riflemen[80] came over to the Polish-Ukrainian side. The Twelfth Red Army no longer existed for any practical purpose, and remnants of the Fourteenth Army withdrew in the direction of Odessa. On 9 May, the Polish forces took control of the bridges on the Dniester and reinforced their forward positions at the bridges on the left side of the river. During this time, the Poles occupied Brasław, Tulczyn, Jampol, and in Polesie the town and Rzeczyca railroad terminal.

Piłsudski issued a proclamation at the start of the Kiev expedition. *To all inhabitants of Ukraine. Armies of the Polish Republic have moved forward on my order, penetrating deeply into the interior of Ukraine. I want to inform the inhabitants of those territories that the Polish forces will remove the foreign invaders, against whom the Ukrainian nation had risen with arms in hand, protecting their own against rape, pillage, and violence. The Polish Army will remain on Ukrainian territory only until the time that an Ukrainian government takes charge. At the moment, when a national government of an Ukrainian Republic creates a governing structure and on the borders stand armed units of the Ukrainian people, able to defend the country against a new invasion and a free nation will be able to determine its own future, then the Polish soldier will return to the borders of the Polish Republic, having fulfilled his noble calling of fighting for the freedom of nations. Together with the Polish Armies, there came fighting ranks of Ukrainian sons under the command of chief field commander Symon Petliura, having found shelter in the Polish Republic and assistance in those most difficult days of trial for the Ukrainian nation.*

I believe that the Ukrainian nation will strain every muscle to help the Polish Republic in winning its own freedom and secure the fertile soil of its homeland, bringing happiness and wellbeing, which will benefit all after they return to work and peace. To all inhabitants of Ukraine, regardless of rank, descent, or religious belief, the forces of the Polish Republic promise safety and care. I call upon the Ukrainian people of this land to patiently bear the burdens which are imposed by the hard time of war and assist in some measure the Armies of the Polish Republic in its bloody toil for their own lives and freedom.

A similar appeal was issued by the chief field commander of the Ukrainian Republic stressing that the Polish nation, in the person of Chief of State and Commander-in-Chief Józef Piłsudski, has recognized the independence of the Ukrainian state.

Those who have been repeating the words of communist propaganda about the, *invasion of the Polish lords on Ukraine in order to organize plantations,* should remember that the Polish military command received Piłsudski's orders not to allow former Polish landowners to come into those areas. The Polish forces there did not meet any instances of enmity – just the reverse, they were greeted with enthusiasm driven by hope. A confirmation of these attitudes was the atmosphere under which Polish forces entered Kiev (on May 7th), and the splendid parade which took place on the sunny Saturday the following day turned into a festival of joy.

The top commanders received the following instruction: *It is in the Polish interest to withdraw our forces from these territories as quickly as possible and establish good neighborly relations with the newly established Ukrainian state, and in so doing to secure a greater portion of our eastern border against the threat from the Bolshevik Armies. The occupation of Ukrainian territory by Polish forces must be reckoned not in years, but in months.*

Piłsudski sent General Tadeusz Rozwadowski[81] on a special mission to Bucharest, stating precisely the Polish positions in the following points:

a. Polish policy is not to occupy Ukraine.

b. Poland wants to cooperate with Romania on behalf of Ukrainian independence.

c. One important goal is to separate Poland and Romania from Russia.

d. Poland and Romania should recognize the leadership of Symon Petliura.

Many opinions, comments, and reflections that Piłsudski had can be seen in his letters to Aleksandra Szczerbińska, who at this time was not yet his wife, living with her daughters (Wanda – born 7 February 1918, and Jadwiga - born 28 February 1920) in Warsaw at 70 Koszykowa Street.

The spirit of the army is wonderful. This was a true race, where a forty-kilometer march by the infantry and an eighty kilometer move by the cavalry was a daily occurrence. ... The scattering and destruction of the enemy was achieved. Our own losses were minimal, about one hundred killed and another three hundred wounded. I miss you all so much. I have also suffered a personal loss – very sad and painful. One of my adjutants, Stanisław Radziwiłł was killed. As you know, I liked the man and respected him as a good officer. We found him after a counterattack, stabbed by bayonets and bludgeoned with rifle butts.

On 17 May, Commander Petliura and representatives of the Ukrainian people received Marshal Piłsudski in a ceremony in Winnica. In answer to Petliura's greeting, Piłsudski said:

Poland and Ukraine have passed through a difficult time of oppression. A free Poland cannot be truly free as long as the threat of subjugation through terror is alive. Poland has attained the greatest treasure on this earth, which is freedom, and now we must push those things that endanger that freedom far from our borders. The flashing of our bayonets and our sabers, you should not perceive as the imposition of a foreign will. I want you to see them as the flashes of your own freedom. Your commander in his beautiful appeal promised to assemble a free parliament in a free Ukraine. I will be most happy, when not I – a small servant to my own nation – but representatives of the Polish and Ukrainian Parliaments establish a common platform for an understanding. In the name of Poland, I raise the cry,

"Long live a free Ukraine."

In unofficial conversations, Piłsudski stressed that everything depends on the Ukrainian nation. *The Polish Army will not go beyond Kiev. If the Ukrainians do not unite in the cause of gaining their freedom, then they shall not have it.* In another conversation, he said, *Against the Soviet Ukraine of Rakowski, we place the Ukraine of Petliura. Let the Ukrainians decide for themselves which is the true one. In a neutral Kiev, there should meet representatives from the entire Ukraine. As for Byelorussia, they have no interest in that. In reference to the changes in Allied policy toward Russia, we cannot chase after zig-zags of their policy. We either have a solid peace, or we will fight, and fight so that the chips will fly.*

In reference to the Kiev Expedition, Piłsudski expected that the Bolshevik forces would move from the northern front and then the situation on the front would be eased. This movement did not happen. Just the reverse – the Russians started an offensive on the northern front, and this required the regrouping of Polish forces, as reserves were very slim.

The taking of Kiev by Polish forces caused enthusiasm and even joy among all Poles, excepting the communists. At a session of the Sejm on 4 May 1920, Speaker Trąpczyński[82] read a declaration which was accepted by all the representatives.

On the anniversary of the great day when the May 3rd Constitution was enacted, our eagles bring freedom and order to the people living in Wołyń, Podole, and Kiev. They bring the blessings of peace to people and the possibility of working in peace and the assurance that no one will seize the fruits of their work. ... It is the task of the Polish soldier not to interfere in the internal matters of other nations but to create such borders for the Polish Republic which would in an adequate measure secure the state, making any new war unlikely. In this time that the Polish armies are marching east, the Polish nation should be filled with pride. The nation should believe and give encouragement!

The Sejm sent the following telegram to Piłsudski.

News about the excellent victory that Polish soldiers have achieved under your leadership has filled the entire Polish nation with joyous pride. For this heroic and bloody effort, which moves us toward the longed-for peace and puts new foundations under the might of the Polish state, the Sejm in the name of the Homeland sends to you our Commander-in-Chief - and to the heroic army – our sincere thanks.

In connection to an invitation to a celebration in Warsaw, Piłsudski wrote, *If such is the will and desire of Warsaw, I will consent to it, even with pleasure. Not only that an ovation will be given, which was well de-*

served, but I think it will be beneficial to the work at the moment.

On 18 May at 4:00 pm, Piłsudski was greeted at the Warsaw railroad station by the Chief of the Ministers' Council Leopold Skulski,[83] Chief of the City Council Ignacy Baliński,[84] and the Ukrainian General Mychajło[85] At the church of St. Alexander on Three Crosses Square, a Te Deum was sung and Piłsudski was greeted by Speaker of the Sejm Trąmpczyński with Cardinal Aleksander Kakowski representing the clergy.

At a ceremonial session of the Sejm Trąmpczyński said:

The Sejm greets you, Commander-in-Chief, through my lips, as you return from Bolesław Chrobry's[86] trail. From the time of Chocim, the Polish nation has not had such a triumph of arms. But it is not the triumph over a defeated foe or national pride that swells our hearts. History has not yet seen a nation which was in such difficult conditions as ours, to recreate its own statehood. In such a moment, the victorious march on Kiev has given the nation a feeling of its own strength, reinforced its faith in a future of freedom, made possible its spiritual activity, but most of all reestablished the basis for a favorable and lasting peace, which we so all desire.

Through this feat of arms, you have testified not only to the bravery of Polish arms, but you have taken from the breast of the nation its greatest longing and turned it into a banner, its knighthood in the service of freedom for the nations. In vain did our enemies place faith in the differences among political parties in Poland. All of Poland is united in its desire for the people, freed by our army, to decide their own fate, the form of their statehood and the shape of their government. Our army, on the strength of its bayonets, has carried freedom to peoples long under the yoke, it carries peace to people of good will.

In you, Commander-in-Chief, beyond party differences, we see the symbol of our beloved army; an army of such strength, such that our nation did not have even during the times of greatness. The victories gained by this army under your command will influence our future in the East. Today, the whole world sees and knows that Poland is no longer defenseless. All hail to the Commander-in-Chief of our army.

These words had an even greater significance in that they were spoken by a politician from Greater Poland, who had earlier showed, perhaps not hostility, but definitely reticence toward Piłsudski.

Meanwhile, the fact that a free Ukraine was established as an ally of Poland created a great consternation in Russia. On appeals from the former Tsarist general, White Army soldiers joined the Red Army en-masse, as not to permit the "breadbasket" to be separated from "Mother Russia." At the same time, the Bolshevik high command started to operate in a way much better thought out than Piłsudski expected. He had expected that the Russians would move a greater portion of their forces from the north to save the situation in the south and abandon the earlier planned offensive.

Things moved in a different way. Tuchachevsky, whose abilities for strategic planning had revealed themselves earlier at the Tsarist military academy, knew the art of war and did not change his plan. On 14 May, taking advantage of the favorable situation on the northern front, seven divisions of the Fifteenth Soviet Army moved against the segment defended by three divisions of the First Polish Army. At the beginning of June, after lengthy and bloody battles, Tuchachevsky's forces were pushed back to their starting positions, beyond the Rivers Berezyna and Auta. However, the situation on the Ukrainian front developed unfavorably for the Polish forces. The new Russian commanders on this front, with Stalin as political commissar, were given powerful reinforcement by the horse army under command of Siemion Budionny. This army, famous for smashing Denikin's forces, was well trained, boldly and expertly led, and had four divisions of cavalry. It was well equipped with heavy machineguns mounted on "taczanki" or two-wheeled carts.[87]

Piłsudski, who was accused without basis by communist propaganda with overvaluing and over-building the Polish cavalry, did not spot the threat connected with the appearance of Budionny's horse army. This matter, and the theoretically correct assessment of the diminished role of the cavalry in modern warfare, Piłsudski best explains in the text of his book, *Rok 1920* (*The Year 1920*).

> *Budionny's cavalry was moving up. I had relatively concise and accurate intelligence about it. It moved in a long march, from somewhere near Rostov on the Don River. ... As I already noted, I did not appreciate the significance of this new enemy. The cavalry, as we know, has lost a lot of its significance in war... The horses were passed to the artillery, and the riders were hurriedly turned into infantrymen. It seemed impossible to me that even a haphazardly equipped infantry with the addition of machine guns and artillery would not be able to defeat cavalry with firepower. After all, I had personal experiences, in 1916 when a brigade of the Legions was attacked by Russian cavalry on the fields near Kostiuchnowka and Wołczeck. Having hardly any artillery, as only one battery was firing, the fire from the infantry and*

machine guns simply blew away the charging horsemen...

With disbelief I saw the method applied to the use of cavalry, resembling that of the nomads, in a way that recalled olden times, so well-known to our forbears from the Tartar raids. Their horsemen moved, as to say, without an organized rear, feeding people and horses from the land like locusts, consuming that which was found along the way ... this cavalry, formed into a self-sustaining army, seemed to me then, and still seems, a strategic nonsense. I did not attach to it any great significance or to its successes on Soviet fronts, about which I had received information. I attributed these successes to the internal degeneration of the forces fighting against it, rather than to the methods it used in warfare.

Piłsudski was correct in his assessments, but as a result of the exceptional circumstances and the inadequate forces available for defense, Budionny was able to break through into the Polish rear. There, unopposed, he attacked the field hospitals, cut off the supply of food and ammunition, murdered the civilian population, and raised fires. All of this created a psychosis of fear and the conviction that Budionny was everywhere. In these circumstances, Piłsudski decided that more important than holding on to Kiev was to eliminate Budionny's horse army from the war. Ryz-Śmigły, who was stationed in Kiev, received orders to concentrate his forces in the area of Żytomierz and engage Budionny in a decisive battle.

Fighting against the growing Polish forces, Budionny managed to evade encirclement in turn at Żytomierz, Zwihl, and Równo. As Piłsudski wrote in his book, *Rok 1920 (The Year 1920)*, *Budionny's cavalry became some kind of legendary, invincible force. And it could be said that the farther they were from the front, then the stronger and more pervasive was this suggestion, without applying any logical reason. In this way, the most dangerous front for me was beginning to form - the internal front.*

Anticipating a general offensive of the Soviet armies in the north and under strong influence of the "internal front," Piłsudski decided, *on our own, without pressure from the enemy, to move the entire northern front back to the approximate line of the German trenches in the center, and simultaneously form strong maneuvering groups on both flanks.* Unfortunately, this had a fatal influence on Polish public opinion. There was an immediate loss of fighting spirit. The army had no moral support from the population. Instead, in Polish and foreign newspapers, reports appeared with insistent propaganda supporting peace. In the Sejm, some of the parties and many representatives also tried to outpace each other with peace proposals. The Army felt abandoned.

Chapter 17
Poland in Mortal Danger

In June of 1920, plans for organizing a "Polish Soviet," "German Soviet," and a "Hungarian Soviet" were being discussed in Moscow. On 2 July of that year, Tukhachevsky announced the following order to the twenty divisions under his command: *Soldiers of the Red Army, remember that the western front is the front of world revolution. The road to world revolution leads over the corpse of White Poland.*

On 4 July 1920, Tukhachevsky began his six-week offensive, commonly known as the "March beyond the Vistula." *To avenge the defiling of Kiev, the Red Army begins a mortal struggle with the armies under the White Eagle ... We will drown the criminal government of Piłsudski in the blood of the crushed Polish Army.*

The aims of the Bolshevik "march" were no longer camouflaged by any of their favorite slogans which referred to peace, social justice, or progress, though from statements made later by Tukhachevsky. We know that the Bolsheviks were convinced that in Poland, as well as in the other Western countries, *the revolutionary movement is growing and it is only sufficient for the Red Army to move onto Polish soil for the masses of workers and peasants to rise and obliterate the hated government.* This opinion, founded on information provided by Polish communists and quoted from Tukhachevsky, turned out to be wishful thinking drawn from an over-excited imagination.

On the other hand, Gen. Sergeiev, commander of the Fourth Soviet Army, had little faith in the revolutionary inclinations of Poles. He wrote about this very circumspectly and cautiously: *The possibility of a Polish revolution breaking out could have been taken seriously only in the political offices, and those must have been far from the front lines. The army had little faith in this, and it seems that the attempt to form a Polish Red Army in Bialystok was sufficient proof that our sources of information had a much too optimistic a view of the situation in Poland.*

Piłsudski presented the situation in the following way. *I have no fear of the famed Bolshevik propaganda machine, which some have already made into a scarecrow. It has no influence over Poland. We, as neighbors of the Soviet Republic, have had ample opportunity to assess the results of the communist experiment. In Poland, even people — to put it more politely— who are among the most radical, are frightened of the gulf into which Bolshevism has pushed Russia. ... The European nations farther removed from the Bolshevik hearth may still believe in the beauties of the system that Le-*

nin had introduced. But we who can look at it up closely, have already made up our minds and are frightened of the awful situation created in Russia by Bolshevism.

At the time, the Bolshevik offensive moved forward, the Polish army had about seven hundred thousand personnel in its ranks, with about three hundred thousand stationed in front line units. The Bolsheviks had almost eight hundred thousand men on the western front. Recalculating these numbers to actual fighting strength, it appeared to Piłsudski that the sides were assembled at one hundred thousand Polish sabers and bayonets versus one hundred and twenty thousand Russian sabers and bayonets. Tukhachevsky's evaluation put the proportions at 100 to 160 in favor of the Russians.

The Polish left flank of the north-western front began to yield under the pressure of the Bolshevik push. Polish units in that area began to withdraw, causing neighboring sections to do the same. The Soviet plan included the assumption that Polish forces defending the section between Dzwina and Berezyna would be destroyed. But it did not go easily. The Polish 33rd Infantry regiment counterattacked seventeen times within sixteen hours. In many locations, fighting continued to the last man.

The cause of the Polish disaster and the unprecedented reversal during which the Polish forces withdrew six hundred kilometers within one month was due neither to Polish weakness nor Bolshevik strength. The main reason was tactical errors committed by commanders on the North-Western Front. On 5 July, the commander of that front, Gen. Szeptycki,[88] gave the unfortunate order to withdraw, indicating a place where the new defensive line was to be established. This line started in Niebyszew and ended in Koziary. In this case, let us quote the words and opinion of the Marshal which he wrote in his book, *The Year 1920*.

> *When I try to analyze the Polish-Bolshevik War from the viewpoint of trench warfare, I find in both my recollections and in documents, the internal disagreements that were present within our army on this very point. Then I, as Commander-in-Chief, decided not to engage in trench warfare because I saw no benefit for us in using this method. Still, among my subordinates and among our people, there was a tendency to adopt the view of faites une ligne forte (make a strong line).*
>
> *Many people have been strongly impressed by the past European war, so they have consequently interpreted my attempts to introduce maneuver and movement into our war as an insufficiently developed strategy. This strategy is at odds with the might and strength of the recent king of the battlefield — the strong and deep line of*

*trenches. Unfortunately, our situation permitted only a very thin and
weak line of trenches. We could not feed and supply this trench line to
have it attain a sufficient strategic importance — we had neither the
industry nor the manpower.... In our case, the idea of the trench line
had to be taken down from the throne. But the idea kept returning,
of putting the inseparable sister of the trench in its place, the fixed
front line which was in direct conflict with the warfare of maneuver and movement which I introduced.... Because of this, there have
been many shrugs of the shoulders around me, and behind me many
whispers of dissatisfaction and whispered hurtful comments about
the Commander-in-Chief's antiquated romantic notions.*

After a few days of the Soviet offensive, Piłsudski became aware
that it was taking place on a set pattern, where the best units of the Red
Army attacked our units at their weakest points and began flanking maneuvers. This caused our withdrawal to another defensive line. The Polish retreat on 5-6 July caused the loss of Vilnius, Lida, and Grodno. From
21 July, heavy fighting took place near Zbrucz. Attempts to stop the Bolsheviks on the line of old German trenches, left over from the World War,
and plans to set up a defensive line on the Bug River proved to be impossible to implement.

The goal of the Soviet offensive was Warsaw. In the plans drawn
up by the Bolsheviks, taking Warsaw would mean the end of the Polish
government, and the end of the first phase in their plan to bring revolution to all of Europe. The battles of August of 1920 were to decide if the
Polish Republic would continue to exist. Its army was falling back while
fighting ferocious battles, and as it did so, in a natural and indefensible
way it was also losing faith in any kind of eventual victory. Would the
Polish forces be able to halt the hordes which were growing ever surer
of their power? These were questions posed by nearly all Poles, but the
answers were less confident.

Among the questions regarding the tactics applied by Józef Piłsudski during the war with Soviet Russia in 1920 are accusations that
since he had different ideas about waging war, why did he not remove
those generals who permitted the errors which led to catastrophic results? These kinds of questions can be multiplied, and they have appeared
ad infinitum in many anti-Piłsudski publications. But the most convincing answers to those kinds of questions and accusations are contained in
the Marshal's own writings. *I had a choice. I could change the general on
the front line or accept his understanding of the situation, because I preferred to have a bad solution, but a confident commander. I chose the second option but indicated the necessity of organizing a strategic withdrawal*

according to my own concepts.

Piłsudski implemented changes among the commanders only at the end of July. General Szeptycki was replaced by Gen. Józef Haller,[89] and Gen. Zygadłowicz,[90] commander of the First Army, by Gen. Romer. It must be added that the entire officer corps had a consistent attitude toward the obligatory strategic thought. All the generals routinely held sacred the current military doctrine of: position, cordon, line, trench. Why didn't the Marshal personally go to the front line and take over command?

To be aware of the complexity and difficulty of making this type of decision, one must remember that Piłsudski was not only the Commander-in-Chief, but also the Head of State. There was also trouble in the government. Leadership positions were being taken by weak persons, those with low confidence or even cowards. The Sejm sent plaintive notes to Moscow begging for peace. Piłsudski's absence from Warsaw could have had the direst consequences, which could result in his achievements up to then being for nothing. This is how he summed up the situation. *To restore morale, a move that I wanted to make and to which I devoted much consideration, was to go to the front and take over direct command. With great sadness to myself, I rejected this idea. My main reason for doing this was the feeling that morale in the entire country was wrong for the conduct of war. The atmosphere of panic and fear was so great that after the actual front-line situation, the home front began to be a negative factor in my calculations. I had to admit that my place was in Warsaw.*

Because of the bad internal situation and the disputes which caused the inability to make operational decisions in government matters, a Council for National Defense (ROP) was created on 1 July. It was composed of the head of government as president, the Marshal of the Sejm and nine representatives chosen from the Sejm, the Prime Minister, and three military representatives chosen by the Commander-in-Chief.

On 2 July, a very pessimistic picture of the situation on the front lines was presented by Gen. Szeptycki at a session of the ROP. On the following day, Piłsudski proposed, and after approval, signed two messages on behalf the ROP. These were: *To the Citizens of the Republic* and *To the Soldiers.*

The homeland is in need, he wrote. *The actions of the invaders coming from the interior of Asia are trying to break our armies, to begin a dreadful reign on the resulting cemetery of Poland. We must stand as a solid, united wall in opposing them. Volunteer to join the ranks of the Polish Army.*

In his message to the soldiers, Piłsudski stressed that the result of this war will determine whether Poland will become a strong and free nation or a small and weak country where the enemy will rule. Calling on the soldiers to fight, he stressed that, *those who stand on the front lines are not alone, behind them is the entire nation. No soldier who returns home from a victorious war is without a place of work, whether in the countryside or city... Every soldier, officer, or private must at this moment give the utmost effort that he can, giving his manhood and devotion to the Homeland. This must be done so that glory and blessing surround his name, rather than disgrace and curses of entire generations.*

At this time, a conference of allied nations —the Entente — was taking place in Spa. On 5 July, at a subsequent meeting of the ROP, Piłsudski recommended that a Polish delegation be sent to that conference. *We must explain that we are defending Europe from Bolshevism... The pacifist atmosphere in the country has a bad effect on army morale. When we feed the army on peace, it is difficult to speak of victory.*

After Leopold Skulski resigned as Prime Minister on 23 June, this post was filled by Władysław Grabski. On 6 July, he left for Spa. Working under the threat of disaster and pressured by the Western nations, mainly Great Britain, he signed an agreement under which Polish forces were to withdraw to the so-called Curzon line, located on the Bug and San Rivers. Doing this, he exceeded his authority. Fortunately, the agreement was never enforced. Great Britain offered itself as a mediator to broker a ceasefire, but the Soviets were so confident in their strength that they rejected this offer, stating falsely that they could give Poland more favorable borders than those proposed by the Allies. The Russians had no intention of settling on any borders and treated their proclamation as a trial balloon, thinking that, *if the Poles accept direct negotiations, then they will not be able to count on any outside support.*

On 13 July at the ROP meeting, Grabski reported on the conditions of the agreement signed in Spa. Piłsudski then declared that the Prime Minister had exceeded his authority and asked for his resignation. Several representatives including Dmowski and Chądzyński opposed the Commander-in-Chief. In his reply, Piłsudski said that, *disease has taken over the country. You, gentlemen, give proof of this. If the nation wants to win, it will win.*

The retreat of the Polish forces grew more and more chaotic. At the ROP meeting on 19 July, new and old accusations were leveled at the army and its leadership. Dmowski stated that it was necessary to change the leadership at all levels. He proposed Dowbór-Muśnicki for the position of commander-in-chief. He also considered the following possibility; "if we cannot find our own officers who are suitably qualified, then we should turn to our allies."

Piłsudski stated, *Victory depends three-quarters on the strength and morale of the army and society, and one-quarter on its technical pre-*

*paredness. We need an indomitable will to win. Instead, you present a pic-
ture of demoralizing uncertainty, argument, and disunity. I do not know
what words I am to use to convince you, to put the spirit of faith into you ...
If my death is necessary for this, then I am ready to shoot myself in the head,
if it would make you understand that this is the last moment for salvation
... I know what I need to do — I have a plan, but I do not force it upon you,
but place it at your disposal.*

During this meting at the Belweder,[91] a delegation from the
Poznań region arrived, headed by Fr. Stanisław Adamski[92] (1875-1967).
He was a Sejm deputy and the president of the National Christian Workers' Club. During the years 1930-1967, he was bishop of Katowice. For his
patriotic stance, he was later prevented from practicing this office both
by Hitler's occupation authorities during 1941-1945 and Stalin's government during 1952-1956. In 1920, however, he had no cause, during the
ongoing situation, to look for treason in the army. When he accused Piłsudski, the Marshal turned and silently walked out.

Two meetings of ROP took place on 20 July. Piłsudski nominated Tadeusz Rozwadowski to be chief of staff, stressing that he was one
of the few exceptional generals who had not lost faith in victory. The
French government had sent to Poland their Chief of Staff, Gen. Maxim
Weygand,[93] with a large retinue of officers. Among them was the then
thirty-year-old Captain Charles deGaule. France was assisting by making deliveries of military equipment and ammunition. The transports of
weapons to Poland were, however, being blocked because of Bolshevik
propaganda. Initially, Czech railway men interfered with the shipments,
but on 24 and 25 July, orders forbidding the transport of weapons and
ammunition were issued in Gdańsk and more widely by the government
of the German Reich.

The situation looked hopeless and many Polish politicians saw
their only chance in the ceasefire that might be reached during direct
negotiations between Polish and Soviet governments. The Polish nego-
tiators left Warsaw on 22 July, but when they reached Minsk, they were
repeatedly stopped and humiliated. They were treated in a high-handed
way by the arrogant servants of Moscow. *Where are your authorizations?*
they were asked. *You only want a ceasefire as a dishonest tactical ploy. We
will negotiate only on the conditions for peace.*

The Polish delegation had no authority to conduct peace negotiations, and therefore, returned to Warsaw. In any case, it was obvious that
the Russians wanted neither a ceasefire nor peace negotiations, because
at the time, they were confident of a sweeping victory.

On 30 July in Bialystok, now occupied by the Red Army, the
communists (Marchlewski,[94] Dzierzyński,[95] Próchnik,[96] Kon,[97] and Un-

szlicht[98]) formed the Provisional Polish Revolutionary Committee that would become the government of a future Polish Soviet Republic. This news was proclaimed by the *Goniec Czerwony [Red Courier]*, the "official" publication of this selfsame body printed on 20 August 1920.

On 24 July 1920, a coalition government was formed under the leadership of Wincenty Witos. In addition to Ignacy Daszynski, who was named as vice-prime minister [premier], there were several others who not only represented their parties and groups but had meritorious and professional qualifications. Eustachy Sapiecha[99] was named Foreign Minister; Leopold Skulski, Minister of the Interior; Władysław Grabski,[100] Minister of the Treasury; Gabriel Narutowicz,[101] Minister of Public Works; General Józef Lesniewski,[102] Minister of the Armed Forces. This last nominee was soon replaced by Kazimierz Sosnkowski.

For the first time, at Piłsudski's insistence, one-third of the government was comprised of non-aligned professionals. The time had arrived, and this was perceptible at every step, that the defeats had a weakening effect on the Polish populace. The nation finally began to understand that is was a do or die situation. As nearly one hundred and seventy thousand volunteers swelled the ranks of the army, schools and offices began to look empty. The word *dekownik* [slacker] became a most insulting and derogatory epithet. Volunteers, though not trained, lifted the army's morale. Women flocked to serve in the armed forces.

In the August days before the decisive battles, Polish forces at Warsaw numbered about one hundred and fifty thousand men. Meanwhile, Tukhachevsky brought to this segment of the front line over two hundred thousand troops of his Red Army. Piłsudski did not fear this disproportion of numbers. He believed that in the battle for Warsaw, a well-made and executed strategic plan would prevail. In conversations with the chief of staff of the Entente Council of War, Gen Weygand, Piłsudski did not attempt to hide the seriousness of the situation. In writing about his conversation with the Polish Marshal, Weygand stated that the Polish commander-in-chief gave him the impression of a brilliant intellect, intuitive in the field of strategy, with a specific understanding of the role of action and maneuver.

According to what he had said at the 19 July ROP meeting, Piłsudski had a plan for a decisive battle. His idea depended on halting the retreat and striking Tukhachevsky's left flank with the Polish right flank. Brześć, defended by Gen. Sikorski, was to be the place where Polish forces were to concentrate their counteroffensive. Unfortunately, Brześć fell (2 August), and the Bolshevik forces crossed the Bug River, because the bridge had not been destroyed.

After touring the front lines, Piłsudski returned to Warsaw and found the atmosphere more fearful than when he left. He knew that he had reached a time when final decisions had to be made. Therefore, he determined to spend three days in Anin, where his wife and daughters were staying. "I had to absorb the news about the fall of Brześć, do an accounting of our and the enemy's forces, and consider the possibilities for fighting a battle on the lands near the Vistula River." Attentive observers noted that when the Marshal returned to Warsaw, he was a different man. He was decisive and refreshed.

At the 5 August meeting of the ROP, much time was spent not on discussing the defensive, but on matters concerning coming to terms with the Bolsheviks. From reports of the delegates, it was obvious that by questioning their authority and changing the previously agreed-on purpose of the negotiations — from a cease-fire to terms of peace — the Russians showed a definite lack of good will. There was no point in thinking otherwise.

I *cannot call it anything other than begging. To start negotiations when the enemy is knocking at the door of our capital and threatening the destruction of the government, even before a word about peace is uttered.* This is how Piłsudski summed up the situation, and he had reason on his side not only because victory would soon be his, but because the conditions proposed by the Russians were an insult to the Poles and their aspirations for independence.

The conditions can be summed up as follows:

1. Recognition of an Eastern border on the "Curzon line."
2. A limit placed on the Polish armed forces at sixty thousand men.
3. The creation of a Peoples' Militia.
4. Unimpeded transit for Russian armies through Poland, at any time and in any direction.

These conditions were in agreement with the decisions of the Comintern[103] (deliberations from July 19 to August 7, 1920) where forty-eight Communist Parties of various regions pledged to cooperate and assist the Bolshevik "March across the Vistula."

Chapter 18
The Eighteenth Most Decisive Battle in the History of the World

Piłsudski spent the night of 5-6 August at the Belweder making the final adjustments to his strategic plan. The general outline of the plan remained the same — with the Polish right flank striking at Tukhachevsky's left flank. But the point for concentrating the attack was changed to Dęblin, using the Vistula River for support. The most difficult part was disengaging from the enemy and properly redistributing all the resources that were at the Poles' disposition. *During that night, I sometimes thought,* Piłsudski wrote, *about the great finesse of Napoleon's genius who, though a giant, compared to himself a weak woman straining in labor.* In Piłsudski's plan, Warsaw was to play a passive role, having to endure the pressure that was bearing down upon it.

On 6 August, General Rozwadowski, chief of the general staff, reported to the Belweder with his plan for the retreat, Piłsudski rejected it. After a discussion, Piłsudski's plan was finalized, with its thrusts from the Vistula and Wieprz Rivers. As for the concentrated forces, these could be most easily obtained from the First Army, which was already in the vicinity of Warsaw. Piłsudski, however, thought this unwise because it would further lower the morale in the capital.

> *A specter of frustration rose over Warsaw, powerlessness and cowardly thoughts. The most visible proof was the delegation sent with a plea for peace ... When I considered reducing the passive force, I began to fear whether Warsaw would hold, and if the departure of a part of the forces would cause a loss of confidence in the defenses ... How many times did I try to shrink from this decision, pressed by the responsibility for the nation and its capital.*

Eventually, the Marshal decided to form a strike group from five divisions. He took three divisions from the Fourth Army, and two of the best in the Polish armed forces (the 1st and 3rd Legion) from the Third Army. The entire group was to be reinforced by cavalry regiments. All the divisions that were designated to be in the strike group had been engaged in battle. It was then necessary to make the difficult maneuver of disengaging from the enemy, moving to the place where forces were to concentrate, regroup, and assure sufficient rest and supply.

He has a most difficult task, who despite weakness must show strength, which is to play a decisive role. I had previously decided, wrote Piłsudski, *that I could not leave this burden to any of my subordinates but had to take it up myself. That is why I stopped with the thought that the counterattacking group, whether stronger or weaker, would be commanded by me personally.* From 6 to 12 August, Piłsudski carefully observed how the disengagement maneuver was being performed by the designated divisions. *The decision had been made, now much depends on the strength of the capital's determination. Our divisions at the gates of Warsaw must push back the enemy's attacks until the attack group has had a chance to concentrate its forces, that is until August 17.*

At this point, perhaps in summary, it would be proper to address the still debated point of authorship of the plan for the "Battle of Warsaw." In this matter, Piłsudski's opponents often point to two generals: Tadeusz Rozwadowski, chief of the general staff, and Maxime Weygand, the chief of the French military mission in Poland. The argument of course may be dispensed with the statement that success has many fathers, while failure is an orphan. Yet, in this instance, the significance of the question is much more serious, both from a historical and psychological points of view.

As for history, facts have more weight than their various interpretations. It is a fact that Piłsudski was the commander-in-chief, and he had to approve and execute any approved plan regardless of the intellectual input of the various persons participating in creating that plan. Among the irrefutable facts are statements made by both generals Rozwadowski and Weygand that refer to ideas and proposals that differed from Piłsudski's in reference to the decisive battle with the Bolshevik forces.

It is sufficient to mention the conversation, well known to historians, between Gen. Rozwadowski and Wincenty Witos on 13 August where Rozwadowski expressed the view that the heaviest fighting had moved to the north, and as a result, Piłsudski's strike from the Wieprz River would have no strategic significance in the course of battle. By stressing doubt in the effectiveness of the maneuver from the Wieprz, Rozwadowski proved that he was not the author of the plan.

General Weygand was even more unequivocal in the matter of the plan. A man of caution and adverse to risk, he stuck to the doctrine of the time and proposed a strong, united front on the line of the Bug and Vistula Rivers. When the Poles did not follow his advice, he frankly admitted, avoiding any undeserved praise, that *this victory, which is the cause for celebration in Warsaw, is a Polish victory; the military operations were carried out by Polish generals according to a Polish operational plan ... the heroic Polish nation had saved itself.*

As for the psychological dimension of the argument about the authorship of the plan which brought victory, one must be surprised by the "inferiority complex" of those authors in the National Democrat [Endecja][104] wing, who thought that ingenious ideas could only come from the heads of Frenchmen or generals schooled in Austrian military academies.

The domestic verbal attacks on the commander-in-chief had their effect on members of the allied powers. Marshal Foch openly criticized Piłsudski for holding the two most important government functions - Commander-in-Chief and Head of Government - simultaneously. Later, Gen. Waygand would write beautiful memoirs about Piłsudski, but in his reports to Foch, he must not have been too complimentary, for the French marshal stated that military command in Poland should be given to a general who could follow the advice of Entente advisors. At the French-British conference in Hythe (8-10 August), further aid to Poland was made conditional on the appointment of a Commander-in-Chief who held no other post. On 11 August at another ROP meeting a discussion was held on "the composition of a delegation and problems of negotiation" with the Bolsheviks in Minsk. *My dear assembly, I cannot bear this nervous stress,"* were nearly the only words from Piłsudski at this meeting. On the next day, he departed for the front lines. Before leaving, he invited Witos, Daszynski, and Skulski to meet with him.

Witos later remembered that Piłsudski was very careful in his choice of words. He said that a trump card was being played and there was no assurance of victory. During the conversation, he pulled an unsealed letter from his pocket and read it in an indistinct and changed voice. On four small pages was the justification for his resignation from the posts of Commander-in-Chief and Head of Government. Piłsudski gave the task of announcing this resignation to Witos (after the war it was archived with Piłsudski's other correspondence).

On 12 August, Piłsudski had a long meeting with Rozwadowski, Sosnkowski, and Weygand presenting the general disposition of the Polish forces. Of the twenty divisions, fifteen were to play a passive role on the Warsaw defensive front. These divisions had artillery and aircraft which together should blunt the enemy attacks. *The forces which I am concentrating for the attack must have some rest and time to absorb replacements. In addition, I must have time to inspect them.*

On his way to Puławy, Piłsudski stopped to visit his family. His wife wrote, *He parted from me as if he were going to his death. He was bothered by my unshakable faith that the battle would end in our victory, and that he would be unharmed.* 'The result of every war,' my husband said, before leaving, 'is unsure until the end. All is in the hands of God.*

On 13 August Piłsudski was in Puławy and immediately started to visit the units that were to take part in the main assault. Thousands of volunteers were joining these units. The army's morale was raised by the enthusiasm of these volunteers, several days' rest, the order commanding them to go on the offensive, and the presence of the commander-in-chief. Care was given to clothing and properly equipping the army. On the night of 14-15 August, the Marshal wrote to Gen. Rozwadowski that *the entire army is entering a trance.* The soldiers who have been in a state of low morale during the retreat recovered when the replacements doubled their ranks and when the penetrating gaze of the commander-in-chief met theirs.

Piłsudski was pleased by what he saw during the inspection. He saw that there was only a deficiency in equipment and supplies. Various divisions had German, Austrian, and French weapons, and it happened that battalions with French rifles were assigned to divisions with German Mausers or Austrian Manlinchers. In Firlej, nearly half of men in the divisions that passed before the Marshal had no boots. Knowing that General Weygand was not an uncritical admirer of Piłsudski, it is worthwhile to cite his comment. *During the three days that the Marshal spent among the troops, he electrified them, he passed from his heart to the ears of the troops the faith and the will to overcome all obstacles. No other commander of Polish armies could have inspired the men to such an aggressive offensive that continued to the German border while destroying four Soviet armies along the way, armies who had thought themselves to be victors.*

The Commander-in-Chef's orders, read to the ranks on 15 August, announced the beginning of the attack and asked the army to *concentrate all its will and energy, so to surprise the enemy by quick action, and win the battle through the sheer marching strength and manhood of the Polish soldier.* The orders also repeated the 3 August decree *regarding the advancement of men from the ranks to officer grade for action in the face of the enemy.*

That day, Piłsudski moved his headquarters to Dęblin. Messages arrived from Warsaw telling of the critical situation and requesting an immediate counterattack. There was also the news that Budienny's Horse Army had attacked the Polish Sixth Army which then began a retreat toward Lwów. This was good news, because Budienny could have been a threat to the attack groups from the rear. Piłsudski decided to begin his attack on the next day at dawn. He had forty-three thousand infantry and four thousand five hundred cavalry, one hundred and seventy-nine artillery pieces, and eight hundred machine guns. In the operational orders issued before the battle, the Marshal forbade any "looking around to the flanks." Each division was to attack in its designated sector with maximum speed, without looking if the neighboring divisions were keeping up. In reference to contemporary accepted strategy and tactics, this was another "heresy" committed by the Marshal, where he outpaced military theory by twenty years.

> *On August 16, I will be at the crossroads Deblin-Kock-War-saw-Lublin. I address your attention to the absolute necessity of conducting the entire operation in the dimensions ordered. ... All units must understand that this battle will decide the fate of the war and of our country. The desired outcome will result only from the greatest effort of every officer and soldier.*

At this point, it would be worthwhile to mention the assessments of the situation as stated by Poland's enemies. The commander of the northern front, Soviet Marshal Michail Tukhachevsky, in his book *March Past the Vistula* wrote: *Meanwhile, our offensive went on without pause. It was clear that this was no time to hesitate or rest, but that the time had come to finish off the campaign with a single stroke. More than once, instructions were issued in this regard, stressed on August 12 in the directives issued by the general commander about the necessity of taking Warsaw as quickly as possible. The orders from comrade Trotsky were of this type. ...*

In choosing the main direction of attack, one thought not only of its tactical value during the fighting, but also about the transport capabilities of the enemy. Turning at the center in the direction of Warsaw was a task beyond our capabilities. We had to contend ourselves with breaking one of his flanks, the right or the left. Attacking his left flank, we could run afoul of his transport links to Gdańsk. Taking into consideration that the revolutionary movement in Germany was disrupting the normal deliveries of weapons and ammunition to the Polish Army from France, that the main transport route was the connection through Gdańsk, the maneuver not only placed us on the flank of the core Polish grouping but also threatened the main line of Polish transport. Another advantage to this direction was that for our units to execute this move we did not have to reform, thus gaining time, and did not have to change our main communications route. This line ran from Vilnius to Lida toward the southwest.

The Bolsheviks were convinced that the Polish armies were already scattered, demoralized, and incapable of further resistance. The official communiqués issued by the Soviet leadership forecasted the taking of Warsaw on 15 August. Tukhachevsky described the morale of the Polish army as follows: *Continuing defeat and continuous retreat broke the Polish Army's ability to continue fighting. This was no longer the army with which we had to contend in July of this year. Total demoralization and disbelief in any chance of success weakened the ability of the officers and men to fight. Retreat was often initiated for no good reason. The army's rear was teeming with deserters.*

The battle for the Polish capital started on 13 August 1920 in the evening hours with the attack by the 21st and 27th Red Army divisions on Radzymin. These were among the best Soviet divisions and had earned fame by scattering Kolczka's army and had advanced through Russia shouting *Dajosz Warszawu! [Give Us Warsaw!]*. To make the decisive attack on Warsaw, the Soviets designated the Seventeenth Infantry Corps and the famous cavalry corps led by Gay-Chan. In the first phase of the battle, the Poles could oppose them with only four and a half divisions. A break in the front line could mean disaster and constitute a direct threat to Warsaw, which, according to the Marshal's plan, had to hold out until at least 17 August.

Despite heroic defense, on 14 August, the Russians took Radzymin and the Red Army moved to within a striking distance of the Polish capital. Two Soviet divisions entered Radzymin with all their supply trains and support. Individual brigades made it as far as Słupno and in the direction of Jabłonna as far as Górka Radzymińska. On the road to Nieporent, Soviet patrols captured Polish couriers and paralyzed motor traffic. It is a wonderful paradox that this undeniable Soviet success contributed mightily to their defeat. General Haller, who had regrouped his Fifth Army and according to plan was to enter the fighting only on the following day, on hearing about the situation in Radzymin decided to counterattack with the main strength of the First and Fifth Polish Armies. Fierce fighting continued over the entire day on 14 August. Radzymin changed hands several times. Polish counterattacks used up battalion after Polish battalion.

In the Volunteer Infantry regiments, consisting of students from Warsaw schools, losses were nearly seventy percent. Fr. Skorupka, fell at the head of one of the battalions, still clutching his processional cross. General Żeligowski hurried to find new forces so that the counterattacks (which lasted to 15 August) could plug up the gap at Radzymin. From the nearby hills, the Russians could see the towers of the Orthodox Church on Saski Square in Warsaw. [Had a defeat happened then, this would never had been renamed Victory Square, where Pope John Paul II gave his long-remembered homily].

Lord d'Abernon, who called the battle for Warsaw the 18th most decisive battle in the history of the world, wrote the following about the Bolsheviks. *Their only faith was the belief in destroying the existing order, their only policy was to destroy all that exists according to our laws... It is difficult to estimate the importance of the events in past centuries in comparison to the battle for Warsaw, but it can be safely assumed that had the Soviet army broken through the Polish resistance, Bolshevism would have surely taken over all of Europe.*

In Warsaw, where hearts quivered to hear the artillery and rifle fire, the embassies of allied nations prepared to evacuate their staffs to Poznań. Among the few diplomats to remain in Warsaw was Papal Nuncio, Cardinal Achilles Ratti, later Pius XI, who was nicknamed "Papa Polacco" because of his obvious sympathies.

The decisive day in the battle for Warsaw was 15 August. Throughout the night both sides brought in reserves and regrouped forces, so that in the morning, the decisive engagement could take place. Piłsudski received urgent messages and analyzed the situation on the entire front, including Radzymin. He knew the atmosphere in Warsaw and decided that he would start his own counterattack a day early, on 16 August at dawn. This attack, according to plan, was to change the situation to Poland's advantage, but Warsaw had to mount its defenses. This was a condition for victory. Command in the Radzymin sector was taken over by General Żeligowski. The defensive-attack maneuver he prepared was as follows. After the main forces of the 10th Division gathered at Neporęt, he would strike through Beniaminów and Wołka Radzymińska toward Aleksandrów and Mokre, bypassing Radzymin from the north. Among the hastily assembled forces that Gen. Żeligowski gathered was the 28th Infantry Regiment. The first battalion of this regiment, which took the leading position on the march-out for the morning attack at Kąty Węgierskie, was led by Lt. Stefan Pogonowski.

During the battle for Warsaw, there were many heroic deeds and sacrifices - the plan was ingenious, and its executors were magnificent. All of this is true, yet there was undeniably a miraculous component to this battle - the eighteenth most important in the history of the world. This miraculous moment took place on 15 August at 1:00 am in the morning when Lieutenant Pogonowski, moved by a difficult to explain premonition, committed his battalion to battle without waiting for the appointed time. Later analysis confirmed that his bravura attack found the most sensitive spot point in the Russian army — a staff headquarters in the process of regrouping.

The surprise of the Bolsheviks was complete. Pogonowski scattered a large enemy unit in Mosty Wołczańskie, where a conference of commanders was taking place, and struck at Wołka Radzymińska where a Soviet division was based. The Bolshevik regiments, hearing the sounds of fighting in their rear, started to withdraw backing almost literally right onto the bayonets of a much larger Polish force. The Soviets did not realize that the very effective attack was executed by a single battalion. Lieutenant Pogonowski fell in the fighting, his death was not only heroic, but also the most meaningful sacrifice of the ongoing battle, if not the entire war.

Intense fighting continued through the day on 15 August on all the segments of the front. In the evening, the town of Radzymin was in Polish hands for good. *The city is rather pitiful*, wrote Gen. Żeligowski, *it is situated between the first defensive line, a line that is not very good, and the second line of defense which is very good indeed. For three days, bloody and intense fighting continued; not on the first line, not on the second, but somewhere midway between the two*. The Soviet forces were stopped on all segments of the Warsaw front, but the battle for Warsaw did not guarantee a Polish victory. The Russians were sure that their side would be victorious. Their plan was still in action. It was based on three points 1. continue attacking Warsaw until taken 2. cut off Poznań, a center of reaction 3. cut the supply line from Gdańsk.

On 13 August, Tukhachevsky informed his staff that he was worried about the left flank and asked that Budienny's Horse Army turn away from Lwów and move toward Warsaw as soon as possible. Budienny did not execute the order, and Tukhachevsky asked Trotsky to intervene. Later, Soviet politicians and historians tried to use Budienny's insubordination to excuse their defeat. This thought was also held by some Poles. The truth is that Piłsudski considered the threat from Budienny's forces and proved that the cavalry force could not have made a meaningful contribution to the battle even if it proceeded to execute the order immediately on 16 August. It was because on that day, at dawn, Piłsudski made his decisive strike. On the first day of the attack, Polish divisions moved thirty kilometers without encountering the enemy. The small Bolshevik units that met the Polish forces scattered without giving hardly any resistance. This easy march, nearly without opposition, was worrisome to the commander-in-chief. Was there something the enemy was hiding?

He later wrote, *I did not understand what was dream and what was reality. Was I dreaming then, or was it some nightmare that was drawing me in with an unstoppable force, bringing its monstrous paws to my throat. Or was I dreaming now when five divisions have easily and without resistance moved over the same terrain which just recently, in a deathly fear, was yielded to the enemy. Though this was a happy dream, it did not then seem real. After a month during which we expected overbearing force, the fear did not want to pass. The happy dream did not seem real.*

The entire day of 16 August, the commander-in-chief spent in his automobile, among the 14th Division which easily passed Garwolin and was at the rear of the Sixteenth Bolshevik Army that was attacking Warsaw. On 17 August, Piłsudski's attack force still did not meet any large enemy force. Piłsudski spent another day in his car.

Drinking tea, I jumped up when I finally heard the sounds of life, the sounds of reality, the dull thud of cannon coming somewhere from the north. The 14th Division was fighting in the vicinity of Kołbiela.

Resistance was being offered by two Soviet divisions (57th and 58th) of the so-called Mozyrska Group. They had been scattered at Włodawa and Brześć by the 3rd Legion Division. On August 18, larger Soviet forces started to gather at Węgrów. The morale of the Red Army troops was poor, and when the 21st Polish Division attacked, three Russian divisions began a disorderly retreat toward Drohiczyn. Eventually, they were met by the First Polish Army which had gone over from defense to pursuit. The Soviet divisions then changed direction and continued to retreat toward Bielsk Podlaski. Their way was blocked by the 1st Legion Division. At that time, the Sixteenth Soviet Army, just recently a deadly threat to Warsaw, virtually ceased to exist; it was as Tukhachevsky liked to say, "blown away." A similar fate awaited the other Soviet armies. So ended the "March beyond the Vistula."

Piłsudski returned to Warsaw on the evening of 18 August to complete the necessary regrouping and determine the next actions to be taken by the Polish armed forces. Piłsudski thought that the Bolsheviks might yet try to organize a counterattack on the line: Minsk Mazowiecki-Siedlce. When it turned out that the Russians were only interested in withdrawing their forces, he decided to concentrate on eliminating as much as possible of the enemy manpower and material from the war.

On 19 August, the Bolshevik government at the Kremlin was not aware of the magnitude of the disaster but were worried by the lack of success. They issued a communique stating: *In connection with the universal and historical significance of the Polish front, the Central Committee considers itself authorized to call all communists of the world to join in the heroic struggle.* The communiqué was signed by Lenin, Krestyński, Trotsky, and Bucharin.

Chapter 19
The Victory Must be Complete

In his message to the Polish nation, Marshal Piłsudski encouraged the people to fight the fleeing enemy. May the invader's foot never leave the Polish lands alive. For those who fell in the defense of the homeland, for the ruined harvest, for the plundered homes - may your fists - armed with scythes, pitchforks, and flails - punish the Bolsheviks. Those taken alive should be given into the hands of the civil or military authorities.

On the night of 20-21 September, Piłsudski went to Siedlce, where the headquarters of the Commander-in-Chief had been located. He divided the Polish forces into five armies. The Second, Third, and Fourth Armies were the group of the center front, under the personal command of the marshal. He sent those armies to the east, letting then spread out like a fan in order to take the most distant road crossings and railways centers, cutting off the Red Army as it retreated toward Brześć, Białystok, and Ostrowiec. General Haller was pursuing the enemy in a north-east direction on the Warsaw-Wyszków-Ostrów-Łomża line.

The task of the Fifth Army was to destroy Gay-Chan's cavalry and those Soviet divisions which were cut-off from the east in the area of Mława and Przasnysz. The lines of Bolshevik retreat were narrowing. The enemy was feeling in panic. It was not just a disaster, but an unprecedented rout. Those Soviet divisions which were unable to move east or into East Prussia threw down their weapons, surrendered, or scattered. By the end of August, the Red Amy lost one hundred and fifty thousand men, three hundred and twenty one artillery pieces, one thousand and twenty-three machine guns, two hundred and sixty-eighty field kitchens, several thousand horses, ten thousand wagons with supplies and ammunition, a large number of motor vehicles, and considerable rail rolling stock.

In only a few places on the territory of the Polish Republic was the enemy still a threat. Budienny, after unsuccessfully trying to take Lwów by storm, finally moved to support the Bolshevik "March to the Vistula" (22 August) but when he realized the scale of the Red Army's disaster, he tried to find temporary relief and fresh supplies for his cavalry by attacking Zamość. Despite a ten-to-one superiority, he was not able to break through the Polish defenses. On 31 August, the city was relieved by a pursuit group led by Gen. Stanisław Haller. The Red Cavalry tried to retreat but was soon surrounded. This time, despite repeated charges, it could not break out of the encirclement and was crushed. Only small fragments of this army evaded death or capture, but among those who slipped away were Budienny and his political Commissar Józef Dzugaszwili (Stalin).

The battle for Warsaw was over, but the war continued. The Soviets hurriedly rebuilt their armed forces and were helped in doing so by the Germans who (acting in a manner contrary to the Geneva Convention) released tens of thousands of Russian soldiers who had saved themselves by fleeing into East Prussia. "Our friends want us to take a strictly defensive posture in the East. I consider this absurd," said Piłsudski. "There are two solutions: to go forward until the enemy is totally shattered ... or to stand on an illusionary eastern border and make peace quickly. Society must make this choice."

The Polish Peace Delegation sent from Warsaw before 14 August was quartered in Minsk and completely cut-off from the flow of true information. It had no idea how the situation was changing. At the meeting of ROP on 27 August, new conditions were set for the eventual armistice (on the line of trenches Horyń-Zbrucz) and a demand issued to move the negotiations from Minsk to Riga. Meanwhile, Poland's western allies still naively believed in the peaceful intentions proclaimed by Bolshevik Russia, while accusing the Poles of imperial ambitions.

Władysław Branowski, who spoke with Piłsudski at the end of August, wrote: The Lithuanians are maintaining apparent neutrality, but in reality, have actively assisted the Bolsheviks with whom they signed a peace treaty. ... While the Russian armies had freedom of movement on Lithuanian territory, Polish forces were being hamstrung in their pursuit and strategic movements by constant warnings from their High Council ... Piłsudski, then residing in Łapy with the chief commanders, made occasional trips to Warsaw, mostly incognito, absorbed by the situation at the front. He, however, did not neglect the international situation in face of the constant interventions by representatives of the great powers, who interfered in the free execution of his strategic plan.

During one of these short visits in Warsaw, I was suddenly called to the Belweder. It could have happened in the last days of August... I found Piłsudski in splendid form and in a much better physical state than he had been in July and August when he was thin and jaundiced and was in a mood that was not so much depressing, but death-like. Now his face was tanned, martial, radiating energy and good physical condition. From his appearance, I understood that the situation at the front was favorable. Because Piłsudski was generally in good humor, he expressed his comments angrily, unequivocally, and not without a certain irony. Without preliminaries, he asked that I listen carefully to him, because time was running short.

You must make haste on all sides. I have had enough of these friendly games that come from everywhere in the form of advice and admonitions. ... At this time, our friends are aiding the Bolsheviks through their silence, while their shouting is hobbling our operations. To whip the Bolsheviks once and for all, Rydz Śmigły must take Grodno and push them into the Pinsk marshes, and the quicker the better, because the Entente is interfering with their representatives and commissions. They tell us that the Bolsheviks have a sincere desire for peace and add that peace must be made as soon as possible, but we believe that true peace can only be made after victory is complete. We must take Grodno and put men into the German trenches. That line is our defensive line in the East and this will make it easier to get along with Lithuania. Curzon's line, which is being spoken of again and is again proposed, will force us to maintain a warlike stance. The Entente has forgotten that Grabski's signature at Spa is no longer valid, for since the Spa conference, and from the time we have been threatened, Poland has had to conduct the war alone. Speaking of Entente aid, we have not received one rifle, so it would be an exaggeration to speak of help in achieving victory."

In a message to the army from the ROP, Piłsudski wrote: *The history of Poland and the history of Europe will record your deeds in golden letters, and the Homeland will be grateful for many generations.* The Marshal was in good health; *We must take Grodno and ask the Entente — allow us to defeat your enemies.*

Finally, at the ROP meeting on 8 September, Piłsudski was allowed to cross the line of demarcation. This permitted the preparation of a further offensive against the Bolsheviks who, during the interruption in Polish army operations, had reorganized their scattered forces and prepared for a counterattack. On 10 September, Piłsudski met with the army commanders in Brześć on the Bug and presented the points of the operational plan for the next offensive. If we want to have peace before winter sets in, he said: and all Poles are dreaming of this, we must make a most energetic effort and defeat the enemy once again. In this way, we can force him (the Russians) to treat the peace negotiations seriously. The Marshal stated the he would direct future operations himself and personally command the army with which he made the maneuver from the Wieprz River.

We have little time to prepare and conduct our offensive. It will be necessary to move the army with unusual speed, and therefore, I will ask for an effort greater than ever before, during the march, and

*in battle. The operational plan must remain under the tightest secre-
cy. Commands must be issued in a way to confuse our opponent as to
our intention and time of attack.*

The precision with which his orders were carried out is borne out
by the fact that, until 17 September, even Polish field commanders were
convinced that the preparations were meant for a march on Kovno.

Despite victorious battles, the war continued, with the Bolsheviks losing no faith in their future European and world-wide conquests.
At the 9th Party Conference on 22 September 1920, Lenin struck the podium with his fist as he loudly proclaimed: *The diplomats who are counting
on our weakness have been disappointed in their calculations, as we have
proved that Poland would not defeat us, and we are not far from victory.*
The 'great leader of the international proletariat' had no idea that three
days earlier, Piłsudski gave the order for the start of a great offensive and
Polish forces moved to attack. On the night of 25-26 September, Polish
forces took Grodno and Wołkowysk. The Fourth and Fifth Polish Armies
crossed the Bug River and took the towns of Włodzimierz, Kowel, Łuck,
Dubno, and Równe in sequence. The Bolshevik forces in Wołyn withdrew
to Horyń and Styr. The flanking group of the Second Army moved from
Augustów, and after crossing the Niemen River, near Druskienniki, took
the rail station at Porzecze on the Grodno-Vilnius line.

On 25 September, Piłsudski issued a new order for the army to
start marching as quickly as possible toward the Mosty-Lida line. The
Second Army is to strike the enemy near the Szczana and upper Niemen
Rivers. Piłsudski was not satisfied by the reports and reconnaissance he
was receiving. He spent nearly all his time in an automobile driving up
and down the front, checking the situation and making his own inquiries.
He wanted to verify the information that he would later use in making the
more important decisions. The Soviet armies were in retreat everywhere.
The Polish army was pursuing. On 1 October, battles would start for the
possession of Mołodeczno and Święciany.

An important matter at this time was the problem of Vilnius. None
of the attempts to establish cooperation with Lithuania worked. Colonel
Adam Koc noted in his memoir a certain incident that was fraught with
consequences. *The Marshal said that Gen. Żeligowski and his group would
execute an operation toward Vilnius, and for this purpose, ordered that
three thousand soldiers, volunteers from a division formed of inhabitants
from the borderlands, be detached for this duty. I did not have that many
soldiers of this particular background and tried to explain.*

There and then he exploded, writes Koc, *I felt as if thunderbolts
were striking my head, and lightning was flashing from the interior of the*

car. Only after a few moments, Koc realized what was being asked of him. Per the order, citizen commander, he answered Polish Legion style, General Żeligowski will receive three thousand soldiers from me from the borderlands. Piłsudski's anger evaporated as quickly as it came. Laughing he said, *Well done, my boy, well done.*

On 2 October, on departure from Lida, Piłsudski presented this matter to the officers of the Bieloruss-Lithuanian division. As head of the nation, I must take into consideration the coalition powers and their will which is not always fair to me. We paid in blood for the Curzon Line that was imposed on us. Poland was to end somewhere near Grodno. You are from those parts, you have weapons in hand, go to your homes. In Vilnius, there is youth that will want to help you. For your actions I, as head of nation, cannot be responsible, nor can I give you any orders in this regard. Do what you will on your own account and responsibility. General Żeligowski will take over command.

The "rebellion" generated enthusiasm among the soldiers who had homes in those parts, but also much doubt among the officers and politicians. The "rebellious" Byeloruss-Lithuanian division was part of the Polish Third Army led by Gen. Sikorski. On 8 October, the units in rebellion moved toward Vilnius. General Żeligowski informed the army staff with the following message: *Understanding that the armistice lines agreed to by the Kovno government are drawn to our detriment, and that we, the inhabitants of the Vilnius, Grodno, and Lida lands, and our country, together with Polish Vilnius, will be given to the Lithuanians, I have decided, with weapons in hand, to defend the right of my Homeland and have taken over command of soldiers who make their homes in these lands. Not wanting to go against the prompting of my conscience and the feeling of a citizen's duty, I therefore, with regret, resign my rank and command of the group. Disciplined in their training and faithful to the idea of liberating their Homeland, the soldiers still obey my orders. Meanwhile, please give direct orders to the other units.*

On 9 October, Żeligowski and his "rebellious units" took Vilnius without firing a shot. Then from 10 to 18 October he took: Święciany, Wilejka, Kojdanów, Mołodeczno, and Radoszkowice. In this way, a new country was created under the name "Central Lithuania." In Piłsudski's plans, this was to be a departure from previously announced plans for a federation of Poland and Lithuania. The right-wing parties on the Polish and Lithuanian sides effectively blocked such plans. The Marshal's idea, to make of Vilnius something that would link and not divide Poles and Lithuanians, turned out to be undoable.

The offensive along the Niemen had a beneficial result for Poland also on the southern front. The forces defending Lwów went onto the attack, and after pushing the Bolsheviks entirely out of Galicja, crossed the Zbrucz River, entering Russian Podole. The final armistice line on the day that operations ceased (October 8) on the entire front, ran from Dyneburg near Minsk through Słuck-Olewsk along Dzwiny-Zwiahel-Chemielnik-Dereznie.

Piłsudski issued a special order to his soldiers: *Two long years, when Poland first existed, we had spent in bloody toil. You are finishing this war with magnificent victories and the enemy, broken by you, has at last agreed to sign the first and main principles for the long-desired peace. ... The peace has not yet been made in a finished form. The Polish soldier must wait for it with arms at rest, patiently and in reserve, but ready at any time to stand in the defense of the fruits of this victory, should the enemy reverse himself before the final terms are sealed. This patience and reserve I most strongly demand from you.*

The eventual re-commencement of military operations against Bolshevik Russia, Piłsudski made conditional on the conduct of the peace conference in Riga, and on the attitude of the Polish nation and its allies, but also on the attitude of the Byelorussians, Ukrainians, and other nations fighting against the Bolsheviks for their freedom and ours. According to agreements into which Poland entered with the Directorate of Semen Petliura and the Russian National Committee (later the Unity Committee under the leadership of Borys Sawinkow and Dimitri Filosof), there remained on Polish territory Ukrainian and Russian Units.

The doubts connected with the interruption of military operations and the later unfortunate Peace Pact signed in Riga, have become, as often takes place in such circumstances, a matter for many historical and editorial deliberations.

Piłsudski only voiced his opinion on this subject once, during a speech given in Vilnius on 24 April 1923. *The Bolshevik Army had been completely defeated along the entire front line, and there was no barrier stopping me from reaching as far as I wanted. The thing that held me back was the lack of moral strength in the nation.*

In his book, *Zwyciestwo Prowokacji [Victory of Provocation]*, Józef Mackiewicz argues that the above cited statement by Piłsudski is "foggy and indefinite" and that the cause of the Polish offensive halting was the same as in autumn of 1919.

In April 1920, command over the remainders of the White Army was taken over by Wrangel. In an interview published on 14 October 1920, (in Wola Rosii [Russia's Will]) he stated: *Poland should enter into an understanding with us and put up the maximum number of soldiers on the front line; if this condition is fulfilled, then by spring of 1921, we will see the eventual collapse of Bolshevism*. Mackiewicz believes that the suspension of hostilities in October 1920 was due to a fear that the "White Reactionaries" might defeat the Bolsheviks.

It is difficult to settle these kinds of arguments, but it cannot be denied that Piłsudski had a strong dislike toward Wrangel. But it must also be realized that Wrangel deserved the opinion that Piłsudski had of him. Wrangel was a typical Russian chauvinist, who held an antagonistic stance toward the aspirations to independence among the nations formerly under Russian domination. France and Great Britain supported Wrangel and demanded that Poland support him as well; they had no understanding of Piłsudski's plans for a federation of nations but imagined that it was not only realistic but necessary to rebuild Russia within borders approximate to those that existed in 1914.

The continuation of the war and the bleeding of the Polish nation, without any chance of realizing the plan for a federation, would have been madness. But was it not madness to allow Byelorussia and Ukraine to remain as part of the Soviet imperium, with a large Polish population living there? After all, such an empire, sooner or later, would become a mortal threat to Poland and all Europe. Piłsudski was aware of this but could not find a solution to this tragic situation, since he did not have the support of the Western Powers.

Meanwhile, stormy debates raged in the Polish Parliament regarding the constitutional provisions that decided about internal distribution of the power the Polish nation, and the peace negotiations with the Bolsheviks continued in Riga. Piłsudski had no influence on either of these important matters. Partisan groups and parties weighed in on these issues, at times achieving slim majorities in parliament. It was also significant that the Marshal was worn-out, and his health was bad. According to doctors' opinion, it was necessary for him to take a rest cure, but urgent matters at hand required the constant presence of the Head of Government. Individually, cities and voivodships which had contributed to the national effort wanted to host him and lobby on matters important to them. Awarding the city of Lwów, the Virtuti Militari Order for its service to Poland, and its traditional inclusion in Poland, Piłsudski said: *Lwów — whose heart would not leap at the sound of that word. In the time of blackest captivity, after 1863, Lwów was the city that refused to give in; here the Polish heart beat the strongest.*

In the last days of December 1920, Piłsudski caught a very severe cold. At this time, France started to seek reproachment with Poland, which after the defeat of Russia, had become the strongest power to the east of Germany. On 25 December 1920, the president and government of the French Republic declared that they would be happy to have the

Marshal and Head of Nation, Józef Piłsudski, make a state visit to Paris in mid-January. Such a visit would be in the interest of both nations and would allow not only for the exchange of views on various matters, but also make possible a political agreement between Poland and France. A significant obstacle to this was the serious condition of Piłsudski's health. At the end of January, the Marshal declared: *Despite my aversion to pomp and ceremony, I must go to Paris. As for my health, I can command certain things, and I can command health in my body.* He then told about an illness which he battled by strength of will despite an unusually high fever.

Piłsudski arrived in Paris on 3 February 1921. With him were the ministers Eustachy Sapiecha and Kazimierz Sosnkowski. The Polish delegation was greeted by the French government and general staff. Among the many Poles present were Ambassador Maurycy Zamoyski, Władysław Mickiewicz (son of the Polish poet)[105] with his daughter who gave Piłsudski a bouquet of red and white roses, and Marie Skłodowska Curie.[106]

At this point, it may be appropriate to mention the warm, but not well known, relations between Piłsudski and Marie Skłodowska Curie and her family. Marie's sister, Dr. Bronisława Dłuska, was the wife of Kazimierz Dłuski (1855-1930), a brilliant physician who in 1894 was the co-creator and activist in the Union of Polish Socialists Abroad. In the years 1902-1918, he was the director of a sanatorium that treated tuberculosis patients in Kościelisk near Zakopane, and he actively cooperated with the Polish independence movement. Piłsudski often took advantage of the help the Dłuskis' were willing to give, both in France and in Poland, where they had a summer house in Helenow near Anin not far from Warsaw (there was another in Świdr).

From 1921, Marie Skłodowska Curie often visited her sister, but not only to rest. Ewa Curie-Joliot wrote about her famous mother in her book: *From the time that Poland recovered its independence, Marie was engaged in one great project; to create a Radium Institute in Warsaw which would become a center for research and for treating cancer. The project faced considerable obstacles. After the long occupation, Poland was poor. It had no financial resources nor a trained cadre of workers. Marie, because of her intensive work schedule, would not be able to do the necessary preparations and fundraising. Can we say who would be the first to rise to her assistance? Of course, her sister Dr. Bronisława Dłuska, who at present lives in Warsaw and who, despite her age, has not lost the enthusiasm or energy of her younger years. ...*

Universities, academies, and cities have given honorary titles to the great scientist. In 1924, Warsaw had made her an honorary citizen of the city. Many schools have desired the honor of naming themselves after her. Marshal Piłsudski, who met her a few years earlier in Paris when she was part of the Polish delegation that greeted him there, had visited her several times.

After Piłsudski's return to Poland (19 February), a political agreement between Poland and France was signed, and a secret military pact regarding mutual aid in case of aggression by a foreign power. During his stay in Paris, Piłsudski was decorated with the great sash of the Legion of Honor.

As the Paris talks were taking place, on Piłsudski's initiative, Poland was also conducting political and military talks with Romania. As a result of these talks, a Polish-Romanian convention on a "defensive alliance" was signed on 3 March. It was to last for five years and obligated both countries to come to the defense of the other in case of attack. Piłsudski also wanted to form strong alliances with the Baltic countries. Negotiations on this matter were moving along well. Unfortunately, agreements with Finland and Latvia were scuttled because of German and Russian machinations.

Poland's internal situation was unsatisfactory. The state of the economy was worrisome, as well as the socio-political situation. The legislative power of the parliament, which Piłsudski wanted to introduce according to his democratic convictions as quickly as possible, had turned into its own style of self-rule having nothing to do with democracy.

With bitterness, somewhat soothed by satisfaction, on 19 January 1921, Piłsudski wrote his observations into the memorial book of the Parliamentary Reporters' Club about the reasons for the hurried creation of the legislative parliament in February of 1919.

> *When I stood on Polish soil and fate placed into my hands the tiller of state ... I gave the Moraczewski government the condition of announcing within 10 days a procedure for elections, and to Paderewski's government the need to assemble the parliament within several weeks. The Parliament, however, started its rule over the nation like a bunch of unruly boys playing ball. Everything was decided by accidental majority; partisan groups, parties, and coalitions made agreements which then would be broken. Members were trying to outdo each other in proving who was a true Pole and pointing out and reminding each other about their orientation during the war. Some of the "politicians" regarded their fight against Józef Piłsudski as their most important work.*

The Marshal was spared no insult, he was accused of dictatorial tendencies, facts were twisted, various plots and scandals were manufactured, his achievements were questioned. Piłsudski, however, was above the partisan disputes and divisions, and resided alone at the Belweder trusting that things would fall into order, that the best and greatest in the nation would come to the fore.

Another important problem facing the future of the country and the Polish nation was the question of Silesia. Despite statements repeated by Piłsudski's detractors, it is not true that he had no interest in Poland's western borders. In December 1920, as a result of an understanding between Korfanty and the Military Ministry, a secret military organization was called into being, the "Command for the Defense of the Plebiscite" (DOP). The man who had Piłsudski's special authority for activities in Silesia was Michał Grażyński. With great energy and political wisdom, he took on the tasks of organization and mobilization.

On 20 March 1921, the Silesian plebiscite took place. Its results did not reflect the true state of the nationalistic yearnings in Silesia. It became apparent that division of Upper Silesia would be very unfavorable to Poland. Insurrectionist tensions were on the rise. It is most likely true that Piłsudski knew and approved of the preparations for an insurrection in which the Polish government was unofficially involved. It is only necessary to cite a fragment of a teletype exchange between Prime Minister Witos and Korfanty.

Korfanty: *The strike has started ..*

Witos: *Please tell me the amount of provisions in the boxcars. I am also informing you that money for the soldiers has been sent immediately ... you will receive three-thousand Mauser rifles and two million rounds of ammunition. Six armored cars have been assigned for your disposal.*

The Third Silesian Insurrection began on the night of 2-3 May 1921 and had many successes, thanks to the fact that it was well organized, decently equipped, and ably led. During the fighting, aid from Poland was forthcoming. Many volunteers from the Polish armed forces were delegated to help. Piłsudski spoke with admiration about Silesia in his speech in Katowice on 22 August 1922.

Chapter 20
The Riga Treaty and the March 1921 Constitution

The deliberations at the Polish-Soviet conference over the peace treaty started on 18 November 1920 and ran into, as is usual, "difficulties of a formal nature" which, after all, had a decisive effect on significant matters. The bone of contention was who, with whom, and what was to be decided by the peace treaty. According to Piłsudski's recommendations, the Polish side demanded that the treaty should be signed by representatives of four independent states: Byelorussia, Poland, Russia, and Ukraine. In the face of an unbending Russian resistance, the Polish delegation made a basic concession at the very beginning of the negotiations. It agreed that only Poland, Russia, and the Ukrainian Soviet Republic take part in the negotiations. This meant that any chances for creating an independent Ukraine were lost and that the Polish agreement made with Petliura's Directorate was broken, despite the fact that his army did not yet enter into armistice and were still fighting for their rights.

Among the members of the Polish delegation were Norbert Barlicki,[107] Stanisław Grabski, Witold Kamieniecki,[108] Feliks Perl,[109] and Leon Wasilewski.[110] The delegation was led by Jan Dąbski.[111] Leading the Soviet delegation was Adolf Jaffe, and his "experts" were Brodski, Hanecki,[112] and Leszczyński-Leński.[113] Witnesses noted that "Jaffe listened carefully to Dąbski's words, shielding his eyes with his hand, while across the face of Leszczyński, the famous commissar for Polish affairs, frequently drifted the shadow of a venomous smile." These sneers had a basis, for in their willingness to compromise, the Russians were ready to leave the city of Minsk to the Poles, but this arrangement fit into the vision of a federation which seemed to frighten the Polish delegates. They thought that Piłsudski would try to establish an autonomous region, a "Central Lithuania," on Byelorussian territory and that this would damage the concept of incorporation which, thanks to Piłsudski's victories, but against his ideas, they could now realize. The lack of an appetite for Minsk among the Poles must have pleased the Russians but also induced a certain lack of trust. What were the Poles planning? – they must have thought it - but had no intention of forcing Minsk into Poland by force. They did not have the power to do this. A great loss in the Riga peace negotiations was that the Poles did not take advantage of Russian weakness at the time.

It is often accepted as a positive detail of the Polish position in Riga that the text of the treaty was written in the Byelorussian language by the Polish delegates. But why did the Polish side accept the fact that no Byelorussian representative was asked to have a voice in the process? The Riga Treaty established Poland's eastern border and ended the war with Russia, but was it not true what the chief of the Russian delegation (Jaffe) unctuously said: "the signing of the peace treaty with Poland closed the circle of peaceful relations between all the countries which once formed the Russian Empire."

The Polish-Russian border was agreed on in Riga, which was valid until 1939, but remained a "contested" border. Russo-German intrigue took advantage of the national aspirations of the Ukrainians, Lithuanians, and Byelorussians using them as a "fifth column." The Eastern borderlands were never the source of strength for Poland that they could have been. Then and later, disputes arose together with damaged trust on both sides, and these still weaken us, even now when there is no doubt that a condition for victory is the solidarity and work for a common purpose among those who wish to rid themselves of oppression.

It would have been an exaggeration to say that the Riga Treaty was a failure, though it is also true that it was a loss after our victory. The beaten Russians, deprived of their weapons and equipment, were not able to enforce their demands through armed intervention. But Poland was not ready to continue the war, nor even threaten with a warlike stance. They were not able to do this because the Western Allies were not willing to support them. *A nation must want and believe in its own strength*, said Piłsudski; but even if the nation wanted to, it feared the vision of a new Bolshevik offensive and had naive faith in the concept that if the Bolsheviks were left in peace, then they would stay within their own borders.

It must be remembered that the war with Bolshevik Russia (during 1919-1920) had more casualties than any other earlier struggle with Russia. Over one hundred thousand were killed and twice that many wounded, while the country was devastated, and the people exhausted. Sometimes, however, one should not count casualties and give into exhaustion. Poland left the Ukrainians and Byelorussians under the inhuman rule of Russia, as well as Polish communities in the areas of Słuck, Żytomierz, and Kamieniec Podolski. The Russians promised to return all the possessions to Poland, both public and private, that were taken during the partitions, as well as paying sixty million rubles in gold as reparations.

It is difficult to understand why the Polish delegation did not remain steadfast in insisting on the immediate payment of these reparations. The Russians never fully completed their obligations under the Riga Treaty and, other debts aside, still owed Poland several tons of gold ducats. In their own interests, they were much more scrupulous. An outstanding example is the matter of fossils. Before the Great War, a Russian professor (Amalicki) found interesting fossilized skeletons in the area of the Dźwina River and brought them to Warsaw. One of the points in the treaty that was quickly executed by Poland was the return of these fossils. With bitter sadness, Antoni Słominski referred to these fossils, saying that, *we live in the shadow of a political dinosaur,* and he believed that, *there will come a time for breaking its bones and placing them in a museum of curiosities.*

On 17 March 1921, the Legislative Sejm finalized the text of the constitution. During the existence of the Polish Peoples Republic, it was said that this was one of the "most progressive in the world." Piłsudski sat in his box seat in the Sejm and voted against it. In his view, a constitution should not be overly progressive or too democratic. A constitution to be good should take into account the interests of the state and the nation. Piłsudski was an advocate of a division of state power (into legislative, executive, and judicial) and criticized the approved constitution for giving executive powers to the Sejm, emasculating the presidency, and making the government subject to the whims of political parties and groupings.

Remembering the recent wartime experiences, the Marshal was incensed that the army, being in a state of war, was menitioned only in a single description, that went: *the president ... is the executive of the Sejm's resolutions in all military matters. Clearly and briefly: the Sejm commands the army ... In no way could I disentangle myself from this complicated contradiction between the existence of a commander in fact, while he is not existent in the constitution.* In another place Piłsudski said: The president of our constitution is placed in as extreme a false situation as a man can be. On the one side, he is the representative of the Polish Republic everywhere and continuously; but on the other side, he has no right to represent himself, his own thoughts, or his own work.

Fulfilling the office of Chief of State and being aware of his contributions, which were not questioned even by his opponents, Piłsudski knew that he was the most serious contender for the office of the President of the Polish Republic. He must have had no doubts that it was because of him that the president was to play the role of a "democratic figurehead." Could he accept such a role? At the time, he had not made the decision. He traveled around the country listening to peoples' voices and echoes. It was a time when there were at first sporadic, later becoming frequent, affronts, attacks, and insults. It was painful for him to think why the dreamed-of Independent Poland was turning out this way.

In connection with ratifying the constitution on 18 March, the Great Theater arranged a performance for the representatives, social and political activists, and other honored guests. The first act of "Hrabina" and the third act of "Halka"[114] were presented. During the performance, a message from Riga announced the signing of the peace treaty with Russia. The message was read by Prime Minister Wincenty Witos, and the orchestra played the Polish and French National Anthems twice over.

The internal situation in Poland was worsened by the lack of political stabilization. Rule of the Sejm was triumphant. Internal arrangements among cliques, parties, and coalitions, often motivated by career-building, caused consecutive governments to form and fall. During the years 1918-1922, while Piłsudski was Chief of State, the cabinet heads were Moraczewski,[115] Paderewski, Skulski, Grabski, Ponikowski,[116] Śliwiński,[117] and Nowak.[118] Under these conditions, when a government would last only a few months, it was impossible to realize the promised reforms and consolidate the state administration.

In April 1921, Piłsudski received an honorary doctorate from the Law Department of Jagiellonian University in Kraków, and in May an honorary doctorate from the Warsaw School of Medicine.

In mid-May 1921, Piłsudski made an uncomfortable visit to Szczypioryn. In the same place where the Legionaries were interned in 1917 were now the "Sich Rifles."[119] General Bezruczko[120] (1883-1944) thanked the Commander-in-Chief for coming and guaranteeing conditions under which the interned soldiers could govern themselves. Piłsudski spoke with some sorrow, that in the Riga Treaty, the Ukrainian situation could not find a proper resolution. Witnesses to the meeting noted that at one point, the Marshal's voice broke with emotion. Tears appeared in his eyes and after a longer pause, in great silence, he spoke the words, *I am sorry, I am very sorry.*

Genera Bezruczko later moved to Warsaw and from 1924 was a minister in the Ukrainian emigrant government. The "Peace of Riga" was unfortunate and tragic for both nations, but it did not break his faith in the necessity for Polish-Ukrainian cooperation. In 1944 (when he was 61 years old), during talks with the Polish underground, Gestapo agents entered his apartment. When all had been arrested and led out, General Bezruczko made his last stand. His weapon was a cane, with which he felled two of the Gestapo men. But he was killed in this struggle. He deserves a worthy place among the heroes of the solidarity between our two nations.

On the night of 16-17 August 1921, Maria Piłsudska died in Kraków. She had been a faithful companion during the socialist conspiracy and a wife, who until her death, would not consent to a divorce. In deep reflection, the Marshal saluted her coffin for a longtime when it was brought to Vilnius. The place of her eternal repose is the cemetery in Rossa. The funeral obsequies were conducted by the Legion's bishop, Bandurski, while the family was represented by Józef's younger brother, Jan. The long involvement with Aleksandra Szczerbinska –mother of his two daughters - was undoubtedly difficult for the Marshal, but now could be transformed into a formal Catholic marriage. The ceremony was conducted by Msgr. Tokarzewski, at the chapel in Łazienki on 25 October 1921.

At this point it must be noted that despite the complications connected to his first marriage that took place in the Augusburg Evangelical Church, Piłsudski always had a great understanding for the role of Roman Catholicism in Poland. Testifying to this, among other things, is his treatment of a proposal by Bishop Hodur,[121] the leader of the Polish National Church in the United States.[122] Adam Krzyżanowski noted in his memoirs that Piłsudski rejected a tempting offer of assistance, stating that, *he would not divide the Polish nation.* When Hodur made his proposal at a meeting of the Provisional Commission of Confederated Independence Parties, Piłsudski protested sharply, stressing the significance of Roman Catholicism to the entire Polish nation.

During the time the Legions fought in the front lines, Piłsudski was supportive to having field masses and carrying on holiday traditions. The first great mass for the Legions and civilians took place on 30 August 1914 in Kielce. Though strongly associated with the National Democrats, Bishop Augustyn Łoźinski[123] would not give permission for a mass at the cathedral, but it nevertheless took place. Fr. Kosma Lenczowski, a Capuchin priest, said the mass in front of the cathedral. At that time, Piłsudski regularly took part in Catholic services. His full return to the Church took place in February 1916.

Of great significance was the recognition that Piłsudski always expressed toward Pope Pius XI. On 14 March 1922, Cardinal Kakowski gave Piłsudski a portrait of Pius XI, with the Pope's personal dedication. *I send to our beloved brother in Christ, Józef Piłsudski, Head of the Polish State, blessings and feelings of great kindness to Him and to His noble Country, dear to our heart.*

Piłsudski had hope for an improvement in the internal relations of the Polish state through the Sejm and Senate elections planned for 1922. It became quickly apparent, based on initial public opinion surveys, press reports, and behavior of candidates for office in the electoral campaign, that such hopes were in vain. In the programs and declarations announced by the political parties, they didn't care for the independent state as a common good that required dedication and sacrifice from the entire nation. The low state of political awareness, a legacy from the time of partitions, could not counter the effects of demagogues or agents who worked on behalf of foreign nations, who despite having been defeated, did not resign from trying to affect the situation in Poland as they had for ages.

On Tuesday, 28 November 1922, the first session of the new Sejm took place, where Piłsudski gave the inauguration speech. The Speaker of the Sejm, Maciej Rataj,[124] declared a joint session of the National Assembly (Sejm and Senate) in order to elect the President of Poland. Four groups, the PPS, PSL – "Wyzwolenie" [Liberation], PSL – "Piast", and the national Worker's Party nominated Józef Piłsudski for the office of president. He did not give his acceptance.

A contest of submitting other candidates began. In the light of the later conflicts of Piłsudski and Witos, it is ironic to recall that Piłsudski proposed Witos for the office of president. He did not accept the nomination. As for Gabriel Narutowicz, Piłsudski advised him not to seek the position.

During the first vote, the greatest number of votes – two hundred and twenty-two – was received by Maurycy Zamoyski. In second and third place were Stanisław Wojciechowski with one hundred and five votes, and Baudouin de Courtenay with one hundred and three. Others were: Narutowicz with sixty-two, and Daszyński with forty-two votes. It took until after the fifth vote for Narutowicz to become the president of Poland. He gained two hundred and eighty-nine votes, that included all those cast by the national minorities. His opponent was Maurycy Zamoyski who gathered two hundred and twenty-seven votes. Immediately after the voting, an action conducted by the right wing began, aimed to force Narutowicz's resignation before the oath of office could be administered.

On Sunday, 10 December, Narutowicz visited Piłsudski at Belweder Palace, and a few hours later, the Piłsudskis returned the visit by going to see him at Łazienki Palace. On the following day (Monday), the swearing-in ceremony took place in the Sejm. Narutowicz's carriage was greeted by angry shouts and insults from the crowd. The benches normally occupied by the right in the Sejm were empty. On Thursday, 14 December, at noon, Narutowicz was received at a reception at the Belweder Palace as the head of state. In greeting the president, Piłsudski said that he receives him in the same Legion uniform in which he entered the Belweder four years earlier. He would leave wearing the same uniform. He also declared that in addition to the standard official protocol, required by law, he would ask for an additional document to be prepared, listing the personal expense account, receipts for the discretionary fund, and an inventory of the property belonging to the state.

After the formalities were concluded, the Piłsudskis and the Marshal's sister (Zofia Kadenacowa) received their guest at lunch. Making a toast, Piłsudski stated that he was extremely happy that it was his privilege to be first in Poland to raise a glass in the presence of Poland's First Citizen and his family.

As the only Polish officer in the active service who never had to salute anyone, I give my salute to Poland, which you represent, making this toast: 'Long live the first President of the Polish Republic.'

In his toast, President Narutowicz said: *There are people in history who may not be judged by their contemporaries, because they have not been able to take into account all of those persons' contributions. You are one of those persons, Marshal, ... If there is anything that gives me hope, it is the faith that you will not stop lending us your strength. The most deserving citizen of the Polish Republic, who raised it from the dead, rebuilt and defended her from enemies, Long Live Marshal Piłsudski.*

The Piłsudskis now moved to 70 Koszykowa Street into the apartment that was long occupied by Aleksandra. On 16 December, Saturday, Piłsudski went to the General Staff building. During the previous two years, he opened the annual displays of paintings at the Zachęta Gallery. This year, he was not present. Staff of the Zachęta did not expect a visit from President Narutowicz, since at the time he was paying a visit to Cardinal Aleksander Kakowski. After that meeting ended early, without notifying the police or the government security detail, Narutowicz decided to visit the Zachęta. Waiting there was Eligiusz Niewiadomski, a painter and art historian, who killed the president with a pistol shot. Piłsudski learned about it a few minutes later, when Marian Zyndram-Kościałowski ran into his office shouting "Commandant, they killed Narutowicz!" Piłsudski ordered them all to leave, as he wanted to be alone.

The death of the president was a shock for the entire nation. Even his most ardent critics were silent. On an overcast and foggy day, Narutowicz's body was taken from the Belweder to the Cathedral of St. John. Silent crowds followed the casket and filled the sidewalks. In the procession, Marshal Piłsudski walked with his wife, members of the government and the episcopate, speakers of the Sejm and Senate, the diplomatic corps, and representatives of the armed forces.

On 20 December, the National Assembly chose a new president – Stanisław Wojciechowski.

On 31 December, Piłsudski gave an interview to the Warsaw daily, *Kurier Polski.* The President's assassin was given the death sentence and a reporter (Ignacy Rosner), considering Niewiadomski's declarations before the court that he wanted to kill Piłsudski, asked mainly about this matter. The Marshal replied:

184

I am sorry that Niewiadomski did not write to me. I would have no doubt come to collect this Polish bullet ... With my luck, it would probably have passed by me harmlessly. It is a great sorrow that my friend has been killed. But this is an example of a mental aberration that can affect one person after another. It is the spirit of the East. This stigma of a foreign spirit exists in all the former zones of partition, but most dangerous is the stigma of the East.

Then Piłsudski explained that he advised Narutowicz twice that he should not to be a candidate for the office of president.

Under European conditions, the election of a president creates a great curiosity, and all want to know who is this person? They want to know the truth. In our situation, there is a search for lies, and on this, politics are built. I have known the Narutowicz family for a long time. They were of the nobility from Kowieńszczyzna. But now I hear that Narutowicz came from a Jewish family.

Piłsudski continued, saying that he did not always approve of Narutowicz's methods as Minister of Public Works, but as Minister of Foreign Affairs, he was the only minister in that position who understood the duties of the office as regarded the nation as well as the Head of State.

Here, one must remember that Piłsudski was not immune from assassination attempts. Some were never explained and will probably forever be a mystery, but there was one attempt, which in connection to Narutowicz's death, must have given the Marshal a pause. It took place on 25 September 1921. Piłsudski had returned to Lwów for the opening of the Eastern Trade Fair. As he and Voivode Kazimierz Grabowski were driving away from the City Hall, Stefan Fedak ran up and fired three shots at the Marshal. The bullets went wild and the voivode alone was hit. He was taken to a hospital while Piłsudski, per the established plan, went to a gala performance at the theater. It is of great significance that the Commander-in-Chief used his influence to ask for leniency for the assassin. For his offense, Fedak received a sentence of six years in prison.

Chapter 21
Efforts to Organize the Government of the Polish State

After Narutowicz's death and considering the possibility of his own death, Piłsudski decided to write an honest unqualified opinion about the qualifications of the generals. In seventeen points, he listed and described the obstacles which he encountered in his work. He wrote that the million-man army was organized too rapidly, with a heterogeneous quality to the officer corps; and about the ambitions of politicians "running wild," the caprice, friction, and mutual dislikes, that the war was conducted by feel and that there were moral and material insufficiencies. Piłsudski's opinions about the generals, given here in fragments, are especially interesting, because they have a ring of truth about the subjects but also about the opinion writer, his wisdom, penetrating intellect, and ...generous sense of justice.

> *General of the Army, Józef Haller. With his abilities to raise morale, he could possibly be the Commander-in-Chief, but unfortunately for only a short time. He is exceptionally difficult to his personnel. He would quickly lose respect because of his demagoguery and seeking popularity at any price. He is talkative and cannot keep secrets. He is overly sensitive to flattery. His range of command – a regiment at most.*

> *General of the Army, Tadeusz Rozwadowski. A very able and quick-thinking head. Has great professional knowledge and lively intelligence. No ability for organizing and administration. He tends to forget about the factors of time and space. Is very good in matters requiring diplomatic work. He is not suited for any kind of command. In times of difficulty, he is the only one who will maintain a healthy optimism, a soldier's fitness, and good humor. Very hard for him to keep a secret. For his deeply felt sense of honor, he would easily sacrifice everything.*

> *General of the Army, Stanisław Szeptycki. Ambition combined with a weak character. His good side is that he can struggle with himself. He is difficult to his subordinates, easy to offend. In times of difficulty places blame on his superiors and subordinates. He is suitable for inspecting armament or an army. His range of command is an army which technically he can manage. He is not a suitable for chief of staff, I would not recommend him to my own enemy.*

General of Division, Władysław Sikorski. Intelligent, lively intellect, a light character with great ambitions. Has a very easy way of relating to people. An excellent organizer. He knows how and likes to command; with his flexibility he can manage in almost any situation. He has an excellent operational eye and is deserving of a higher command. Pleasant in his manner, a bit too eager in seeking popularity, can easily promote his own private interests.

General of Division, Edward Śmigły-Rydz. Strong will, calm and steady, well in control of his character. In this area he has never disappointed in any instance... and I gave him the most difficult assignments during the war. As for his own surroundings, he is capricious and comfort seeking. He is not frightened by bold concepts in his operational work, nor does he break down during difficulties. I would recommend him to anyone for commanding an army. He is one of my candidates for Commander-in-Chief.

General of Division, Kazimierz Sosnkowski. A wide-ranging intellect, great ability, but has little preparation from an operational point of view and is unsure of himself in a larger game. His character is not too strong, and it is easy for him to lose faith in himself during difficulties and disappointments. Has a great ability of relating to others. Has an immeasurable capacity for work without physical weariness. He is a candidate to command an army. He has been the Minister for the Military and can asses the military capability of a state's armed forces under various circumstances and can appreciate factors that are not strictly military in character. The only candidate for Chief of Staff for the Commander-in-Chief. After a great deal of preparatory work in operations, could be a candidate for Commander-in-Chief.

Piłsudski's opinions about ninety-five generals, written out in longhand, were placed in an envelope marked to be opened in case of the Marshal's death by the President of the Republic or a general who would assume command in case of war. The envelope was signed by Piłsudski and Alexander Prystor, who was then the chief of the personnel department in the Council of War.

On Piłsudski's recommendation, Władysław Sikorski became the prime minister, while Kazimierz Sosnkowski continued as the Minister for the Military. Sosnkowski nominated Piłsudski to be Chief of the General Staff. When the Marshal took on this job, he and his wife moved to the official residence on Saxon Square. The apartment was on the second floor (with windows opening onto the Saxony Gardens) and had a direct corridor to the Chief of Staff's office.

Wacław Jędrzejewicz, in his *Kronika Życia Józefa Piłsudskiego [Chronicle of Józef Piłsudski's Life]* mentions that one time, the Marshal was receiving reports on the military and economic situation in Soviet Russia, when into the office ran Wanda and Jagodka [little Jadwiga]. They stared to whisper something apparently important into the Marshal's ear. He listened to them very earnestly and then said, *Now say hello to the gentleman and go to your rooms.*

Jędrzejewicz noted this idyllic scene with the daughters and then contrasted it with the changes that affected Piłsudski's psyche after the death of President Narutowicz. The Marshal was becoming more severe, demanding, and in conversations often bitter and brief. His method of expressing himself also underwent changes. Adam Krzyżanowski states that, *young Piłsudski's wording was delicate and elegant*, but now was often polluted by insults, epithets, and accusations, which he threw at his foes. Piłsudski himself said that by using sharp words, he is protecting his opponents from sharp deeds which they deserve, but he detests those more than the words.

On 23 April 1923, Piłsudski wrote the following dedication on a photograph given to Kazimierz Sławiński, a professor at Vilnius University.

In those most difficult moments, when one does not feel like working, but to live and to work is one and the same – I always draw strength to continue working and living when I think about Vilnius University, as an eternally living proof that the ideal elements of human nature are everlasting and are able to transform into the material proof of their power.

On 9 June 1923, the President of Poland acceded to Piłsudski's request and relieved him of the post of Chief of the General Staff. During this time (June 11), President Wojciechowski opened the envelope with the opinions about the generals. After familiarizing himself with the contents, he placed them in a new envelope marked with the words, *To be opened only by Poland's President with consent of Marshal Piłsudski. In the event of his death it may be opened by the president or with his consent by a general appointed Commander-in-Chief during time of war.*

Piłsudski's decision to resign as Chief of Staff was not an easy one. The Marshal remained a strong influence after Narutowicz's death. He thought, and not without reasons, that moral blame for the assassination belonged to the National Democrats (ND's). Meanwhile, the leaders of the National Democrats felt no responsibility or embarrassment. They were the strongest party in the Sejm and were successful in their struggle for control. One of these successes was the so-called "Lanckorona Pact" signed on 17 May 1923, wherein the People's National Union (the NDs), the Christian Democrats, and the Polish Peoples Party "Piast"[125] pledged themselves to mutual cooperation. As a result of this pact, the Sejm created a new government with Wincenty Witos as prime minister.

Most of the important ministries were taken over by representatives of the right. Władysław Grabski became Minister of the Treasury, Gen. A. Osinski became the Minister for the Military, and the Foreign Minister was M. Seyd, later replaced by Roman Dmowski. These were people whose hand Piłsudski would not shake. At the farewell meeting which took place in the offices of the General Staff on 13 June, Piłsudski said:

> *As I leave, I make to you gentlemen my last recommendation. It is the honor of service ... The honor of service is as the soldier's banner, with which he parts as he would with his life ... Without honor, military service is always without a soul and loses its power.*

Just as Piłsudski predicted, the internal situation in Poland during 1923 worsened in all of life's categories. The government lacked the necessary authority to execute its edicts. Strikes spread from one industry to another. Inflation started to take on catastrophic dimensions. Bloody confrontations with workers took place in Borysław (6 November), in Tarnów (8 November) and – most tragically – in Kraków where forty-two people were killed. As a result, the government of Wincenty Witos resigned, but this did not change the situation. At the head of the new government stood Władysław Grabski.

One matter to which Piłsudski always paid careful attention, even when he did not have a post in the government, was the organization of the armed forces during times of war and peace. The Sejm was currently discussing a project submitted by Gen. Sikorski, whom Piłsudski accused of improperly positioning the future Commander-in-Chief (General Inspector of the Army in times of peace) in relation to the government, the Minister of the Military, and the Chief of the General Staff.

Piłsudski conditioned the correct solution to this problem on his own return to the armed forces and taking over the post of General Inspector of the Army. The Speaker of the Sejm, Rataj, noted a conversation with Gen. Sikorski, during which it was decided to postpone the resolution on the top military administration, in order to avoid the sensitive matter of recalling or not recalling Piłsudski to the army. In a formal bow toward Piłsudski, but not without an allusion that his political role was treated a thing of the past, was the brief resolution of the Sejm from 28 June 1923, whose full wording was as follows: "Józef Piłsudski, as the Head of State and Commander-in-Chief, did a great service for the nation."

After World War II, propagandists who worked for the communists used the expression "spittle covered dwarf of reaction." They were not being original, they plagiarized Piłsudski. The Marshal used those words on 3 July 1923. Speaking to his friends at a banquet in the Raspberry Room of the Bristol Hotel, he remarked at the very start that, for more than five years he was not free and, *had to live surrounded by monstrous tales and legends which were far from the real, humble man, standing here.* In November 1918, he came to Warsaw, returning from Magdeburg. In the space of a few days, without any special effort, he became a dictator. Millions of people submitted to him, millions of people raised him up. A future historian will have much to consider how it happened, why it was he... *I was the commandant of the First Brigade, and I returned from Magdeburg. As its first step, the newly reborn Poland accepted as its symbol, rightly or not, a man wearing a gray, rather worn uniform, soiled during the stay in the Magdeburg prison.*

Piłsudski went on to say that he was dictator[126] for several months but always aimed to have the Sejm meet so he could hand over power and form the legal basis for a Polish state. On 10 February 1919, he opened the session of the Sejm in the same uniform of the First Brigade Commander and was nothing but what he was earlier. A few weeks later, another historical event took place. He was unanimously chosen as the Head of State and Commander-in-Chief (February 20, 1919). They placed everything in his hands, including the office of Leader, with a reference to Kosciuszko, whose name would cause many to cry, and who despite having passed on, will live forever.

I was placed on such a high pedestal, as no one had before, that I would throw my shadow across everything, as one standing in the light. But there was a shadow beside me, there were many shadows. A spittle covered dwarf, on crooked legs, expelling his dark soul, spitting at me from every direction, not sparing anything that should be spared – family, relationships, persons close to me. He observed my steps, making apish grimaces, turning every thought to the opposite – this monstrous dwarf followed me like an inseparable companion, dressed in flags of various types and colors – once of his own country, then those of a foreign power – screaming phrases, contorting his awful face, inventing incredible stories, this dwarf was my companion, inseparable, during my ill and good times, happiness and sadness, victory and defeat.

The nonsense and dastardly deeds of which he was accused, Piłsudski explained through examples:

First, the nation's representative steals the royal insignia, the Sejm commissions investigations (an allusion to a commission created on 4 May 1921, on a resolution introduced by representative Skarbek, to investigate if the old royal insignia were hidden in Włodzimierz Wołyński on the Marshal's orders).

Second, the nation's representative betrays the Homeland during time of war and makes a pact with the enemy (an allusion to rumors that Piłsudski established telegraph communication with Trotsky). Where is the punishment for such a representative? Was there an attempt to bring him to justice? No, there is none. It was only spittle, internal excrement, an incredibly ugly phenomenon of the human soul.

This monstrous dwarf, born of the familial swamp, beaten across the face by each of the partitioning powers, was sold from hand to hand, and paid. Those were the ones who wanted to lower to their level anything that would be held up high.

This spitting was blessed with great words and slogans. It was the nation's work, work that was supposedly patriotic.

When asked by representative Anusz why he left his position, Piłsudski answered:

I respect history, I respect it for myself, I respect it for children, I respect it for the future historians, who would also spit in my face, had I cooperated with the monstrous dwarves who tried to drag me down.

"To the Belweder," he said, "went a different man, legally elected. That gang, those criminals, who tried to hack at my honor, decided to draw blood there. The president was murdered by those very people, who once threw so much dirt at me."

At the end of his speech, Piłsudski drew a parallel to Prince Józef Poniatowski, whose statue was recently placed on Saxon Square. *Prince Józef could have asked where his successors were, the main Polish leaders. He himself died in the mud (October 19, 1813). It was my honor to be the Commander-in-Chief of Poland. I was looking for honor and it was that I had to find it in the mud. This is the fate of all the Polish commanders. When I look upon that statue, I say: 'And I go to the mud...' Elsewhere the Commander-in-Chief, who has been victorious, is respected, he his given honors and appreciation ... In our country, this is different – the commander must go into the mud ... I do not want to create a tragic effect. I only want to state that mud exists, and it has significance in Poland. I am not accusing anyone, I am not the prosecutor, I only want to find the truth. As for myself,*

I only want to have a great rest, so that I could be free and happy, as I was among my colleagues in the First Brigade, among friends, who had paid their greatest respects to me through their work.

Wacław Jędrzejewski, from whose work are cited these fragments of the Marshal's speech, was present in the Raspberry Room at the time. Piłsudski spoke from memory, because he never wrote down his speeches. He spoke a long time, slowly and passionately in some moments. Was this speech only an expression of the sorrow in his soul, or as some unfriendly interpreters of Piłsudski want to believe, the beginning of a great political game whose consequences would lead to a coup d'etat and a reckoning with the opposition?

As the author, I am personally convinced that when Piłsudski resigned from all governmental offices and positions in 1923, he had no crystalized plans for returning to governing, and in truth wanted a rest to do some writing and journalistic work. Using the texts he wrote in Magdeburg, he prepared for publication *Moje pierwsze boje [My First Battles]*, and the books that followed: *O wartosci żołnierza Legionów, [The Value of a Soldier in the Legions], Wspomnienie o Gabrielu Narutowiczu [Reminiscence about Gabriel Narutowicz]*, and *Rok 1863 [Year 1863]*. The most comprehensive and undoubtedly most valuable book written at that time was: *Rok 1920 [Year 1920]*. In the reminiscences about Narutowicz are many thoughts and expressions the same sorrow and outrage, about which Piłsudski spoke in the Raspberry Room at the Bristol Hotel. *Those people were happier under the rule of those who stepped on them and beat them across the face.*

Chapter 22
Sulejówek

In mid-1921, Jędrzej Moraczewski, living in Sulejówek about twenty kilometers from Warsaw near Minsk Mazowiecki, suggested that Aleksandra Szczerbińska buy his small wooden house that stood in the middle of a pine forest. Piłsudski had expressed a liking for this house at one time. Aleksandra decided to take advantage of the offer, and during the summer, lived there with her two daughters. Piłsudski would go there during his days off and said that it was a place where he could get some real rest. For a long time, various committees collected money to buy Piłsudski a home. During the time of the Polish-Bolshevik war, a fair sum was collected for this purpose, but Piłsudski decided that it go for Poland's defense. As money came in again, he would designate sums for orphans or war invalids.

Under the influence of his summer stays in Sulejówek, however, he finally agreed that the Soldiers' Committee could purchase a proper home for him, because the one that belonged to Aleksandra was unheated and was not suitable for occupation in the winter. Various efforts were made but prices during this time had risen, and the matter ended in 1923 with a new brick house being built in the center of the pine forest. On a special plaque was the inscription: *For the First Marshal of Poland, Józef Piłsudski, our Commander-in-Chief, this house was built in the year 1923 by the Soldiers of Independent Poland. May the sun of a free and liberated Homeland shine joyfully on the walls of this house and on the life of our beloved Chief for long heroic years.* The names of the generals conveying this gift of the soldiers, Jakub Krzemieński and Tadeusz Rozwadowski, had a special significance.

The Piłsudskis lived in Sulejówek from June 1923 to June 1926, after that they moved to the Belweder Palace. Aleksandra Piłsudski wrote that initially at their villa "Milusin" in Sulejówek, there was a sense of peace. The Marshal would sleep until ten, eat breakfast in bed, then read the *Kurier Poranny (Morning Courier)* and the *Express*. After breakfast, he would go into the garden, look at the flowers, newly planted trees, and the bees. Dinner was punctually at 3:00 pm prepared by Adelcia from Święciański County. Piłsudski did not attach any specific importance to the meals and ate only the things he liked. He did not like *bigos* [*hunter stew*] or meat dumplings. He did not care for any kind of soup. Among the stronger beverages, he tolerated only Hungarian wine in small quantities. He liked sweets and often had on hand Lithuanian biscuits sprinkled with sugar and cinnamon. He drank little coffee but liked strong, hot, and sweet tea.

He would tell his daughters tales and anecdotes from Polish history. He encouraged them to study the past. This encouragement turned out to be ineffective for Wanda became a psychiatrist, and Jadwiga an architect and a pilot during time of war. Her daughter also studied architecture, so did the Marshal's granddaughter – Joanna Jaraczewska. She did not escape becoming part of Poland's history – she married Janusz Onyszkiewicz, press representative for Solidarity in prison. They have five children.

In his married life, as remembered by Aleksandra , Piłsudski was very simple and easy. After dinner, he played with the children or read on the veranda. The home library at Sulejówek had about a thousand books. Piłsudski often read memoirs, letters, and documents. He would repeatedly return to Napoleon's letters and was an expert on them. He would work mainly at night, even until 2:00 or 3:00 am. Usually he would dictate his texts to his wife or to Kazimierz Świtalski. He would speak so fast that it was difficult to keep up with the transcription. At the same time, he would smoke much and walk around the room. He did not care for his dress. He was most at ease in his legionaries' jacket, without insignia, and in plain trousers that were mostly too long. Only when he had visits from unfamiliar and important guests would he put on his Marshal's uniform with accouterments. He liked to play chess and solitaire.

During the years spent at Sulejówek, Piłsudski's income was very modest. By resolution of the Sejm, the Marshal had been granted a guaranteed salary of a thousand zloty per month. He stubbornly refused to take this money, designating all of it for charitable purposes, most often the widows and orphans of legionaries. For his current expenses, he had to rely on income from lectures and publications. Among the few remnants left after the Marshal, scattered around the world, there is a letter on quadrille paper in which he asks his wife to answer him how much money she would need for the holidays. On the back, Aleksandra answered: *Send me as much as you can, if it is too much, then we'll have it for next month*. One can say that these were typical problems for nearly all the middle-class families in Poland, only that the head of this family was the First Marshal of Poland.

In one of the poems written about him by Julian Tuwim,[127] there is one belonging to the various assessments and descriptions then current, that mentions Piłsudski's attitude to the public treasury.

They know that his brow is beetling and his moustache droops,
And that he wears a non-regulation jacket,
They heard that he uses strong expressions,
That he speaks Lithuanian and has his moods,
But they also know that he won't touch "the cash"
This they appreciate
So, they feel a boorish fear, and a dumb respect,
They check him with his heart, as if it was their pocket.

Piłsudski's principled attitude toward public money was universally known and was not questioned even by politicians of the opposition. Even in this matter though, anonymous writers tried to sow distrust and denigrade him through a public trial against the former Head of State. In the *Kurier Poznański*, dated 26 July 1923, it was reported that in 1919 when Vilnius was liberated, Piłsudski demanded that the community buy back the family lands in Święciański County. Then he supposedly ordered that the beautiful manor "Świętniki" be offered to him in gift. The grain of truth that supposedly is within every lie, in this case depended on the fact that in Świętniki, Piłsudski was given a small plot of land, as were other soldiers who participated in the war.

His wife tried to protect the Marshal from too many guests, but despite her best efforts, traffic at Sulejówek increased. Piłsudski gladly received his friends and listened to their news and often said:

I am at rest. For the first time in many years, I have a rest; a rest from the state, from politics, I can breathe easy in the clean air, and on this small plot I can admire nature and be happy in my homestead. ... I am a journalist, a publicist, or a historian, as you please, and I draw high honorariums on nearly the European scale. This impresses me, he said jokingly, but then grew more serious. What incredible tales and lies have been injected by gossip into public opinion about the most important and well-known facts, such as the defense of Lwów or the taking of Vilnius. ... Therefore, I must be grateful to Mr. Witos and company for keeping me out of the army – they gave me the opportunity to work here, in Sulejówek.

In mid-September of 1924, the first copies of *Rok 1920* came out. The book became a sensation and caused an uproar - Sikorski was incensed. He said: *Piłsudski has decapitated all the generals except for Romer, and he has put Szeptycki to torture.* In reply, Szeptycki published his own book, *Front litewsko-białoruski (16 marca 1919 - 30 lipca 1920) [The Lithuanian-Byelorussian Front (March 16, 1919 – July 30, 1920)]*.

During his time in Sulejówek, in addition to his writing, Piłsudski gave numerous lectures and presentations. To do this, he traveled to Kraków, Vilnius, Lwów, Lublin, and many other cities in Poland.

The situation inside the country was appalling. The value of the złoty was dropping continually, the countryside was overpopulated, and the number of unemployed in the cities was over four hundred thousand, which was equal to one-third of those employed in industry. This led to bloody demonstrations in Lublin, Stryj, Włocławek and Kalisz. The National Railways (PKP) reduced their number of employees by twenty-five thousand. Amounts paid as pensions, unemployment, and other types of assistance decreased, while prices of utilities, petroleum products, tobacco, and alcohol rose. A program of reducing military expenditures was introduced. Officers were released from the army, and this had a distinctly political character as it affected mainly the former legionaries.

During 8-9 August 1925, the Fourth Gathering of Legionaries took place in Warsaw. Piłsudski gave the inaugural address. It is worthwhile to quote a major part of it, because it was not prepared beforehand, and perhaps more than any other speech, reveals the Marshal's personality, his style, and truth.

There are some fairy tales that speak about the truth. Truth and fairy tales, tale and truth. If our lives were fairly tale lives, if our experiences were fairy tale experiences, then I had to find a fairy tale for my speech. ... So, I chose the fairy tale about unhappy Cinderella for today. Everyone knows this fairy tale; all have heard it. ... Where there is Cinderella there is work. For whom? Where there is a Cinderella there is the stepmother, where there is the stepmother there are the awful stepsisters! Someone must feed off Cinderella. It was not only the body louse that crawled on the shoulders of the soldiers. From your wayward slovenly bodies, they could not draw a decent meal. ... Just as in the fairy tale, just like that. Because the fairy tale is truth, and truth is a fairy tale....

Do you remember the year 1915? Poland was consumed by fire and smoke. In a storm of smoke and artillery fire, towns and hamlets were swept from the face of the earth. Poland was burning like a funeral pyre; Poland was burning along its length and breadth. Do you remember how the storm of war, rolling across the fields, united Poland?...

Truth must move on and public morality, defended by the tears of children for a thousand years crying over poor Cinderella, demands a miracle. What the hell, must evil always be victorious? ... Gentlemen,

*fairy tale is truth, and truth is a fairy tale! History was what it was, it
cannot be changed. ... Then there is the banquet and stupid Cinderella
forgives her sisters. Incredible! The children cannot cope with this,
public morality is outraged. One cannot live like this; such a life is
offensive! ...*

*I could not make the passage easily, like the mind of a child deal-
ing with the traitorous stepsisters, over those who advertise themselves in the rear and wear "maciejówki" caps on their heads. ... Why
should the lice make a meal of us? They did not want to suffer the
thorns but wanted to take the money. They smeared the roses and
flowers, and roses and thorns with mud. This is what was most difficult to accept into the daily order. But I wanted to believe then, like in
a beautiful dream, that conditions would rapidly change; and together with Poland's rebirth, the Polish soul would also be renewed. ...*

*My gentlemen! I want to end this fairy tale on an historical note.
Why the thorns, why the roses, the queens of flowers and aromas, is
it a false cult? If I selected a fairy tale style today for children, it was
only that the style of the fairy tale is more readily remembered. I have
a specific purpose. May the roses and their aroma, may the thorns
also remain in history as roses and aromas! ... Life is not a romance,
but also it should not be a muddy puddle, in which we would see ourselves and our children, reflected as in a mirror.*

In the first half of November 1925, Piłsudski met with Stanisław
Wojciechowski, who was then the president. He asked that the army and
national defense should be treated in a proper manner. "It is impossible
to demand," he declared, "that the army serve the political parties and
their interests."

The collective celebrations of greeting Piłsudski on the occasions
of Independence Day (11 November) and on his name-day (19 March)
turned into political demonstrations with great significance. General Or-
lisz-Dreszer expressed the feelings of those assembled and stressed that,
they bring, in addition to their grateful hearts, sabers tempered in victory.

Honor is the god of the army, repeated Piłsudski, *Without it, power
wanes. ... I tried to take a principled stand before the president of the Republic, expressing the necessity for preserving the honor of our times, the
honor of our fame, and the honor of our work.*

The great issue that concerned Piłsudski and his colleagues was
the matter of Poland's defense, considering the threats posed by Germany
and Russia. On 17 April, the Rapallo Tract was signed, which was essentially an alliance between Germany and Russia, quite obviously against
Poland. A consequence of this Tract was the "Berlin Agreement" which

specified the areas of cooperation. Stresemann,[128] the German minister, and Chicherin,[129] his Russian opposite, openly suggested the possibility of both countries revising their borders at Poland's cost. Germans were conducting economic warfare against Poland. The Berlin agreement banned any trade with Poland, decreasing Polish exports by forty percent. Unemployment grew, and the financial situation was collapsing. The government had to make some necessary decisions, but the government was merely the executive arm of the Sejm which dictated every move of the government. The strongest party in the Sejm was the Peoples-National Union, a continuation of the National Democrats.

Commenting on the deepening crisis in Poland (in the *Kurier Poranny*, 29 April 1926), Piłsudski stressed that the work of the government must be done individually by responsible professionals. Any attempt to rule by a group consisting of four hundred and forty-four representatives and one hundred and eleven senators will lead to that which was currently happening.

The interview conducted by Conrad Wrzos was later printed in the book *Piłsudski i Piłsudczycy (Piłsudski and His Supporters)* (published by Biblioteka Polska in 1936). The thoughts and information the Marshal expressed during that interview are worth some attention.

The Marshal wore a threadbare shooting jacket and dark trousers. His hair was not cut. Hair on his neck rubbed the collar. His complexion was sallow. His eyes were bright, as if transparent.

Are we experiencing a parliamentary crisis? asked Wrzos.

Piłsudski replied, *We are surely experiencing it, and in a more severe form than the rest of Europe. According to the principles of the parliamentary system, the government rules, the Sejm judges. But if one adopts the practice that the judge is the accused, and the accused is also the judge, then all sense of responsibility will disappear.*

Does the Marshal share the opinion that a strongman who would take on the responsibility of governing could more easily deal with the difficulties?

With the Sejm, or without the Sejm? Replied the Marshal.

That would be for him to decide.

A dictatorship? Interrupted the Marshal. *You want to put thieves into power? ... But I think that under the constitution, the work of a strong government can be effective. The bad habits of the Sejm stem from a bad constitution.*

Chapter 23
The May Breakthrough

After another change of government on May 10, 1929, the Sejm formed a "new" government, again headed by Wincenty Witos. In an interview given that day to the *Kurier Poranny*, Piłsudski stated that he did not consider the cabinet crisis to be over, because Mr. Witos did not take the moral interests of the state into consideration. The selection of friends around Mr. Witos suggests that in this government there will still exist the possibility for bribery and the abuse of power for private or party interests. The military ministers were chosen from among generals whose consciences were bendable, capable of trading favors for position and rank.

> *I was surrounded by paid spies, there was money and advancement for anyone who would betray me, the former Commander-in-Chief. There was a desire, I dare say, for my death ... This lasted throughout the entire time that Mr. Witos and his friends conducted the government.*

This interview was published on 11 May, and it caused the confiscation of the entire edition of *Kurier Poranny* by the police. This created a great outrage among the Marshal's supporters. To understand the following course of events, one must keep in mind that on 8 May, the Minister of the Military, Gen. Żeligowski,[130] started maneuvers in the vicinity of Rembertów. The overall command of the units taking part in maneuvers was entrusted to Piłsudski. The new Minister of the Military, Gen. Malczewski, countermanded this order, but it was only accepted by the Cadets' School in Warsaw. All factors indicate that Piłsudski decided to make a military demonstration to force the president to affect a change of government.

On 12 May at 7:00 am, Piłsudski departed in his car from Sulejówek, promising his wife that he would return for dinner at 3:00 pm at the latest. After stopping at the garrison mess in Rembertów, Piłsudski drove to Warsaw at 10:00 am to meet with President Wojciechowski. It turned out that the president left for Spała. Alarmed by the growing tension, the government recommended the introduction of martial law in the city of Warsaw, in the Warsaw and Lublin viovodeships, and in Siedlecki and Łukowski counties.

The Minister of the Military (Malczewski) announced that Marshal Piłsudski "is not in active service and has no right to give orders to any part of the armed forces." The commandant of the Warsaw Corps (Gen. Dzierżanowski) gave an order that "any armed units crossing the

202

bridges with the Marshal must be absolutely prevented, use of firearms not excluded." President Wojciechowski, who returned to Warsaw during the afternoon, fully supported the actions of the government and issued a proclamation reminding soldiers of the oath they took to obey the rightful authorities, meaning the government and the Minister for the Military.

At 4:30 pm, the president arrived at the Poniatowski Bridge, and with the help of Col. Stamirowski, sent a message to Piłsudski. After reading the message, Piłsudski, together with Gen. Dreszer and Colonels Wieniawa[131] and Stamirowski, walked over to the Warsaw end of the bridge. The exact wording of the conversation that took place between Piłsudski and President Wojciechowski is not known. One can reconstruct it based on various reports, but it was of no major significance. It is sure that Piłsudski stated that he was not against the president, but he requests that the president exercise his power and dissolve the government for the good of Poland. The president replied that he considered this government legal, and that it has the required power and support of the country.

In Wojciechowski's note, photographic copies of which are known from various publications (S. Arski, J. Zieliński), we read the following:

When (Piłsudski) approached me by himself, I greeted him with the words "I stand to guard the honor of the Polish Army," which evidently angered him. He grabbed my sleeve and in a muffled voice said, "Well, well, only not in this way." I shook off his hand and not permitting any discussion said, "I represent Poland here, I demand that you pursue the resolution of any issues you have in a legal way." ... He went around me and turned to the soldiers who were standing a few steps behind me. Fearing that he could persuade them to forego their orders in my presence, I called out, "Soldiers, do your duty," and walked along their ranks back to my car.

From other sources, we know that Piłsudski went back to the group of officers with whom he arrived. He supposedly said to Col. Wieniawa: *This is bad. I will go to Praga, but I will return here.* This was a most dramatic situation – this "meeting on the bridge." Piłsudski and Wojciechowski were friends and close colleagues during the time of the prewar conspiracy. Morality, the law, and politics? President Wojciechowski could have given an order to have the rebel arrested. In case of resistance, supporting fire was available from the machine guns that were set up in advance. World history willingly justifies this type of action. Could such an incident have been justified in Poland? Personally, I don't think so. In Poland, the application of such methods is always accompanied by the loss of authority, even when this authority is supported by law.

In making an appearance at this time, Piłsudski did not have the law behind him, but he certainly was correct, as he was looking out for the common good. It is irrefutable that Piłsudski wanted to cause a change of government, where Wincenty Witos and his corrupt political allies from the National Democracy camp held sway, through a military demonstration that had mass public support. When he found the unexpected resistance on the part of President Wojciechowski and the government, he decided not to fight, but tried to find a resolution of the situation in repeated attempts at negotiation.

The first shots were fired by pro-government forces. Eleven were killed and several dozen wounded among soldiers from the 36th Infantry Regiment who supported Piłsudski. The drama that Piłsudski had to live through depressed him as nothing had before. After reaching Praga and the headquarters of the 36th Infantry Regiment, he was silent for a long time. Then he started to talk with the Colonels (Sawicki and Ziemski) slowly familiarizing himself with the new situation and the thought of an expanding battle. *I came to you, boys. The Poniatowski Bridge is lost. ... Lost, you understand. ... And how is it here?*

Colonel Sawicki explained that the crossing via the Kierbedź Bridge was open, but the Marshal was deep in thought, as if he was not there. At 5:30, the 30th Infantry Regiment, loyal to the government, stationed near Castle Square, started to shoot after ineffectually demanding that the 36th Regiment return to its quarters. Colonel Ziemianski describes how the Marshal, in a low voice, said as if to himself, "And even so it started. I thought this would not happen."

As a result of the fighting, the units which responded to Piłsudski's orders entered the Krakowskie Przedmiescie district. The government, located in the Governor's Palace, quickly moved to Belweder Palace. At 8:00 pm, Piłsudski came to the Royal Castle. Despite the fact that fighting was still continuing, the streets were filled with crowds cheering him. The "First Brigade" anthem was being sung.

Meanwhile, the government was taking desperate steps. *In case the units marching unlawfully toward Warsaw do not heed the orders given them, use bombs and machine guns in order to scatter them.* At 9:00 pm, Piłsudski restarted negotiations with the speaker of the Sejm as an intermediary. Rataj took on this mission, but he did not expect success as the government expected assistance from units coming from Kraków and Poznań. An order was issued that "an attack on the rebels should begin in the morning, for the purpose of seizing leaders of the rebellion without any attempt to spare their lives."

During the night of 12-13 May, Piłsudski received representatives from the workers' organizations and informed them as follows.

I cannot speak for a long time as I am very tired, both physically and morally. I am an opponent of violence, and I proved this when I was the Head of State. I have attempted, after a long struggle with myself, to a test of strength with all the associated consequences. All my life I have struggled with the meaning of that which is called "imponderable" – such as honor, courage, and the inner strength of a man, not to profit from it myself or for those near me. A state cannot be unjust toward those who work for others, a state cannot have too much injustice if it wants to survive.

Piłsudski spent in part of 13 May at the General Staff on Saski Square and in part at the Vilnius Railroad Station. The actions taken by his forces were defensive and did everything to avoid unnecessary bloodshed. In the afternoon, the government forces intensified their activity using reinforcements that arrived from Poznań. Meanwhile, the Railway Workers Union called for a strike. From 14 May, the PPS announced a general strike in Warsaw. Crowds of Warsavian's demonstrated in support of Piłsudski. The 1st Division of the Legion came from Vilnius. Additional government reinforcements were stopped by the rail strike.

With the attempts at mediation having no effect, Piłsudski ordered an attack on the government forces. On 14 May, President Wojciechowski and the government left Belweder Palace and walked to Wilanów.[132] There they reached the decision to resign. Near midnight, Speaker of the Sejm, Rataj, and Lt. Col. Józef Beck[133] went to Wilanów and received the signed documents. Stanisław Wojciechowski resigned the office of the president and Wincenty Witos announced the dissolution of the government.

The Marshal's wife saw her husband on the evening of 14 May, and later she wrote down her impressions.

I was frightened by his appearance. Over two days he had aged by about 10 years. He looked as if he had lost half his body weight. His face was parchment-like, pale and strangely transparent, as if it had been lit from within. His eyes were sunken from weariness. Only once again did I see him in such state – it was a few hours before he died. ... Those three days left an indelible and merciless mark on him, one that would stay with him to the end. He never recovered his former inner peace, nor the control he had over himself. It seemed that some incredible weight was bearing down upon his shoulders.

On 20 May, Piłsudski spent an hour talking with the French ambassador. He spoke about the necessity of having professionals run the government, a government that would bring peace, enable a rational solution of economic problems, and eliminate corruption. It was noted that he gave the impression of a man in control and one who believed in the future.

On 22 May, Piłsudski issued a special order to the army in which he stated:

Soldiers. I am again at the helm as your commander. You know me. Ignoring my own welfare, I have always been among you during the most difficult battles and struggles, in your difficulties and worries. ... May God be merciful over our sins and stay the punishing hand, and we will stand to do our work, which strengthens and renews the face of the earth.

Piłsudski presented his assessments of the political situation of the time in newspaper interviews, published by the *Kurier Poranny*. In an interview from 25 May, he explained the genesis of the May incidents. The Marshal was indignant over the lawless abuse within the government and the steadily decreasing quality of life for the working man. The formation of a government under Witos reminded him of "the infamous government because of which he left the service of the state, not wishing to use his name to support people who took part in the worst crime committed in Poland - the murder of President Narutowicz."

The actions which Piłsudski took only had the goal of having the president dissolve the government. *I still regret that the president put us into an absurd situation on the Poniatowski Bridge, instead of dismissing those who did not dare to show themselves before me. ... I have accomplished a kind of historical fait, something like a coup d'etat, something like a revolution without any revolutionary consequences.*

The second interview was a discussion of candidates for president and fascism. Piłsudski stated that he expects to be nominated as a candidate for the office. As for fascism, he did not think that something like it could find a home in Poland.

I do not believe that Poland could be governed with a whip. I am not for a dictatorship, but the head of state must have the ability to make quick decisions in matters concerning the national interest. Parliamentary plots slow down the most indispensible solutions. ... I am not saying that we should imitate the United States where the great power of the federal government is balanced with the broad autonomy of the various states but may be able to find something of that kind which could be applied in Poland.

Piłsudski continued saying that he had supporters on the right as well as on the left, but to bring about a recovery, one cannot look for it in party politics but in the activities of all honest citizens of the independent Polish state. In interviews from 27th and 29th of May, he spoke about the essence of a strong government.

The essence of power is a decision made at the proper time. The government and the various ministers must be responsible for their decisions but also must have the ability to make the decisions. ... Meanwhile, here the very formulation of a government is dependent on drawn out discussions among the parties, coalitions, cliques, groupings, and the like. Each minister, instead of the ability to undertake a decision, must also have the talents of a speaker and the cleverness to conduct parliamentary intrigues and the tact to satisfy the demands of the representatives.

On 29 May, at a gathering of representatives from various parties, Piłsudski gave a speech about the election (two days later) of the president.

I have given a guarantee that the election would be unencumbered, and I will keep this promise, but be warned that you are not permitted to make any party deals with the presidential candidates. The candidate for president must be outside the party system, ready to represent the entire nation. ... I have declared war on the scum, scoundrels, murderers, and thieves, and I will not let up in this warfare. The Sejm and the Senate have too many privileges and it should be that those who are called to govern should have more rights. ... Give the ability to those in the government to be responsible for what they do. ... It is not important to me how many votes I receive ... I am not pressing to have myself elected... Find other non-party candidates who are worthy of this high office.

At rallies and demonstrations across the country, the populace was demanding the election of Piłsudski as president. During a session of the National Assembly on 31 May 1926, Józef Piłsudski was elected president with two hundred and ninety-three votes. Adolf Bninski, a candidate put forth by the National Democrats and the Christian-National Coalition, received one hundred and ninety-three votes. Immediately after his election, Piłsudski sent a letter where he expressed thanks and gave an explanation.

> *For a second time in my life, my historical activities and work have been legalized in this way. I thank you that this time the election was not unanimous, as in February of 1919. Unfortunately, however, I cannot accept this office, because in my memory stands the tragic figure of murdered President Narutowicz.*

He continued with an apology for disappointing those who voted for him, as well as those who wished for this outcome outside the parliamentary hall.

On June 1926, Ignacy Mościcki[134] became the president of the Polish Republic. Because he had been a person totally unknown in Poland, Piłsudski gave an interview to the *Kurier Poranny* where he informed all about his friendship with the new president, which had begun in the previous century.

> *His thinking*, stated Piłsudski, *will never be forced within the frames of doctrine, and never ever into the frames of the tiny doctrines and stiff formulas, and even more confining rules. … When I vacillated among the choices of people, a technical moment prevailed over a moment of humanism, which also had to be taken into consideration. I believe that in Poland, we have a shortage of technicians in the government.*

In the new government, under Prime Minister Kazimierz Bartel,[135] Piłsudski took over the office of the Minister of Defense. The Piłsudskis moved into Belweder Palace. Nearly every Sunday they spent in Sulejówek.

On 2 August 1926, the National Assembly revised the constitution of 17 March 1921. The president was given the power to dissolve the chambers of parliament and issue decrees that had the force of law. The role of the government was also strengthened.

On 6 August on the anniversary of the march-out of the cadres, the president issued three decrees that fulfilled Piłsudski's demands on the subject of the high command of the armed forces – then an Office of Inspector General of the Armed Forces (GISZ) and a Committee for National Defense were established.

The famous meeting on the Poniatowski Bridge in May 1926 – the Marshal with the President of the Polish Republic Stanisław Wojciechowski – which was followed by fierce fighting.

Marshal Józef Piłsudski, President of the Polish Republic Ignacy Mościcki (1867 – 1946), and Prime Minister Kazimierz Bartel (1882 – 1941)

(Left) Gen. Bolesław Wieniawą-Długoszowski (1881 – 1942)
(Right) Gen. Gustaw Orlicz-Dreszer (1889 – 1936)

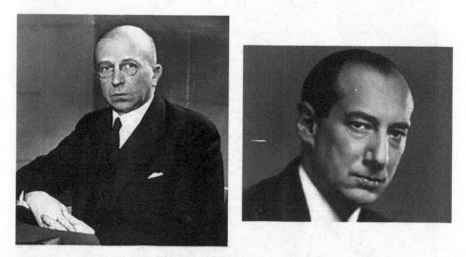

(Left) Adam Koc (1891 – 1969), Commendant of the Union of Legionnaires, one of the founders of the Józef Piłsudski Institute in New York.
(Right) Józef Beck (1894 – 1944), one of the closest collaborators to Piłsudski. During the years 1932 – 1939 he was the head of the Foreign Ministry.

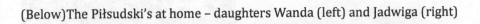

(Left) Aleksandra Piłsudski (nee Szczerbińska) the Marshal's second wife.
(Right) Józef and Aleksandra Piłsudski at Belveder.

(Below)The Piłsudski's at home – daughters Wanda (left) and Jadwiga (right)

(Left) with Kazimierz Bartlem. We all understand that we must fight for our goals, both politically and socially.

(Right) Above the head, there is time for the soul to live, and the man must brace himself to bare it, and then - as the arm of a small child, true, helpless, which he can not think, but smiles cheerfully, palms up like silk, wrinkles smoothes and care to fight the case. The child's impotence is his power.

(Left) Missing the normal manifestation of national life, which is the Polish state, I sought for the factors, the data that the Polish tradition brings with it, in which it feels good, which intensify the forces of the individual and the nation. Because someone else's soul is a dangerous thing.

(Right) Piłsudski's home at Sulejówek. Greatness, where is your name? Of smallness, where are your thoughts? And I often dream in Druskienniki that in just one blissful smile of freedom to rest after work, as in some eternity of the truth about the pleasant laughter of a surprise – to be able to meet with Greatness and Smallness.

Chapter 24
Morning and Evening Auroras

Piłsudski tried to save his deteriorating health with frequent trips to the spa in Druskienniki on the Niemen River, to which he took fancy in 1924. From 1926, this modern medical facility was operated by the beautiful and intelligent Dr. Eugenia Lewika. She was unmarried and a social activist. The Marshal's biographers rarely mention her. Who was she? She was born in Czerkasy in 1896 and studied medicine in Kiev where in 1921 she received her medical diploma. Dr. Lewika was especially interested in modern methods of maintaining good health through exposure to air, water, exercise, and the sun. The doctor conducted some experiments in this field in Denmark and Sweden. Her degree as Doctor of Medicine she received in Warsaw in 1925. That year, she started to organize a modern health facility in Druskienniki.

Eugenia was a proponent of physical education for youth and decided to convince the Marshal as to this approach. Her arguments found fertile soil. Evidence of this is a conversation which Piłsudski had at the beginning of November 1926 with Lt. Col. Juliusz Ulrych, an officer on his staff at Belweder Palace.

Physical education, he said, *cannot be conducted without scientific assistance, without   professional direction. The physical education movement must include both boys and girls, and in the scientific group directing this effort there must be both men and women, representatives of the medical field and science.*

The instructions that Lt. Col. Ulrych received were very detailed and well thought out. On this basis, a Ministry of Physical Education and Military Preparedness was created on 28 January 1927 under the direction of Juliusz Ulrych. On 28 August 1927, a National Scientific Council for Physical Education was created with Piłsudski at its head. Dr. Eugenia Lewika was one of the members. Was it possible that she was a Soviet agent? Or perhaps in the relationship between the aging Marshal and Ms. Lewicka there was something more than understanding and sympathy?

On the basis of rumors, and also other circumstances, all things were possible. Jan Lechoń in the first volume of his *Dziennik [Journal]* (published in London in 1967, p. 186) mentions an anecdote told by Kaden-Bandrowski.

Poland was a woman to Piłsudski, but a woman less than ideal. When he had an outburst against her, he always called her a strumpet. There is something substantial in this. And then, a few years before his death, impulsive romantic infatuation of the Old Man in Ms. Lewicka. This is proof that his political work was only a sublimation of personal feelings and even of sensuality.

When on 15 December 1930, the Marshal left for Madeira, he was under the care of two doctors: Col. Marcin Woyczyński and Dr. Eugenia Lewicka. The circumstances of Lewicka's death on 27 June 1931, are dramatic and not fully explained. Most likely she committed suicide by taking poison. On the day of her funeral, Piłsudski came to the church in Powązki accompanied by Wieniawa and Składkowski. He sat on the side benches close to the rear of the church and then departed.[136]

At the fifth reunion of the legionaries, which took place on 8 August 1926, (Sunday) in Kielce, Piłsudski gave a long speech characterizing his spirit and method of viewing international relations.

On one of the segments of our march was the castle of some margraves in Greater Poland. And it seemed to me that from those walls there rose a phantom of the great margrave, who futilely tried to suppress our forbears' longings for independence.

Drawing on recollections from his Siberian exile, Piłsudski made reference to the significance of auroras.

You can see them when the sun rises and when it sets ... There is the deception of the morning aurora and the falseness of the evening one. How many of those morning and evening auroras had humanity and our Homeland endured. How much falseness and self-deception we have endured when there was no sun, but the sky burned with fire. ... How many false auroras, how many phantoms were behind us, when finally, in August 1914, we marched on the road from Kraków to Kielce.

After reflecting on his reminiscences, Piłsudski presented his comments about the courage of thought and the courage in methods of work.

Our example, for everyone who entertained the false and real dawns despite all the falsehoods, that our fathers and grandfathers have endured, is the example of those who could find light in those

215

*evening auroras and greet the morning auroras with courageous
work. This is proof and a conclusion for all that to think courageously
and to work courageously, is better than talking and playing in the
mud.*

On 2 October 1926, a new government was sworn in. The Prime
Minister and Minister of the Military was Józef Piłsudski. The government was composed of socialists as well as conservatives. The significance of this fact was noted by Speaker of the Sejm, Maciej Rataj, in his
journal. *The presence of extreme conservatives and socialists in the cabinet
means that Piłsudski is a man who wants to establish a social balance in
Poland and assure her peace.*

An event that testified to the fact that Piłsudski had come to
terms with the temperamental landowners was the famous gathering in
Nieświeże. The occasion for this event, which was of great political significance, was the ceremony of placing the *Gold Cross of the Virtuti Militari*
on the sarcophagus of Maj. Stanisław Radziwiłł, a former adjutant to the
Marshal who died during the Kiev expedition. One measure of the difficulties overcome by Piłsudski to bring him near to the many influential
aristocratic families was a saying that started to circulate after the meeting. *It's easy to hit a raven or shoot an owl through the head – but it's a
totally new accomplishment to go from Bezdan to Nieświeże.*

In filling the office of Prime Minister and Minster for the Military,
he was also responsible for Foreign Affairs; and as he competed his official work for Poland, making historic decisions, he also exerted his personal influence on the current problems faced by the Polish state. It is
surely a paradox that one event in 1927 took on a specific significance in
the Marshal's biography with the passage of time. This was the interment
of Juliusz Słowacki's remains in the crypts of the cathedral on Wawel Castle Hill[137] in Kraków. The oration that he gave in connection with the
ceremony (28 June 1927) took place in the courtyard of Wawel Castle
and had the reputation of being his best speech. The text was written
down from memory and it is entirety not known, but it remains as part
of the Piłsudski legend and as such will remain through the generations,
together with Słowacki's poetry and Wawel Castle.

*All that lives must die, all that has died lived once. The law of
death is remorseless and merciless. Often entire generations pass into
eternity, leaving behind only recollections without names or faces.
But the truth of human life gives us other testimony. There are people and there are deeds so strong and powerful that they transcend
death and continue to live with us. Słowacki, as a living truth, is still*

among us. We know as much about him as we do about our closest friends. In this way, the laws of death are overcome. He is alive and he lives among us, and the truth of death has no hold upon him. The overpowering gates of death have closed but not tightly enough to contain him.

Even now, as we bring Słowacki's remains into the royal crypts, we extend his life and he will remain as long as the walls of Wawel can withstand the destruction of time, and the rock by the Vistula, standing there alone, is not dissolved ... Everywhere where there are sharp turns and bends in the road, where people vacillate and little people fear, there are huge solitary stones like road signs, but with names. Słowacki created poetry during times when we ran out of material resources – an army. For the strength of arms which was denied to us, he substituted another power, the power of the spirit ... The proud strains of the harp went up to heaven when the swords were hidden under earth, rusting and wasting away. In Słowacki's work, I found the laws of the soul and of the delight of the soul suffering for pride, for human dignity. He worked like others and thought about the possibility that the spirit could replace the power of the body. And suffering, he doubted, like others, "I have no dignity, I run from suffering." ...

When I now look upon this casket, like all those gathered here, I know that he walks among those stones that, through the names upon then, testify to the chronology of our past. He walks among the Władysławs and Zygmunds, among the Jans and Bolesławs. He walks with a name, testifying also to the great work and the greatness of the Polish spirit. He walks to extend his life, so that he may remain not just with our generation, but with those who are yet to come. He walks as the King Spirit. In the name of the Republic's government, I commend you to take the casket into the royal crypt, for he was the peer of kings.

On 28 November 1918, on the 291st anniversary of the battle at Oliwa, Józef Piłsudski as the Head of State issued a decree concerning the creation of a Polish Navy. Acting on his initiate, on 23 September 1923, the Sejm adopted the resolution which approved the construction of a new seaport at Gdynia.[138] A few months later, ground was broken at Gdynia. The construction work went into full swing in 1926 when the country's leadership was in Piłsudski's hands. The Marshal thought that the new seaport in Gdynia was one of the most important tasks for the new Polish state for both economic and military reasons. Piłsudski visited Gdynia multiple times and was always glad to see the work move forward. Sensitive to supernatural matters, he joked when the weather was bad.

Perhaps I should put a magic spell on the sea. One of my forbears once kidnapped a holy priestess from before the sacred flame and then married her. It was from her that I inherited my unibrow.

In autumn 1926, Gdynia received its city charter, and by 1933, the city already had fifty thousand inhabitants. The new modern port took first place in terms of cargo transferred, outdistancing Gdańsk, but also Szcezcin (Stettin), Stockholm, Leningrad, Riga, and many others. Gdynia became symbolic of Polish possibilities. *It is thanks to her*, said Piłsudski at a ceremony devoted to Days of the Sea, *that Poland is aware how important it is to have the sea as an important part of the country's economy. It is the basis for stabilizing her power, her autonomy, and her future.*

An energetic and tireless executor of the national effort during the building of Gdynia was Eugeniusz Kwiatkowski,[139] who was Minister for Trade and Industry in Piłsudski's government.

As prime minister, Piłsudski concentrated on political matters, in keeping a proper balance among the competences among the Sejm, the President, and the Government. This was not an easy task. The Marshal spoke about this at the next, that is the sixth, Reunion of the Legionaries, which took place 6-7 August 1927, in Kalisz.

We celebrate the tenth anniversary of Szczypiorno, Benjaminów, the tenth anniversary of Magdeburg and other prisons, to which we were sent. We know how it was really, when we sing "not for one or the other was Poland first." I tell you gentlemen, then I talked with people for hours per day ... not being able to reconcile one man with another. ... I had to co-operate with people who would easily curse their brothers, accusing them of faithlessness and dishonor with no hesitation ... I saw legislation going forward and in a constant direction so that foreign agents, bought and paid would be allowed in the upper echelons of government.

Piłsudski continued saying that many of his efforts were foiled by foreign agents, paid for by enemies to do Poland harm. *Poland will go through a difficult time. During the crises – I repeat – beware of foreign agents.*

Piłsudski devoted much time to the matter of defense. As Minister for the Military, he worked from the General Office Building of the Armed Forces Inspectorate on Aleje Ujazdowskie. Zygmunt Szyszko-Bohusz, who was then a Lt. Colonel, described the Marshal's bedroom.

It was a large room with a high ceiling, but rather dark, because the three large windows were shaded by great trees. By the left wall stood a large table piled high with papers and books. In front of it was a small table where the Marshal would sometimes eat his breakfast or play solitaire. Deep within was a regular bed with a nightstand and, on the wall, a large picture of the Virgin Mary of Ostrobrama. On the left side was the open door to the office, through which I saw a large desk, piled with papers, just like the table in the bedroom. The Marshal would not let anyone touch or clean up the mess.

Piłsudski's favorite place to go for a rest was Druskienniki. Long walks by the Niemen River, hours spent on solitary contemplation in the park, conversations with close friends, and much reading, together with baths at the spa – all this regenerated his strength. Yet the state of his health was never good. On Saturday 20 August 1927, Professor Tomasz Siemiradzki, President of the Piłsudski Society of America, came to see him. He described the conditions under which Piłsudski lived in Druskienniki.

He came far to see me and sat me down on the veranda. After a half-hour conversation, a private soldier came in and announced that dinner was ready. The wooden villa, a tiny manor on a hill, was hidden in the forest along the Niemen. From the path and the windows, one could see the opposite shore in Lithuania. His family was in Sulejówek. The table settings were plain, simple, like in camp. An egg salad with meat was served in an excellent sauce. For the second course, poached eggs, then compote, tea, and cakes. There was no liquor. He spoke a lot, with animation, telling about his parents, and I told about mine. Then about his youth, the high school in Vilnius, Siberia, and I related some of my times. In a word, two old friends talking about the past. He so befriended me that I stopped fearing him, though it was difficult to look at those brows and moustache without shivering.

In a relaxed manner, even joyfully, Piłsudski recalled the days in July 1928 spent in Gdynia and on the Hel Peninsula. The occasion was an official one, connected to the launching of three passenger ships, *Wanda, Jadwiga,* and *Hanka,* whose "godmothers" were the Marshal's daughters and the daughter of Minister Kwiatkowski. After the ceremonies were over, there was a little time for a private celebration.

Relations with Lithuania were bad at this time, and this worried Piłsudski as they deteriorated even more. Intrigue by the Germans and Russians together with the unhealthy Lithuanian nationalism, full of complexes, created new disputes and conflicts. In Kowno, Polish activists were arrested, Polish schools and societies were closed. In return, Polish authorities closed the Lithuanian normal school in Vilnius and deported the most vociferous activists of the Lithuanian minority. Under the pretext of a planned Polish attack on Lithuania, a mobilization started in

Kovno, and a protest was lodged in the League of Nations on 15 October 1927.

On 23 November, Piłsudski came to Vilnius in the company of many ministers and politicians from the Eastern Division of the Foreign Ministry. The Polish ambassadors from Moscow (Stanisław Patek) and from Riga (J. Łukasiewicz) were recalled. As the result of a detailed analysis of the situation, on 29 November the government sent a note to the League of Nations and all nations, informing them that Poland had no inimical intentions toward Lithuania and only seeks to establish normal neighborly relations with the Lithuanian Republic. The note asked that the League attempt to influence Lithuania to issue a declaration that it is not in a state of war with Poland and is ready to normalize relations.

In an interview which Piłsudski gave to the Polish Telegraph Agency on 20 November, he said:

> *The state of war which the Lithuanians have declared in regard to Poland is an anomaly and a state of sickness. It is a state as was earlier on wild fields: a brother could not see his brother for years, a dying mother could not bid farewell to her children from the death-bed, not even the smallest kind of business could be conducted.*

Piłsudski continued that he considered the task of calling for mobilization in Poland in response to such moves in Lithuania but decided not to do it and wait for a decision from the League of Nations in answer to the Polish note. In the above quoted interview, Piłsudski appealed to his fellow Poles to behave with gravitas and peace in response to the threat against them, *when the sword is in the hands of madmen*.

Because of the seriousness of the situation, Piłsudski decided to personally go to Geneva to attend the session of the Council of the League of Nations, which was looking into Polish-Lithuanian relations. He departed on 7 December. During this peaceful expedition, he had to appear in civilian attire, but he did not own a suit; and since the founding of the Riflemen's Societies, he wore a uniform. This difficulty was somehow overcome, and he appeared, as per diplomatic protocol, as a total civilian. At a breakfast given by Minister Zaleski, in addition to Piłsudski and Beck, who was his companion, there were the Minister of Foreign Affairs of France – Briand, and a representative of Great Britain – Austin Chamberlain.

On Saturday 10 December, the League of Nations met. There was a less than "diplomatic," but substantial, exchange of views between the Marshal and the Lithuanian Prime Minister – Voldemaras. After forty minutes of murky and complicated discussions by diplomats on the subject of the Lithuanian complaint, the Marshal, who had been listening patiently, rose from his chair and said:

If you gentlemen please, I have come to hear the word "peace," but instead I hear various ruminations. Perhaps these are important, but at this moment, they mean nothing to me. I would like to know if there will be peace, and if the League wants to be part of it? Mr. Voldemaras, I would like to know whether you want peace or war? For if there is going to be war, then the matter is mine; if there will be peace, it will be arranged by the ministers.

Voldemaras, surprised by such a simple statement, was silent for a long while. He concluded that since the cancellation of the state of war depended on a resolution, that he accepted, and that he could only repeat that resolution. Piłsudski stated that this was what he was awaiting. The Marshal's stay in Geneva lasted thirty-eight hours and ended in success, not only because of the easing of tension with Lithuania, but also because of the talks he conducted with many politicians who had influence on the situation in Europe. Piłsudski created a great impression on all of his interlocutors. On Monday, 12 December, he was back in Warsaw, happy that he was able to attend his wife's name-day celebration.

His personal engagement in the conduct of Polish-Lithuanian relations and the appearance at the League of Nations were an external manifestation of Piłsudski's involvement in regulating foreign policy and making it autonomous. The Marshal was aware that Poland's independence was in equal danger from Germany and Soviet Russia. He thought that by conducting a policy of peace that was decisive and not fearful, Poland must counter the intrigues of the hostile powers and prevent their alliance.

Piłsudski considered France to be a tested and natural ally but was against the concepts which later would find expression in the Front Morges,[140] giving Poland only a subsidiary position to France. Despite the failures in realizing the federation program (a negative example of this were relations with Lithuania) Piłsudski saw a possibility for securing Poland's independence by continuing to build up its own power by making treaties with its neighbors and entering into alliances with countries whose interests were threatened by Russia or Germany. Exotic and ineffective in practice, but not without a great vision, was Poland's cooperation with the Prometheus Movement,[141] which coordinated the struggle for independence among the nations incorporated into the Soviet Union.

Chapter 25
A Cure with Complications

Piłsudski thought that in the mid-1920s the Polish State was suffering from a deadly disease, that the moral state of the ruling elites and the "sejmocracy" based on the bad constitution from April 1921 justified a drastic program of treatment. There was to be a moral cleansing of the citizens, especially those involved in the government. This was the motivation behind the May events, which were supported by most of the country's citizens, and which the marshal described as "something between a coup and a revolution, without any revolutionary consequences."

To describe the post-May governing with Piłsudski's participation, and the government that operated in his shadow, the short-hand term "Sanacja" (cleansing) was coined. Over several decades of Communist propaganda, the word "Sanacja" was used practically as a synonym for fascism, anti-democracy, and all other evils that were used to explain the source and cause of the failures that led to Poland's involvement in World War II. The odium associated with Sanacja was intended to diminish Piłsudski's greatness and accomplishments which, even if they were undoubtedly used to gain independence, were to be interpreted as a detriment to Poland during the post-May government.

In the light of facts and honest interpretation that took into consideration Poland's internal situation, as well as the context of complicated interpersonal and international relations, accusations of antidemocratic tendencies aimed at Piłsudski and his supporters cannot withstand scrutiny.

In an interview given to Bogusław Miedziński, Piłsudski said:

> *The question is a very serious and very deep one, because without doubt, parliamentarianism all around the world is diseased. Everywhere they are trying to repair relations in one way or another. As for me, gentlemen, I do not think one could do without elected representatives who are obligated through a feeling of responsibility.*

Piłsudski saw a great evil and an internal threat to the independence of Poland in the particularism inherited from the time of partition, cliques, parties, class-based interests, and the actions by agents working on behalf foreign powers. The solidarity to which Piłsudski and his supporters referred had an emotional and moral character which was not always sufficient for effective reform of the state and its institutions.

One of Piłsudski's closest colleagues at this time was Walery Sławek. The Non-Party Block of Cooperation with the Government (BBWR), which stood outside the ideological and party squabbles, was organized by Sławek as a new form for mobilizing public opinion during the elections. In the elections that took place in March 1928, the BBWR gained one hundred and twenty-two of four hundred and forty-four seats in the Sejm and forty-six of one hundred and eleven in the Senate.

At a meeting with politicians, in a two-hour speech, Piłsudski presented his basic thoughts on how the government should function. He concluded that being an advocate for a legal construction of the state, he was seeking to reach a solution for the third time that would give expanded powers to the president. Changes to the constitution must be made and that required time. Poland cannot follow Russia and Italy by ridding itself of the parliamentary system.

On 27 March 1928, the Sejm began its session. Felicjan Sławoj-Składowski,[142] a decent man, good citizen, and former soldier, who was vociferously maligned at the time, was also an excellent administrator and writer. In his Strzępy meldunków [Scraps of reports] he left a record of the situation in the Sejm at that time.

The Marshal took the proclamation opening the Sejm from the hands of Lt. Zaćwilichowski that was rolled into a scroll and entered the Sejm chamber. … The entire Sejm froze in anticipation. … Suddenly on the left side of the room, between the first and second set of doors leading out into the hallway, in the back rows, a group of representatives started to shout, 'Away with the fascist Piłsudski government!' The Marshal stopped unrolling the paper and spoke toward the screaming communists, 'You gentlemen will be taken from the room!' … but their yelling grew louder. 'Throw them out!' said the Marshal, turning to me and pointing at the communists. I ran out into the main hallway … 'Boys, the son of a bitch communists are interfering with the Marshal's speech. We'll toss them out.' I looked at the pale faced communists and pointed them out to the policemen. At that moment, the entire Sejm started to shout and move from their places … The place was jammed. My police could not remove the communists, as the passageways were clogged while a row of representatives was holding on to them… Fortunately, at that moment Jaroszewicz brought in another ten policemen … As I left the chamber, I looked at the Marshal. He stood there peacefully leaning on his saber, alone, and calm among the chaos of shoving and fighting.

These were experiences that, no doubt, had a negative effect on the Marshal's health. He was only sixty years old at the time but often spoke about death and expressed the wish that his heart be placed in Rossa among the soldiers who fell during the Vilnius expedition in 1919.

At the end of June 1928, Piłsudski resigned from the Presidency of the Council of Ministers. The office of prime minister was again taken over by Professor Kazimierz Bartel. The Speaker of the Sejm, Ignacy Daszyński, wanting to calm the conflicts, asked that the Sejm be dissolved, and new elections held, or that a majority coalition consisting of the BBWR, PPS, and PSL "Wyzwolenie" be formed. Piłsudski approved of this idea but it was never realized. At the time, the government had several successes both in the economic field as well as in the socio-political sphere. However, the generous compromises given by Bartel and a premature resolution by the BBWR to change the constitution at the autumn Sejm session (from 31 October 1928 to 25 February 1929) caused a coalition to form between the left and the center politicians creating the "center-left." The PSL "Piast" party, the Christian Democrats, and the National Workers' Party, not choosy about the means of doing business, began an unceasing battle with Piłsudski and the Sanacja. The situation was complicated by the international economic crisis, which was just beginning. This radicalized the masses and provided fertile ground for all kinds of demagoguery.

Piłsudski was now tired and ill more frequently. In his own statements, that often were rather un-parliamentary, he warned that he would not permit Poland, *to be trampled by the parties*.

In March 1930, Walery Sławek became head of the new government. Władysław Baranowski, the Polish ambassador in Sophia, who returned during that time and visited Piłsudski in Sulejówek noted that:

> "*I saw a real grandfather, a wasted, thin old man bent in half, with dull eyes and a balding head. ... 'I am tired. Strangely tired,' complained the Marshal in a quiet voice.*"

Meanwhile, the political activities of the "center-left" against the government grew in strength. After the congress in Kraków (June 1930), they directly called for sabotage to all service for the government and the overthrow of dictatorship. In August 1930, Sławek resigned and Piłsudski once again assumed the office of prime minister. In an interview given to Miedziński (26 August), he spoke about the difficulties, which confronted every head of government in Poland. These difficulties are due, among other things, *to the badly composed and written constitution. The representatives should not rule but legislate laws and establish con-*

225

trols so that they are observed. Meanwhile, the representatives only want to rule and to show that they are more intelligent than others, while they talk nonsense.

On 29 August 1930, President Mościcki issued a decree that dissolved the Sejm and scheduled elections for 16 November.

On 9 September the police arrested eighteen former representatives. Among them were several who were undoubtedly traitors, acting against Polish national interests, but many of them had unsullied reputations, social passion, and good will. Their imprisonment in Brześć, and especially the bad treatment they received, caused understandable and justifiable public outrage. Piłsudski made a statement that, even before the dissolution of the Sejm, there were many complaints about the lawless behavior of the representatives, but he protected their immunity. After the Sejm was dissolved, the law and could go after these gentlemen for their infractions. Piłsudski went on to explain that the investigations and lawful process in the matter of the former representatives were initiated without any prompting from him. There exists much information to support the fact that the statement is correct.

During the November elections, of the four hundred and forty-four seats in the Sejm the BBWR received two hundred and forty-seven, the left and center one hundred and two, the Nationalist Party sixty-two, and the national minorities thirty-three. Piłsudski judged that Poland would have about five years of peace, years that must be wisely used.

On 28 November 1930, he resigned as prime minister. He said that "he had overexerted himself so badly and was so upset, that it's fearful to talk about." On 4 December, the entire cabinet resigned and a new government formed under the leadership of Walery Sławek.

Piłsudski was totally exhausted. *I cannot work any longer. It is winter, and I am at the threshold of death. ... I have managed to deal with the worst of it, the representatives. Mr. Sławek will deal with the second evil, the laws regarding the functionaries. All the troublemakers must be removed ... I have always admired my father that he was able to work for eighteen hours a day. I could only survive that for thirty years. Now I am tired.*

After long discussions and consultations, it was decided that the best place for a rest cure would be Madeira.

On 13 December 930, Piłsudski gave the last interview of his life. In a long conversation with Tadeusz Świecicki, he again stated his comments on the subject of organizing the government, especially the office of the president. He reiterated that the office of the president is held by one man, while the government has fourteen members, and the Sejm and Senate together nearly six hundred. The president must be independent and must have the authority to regulate the entire government apparatus. As in the United States, the president should be elected by the whole of society. And when the governmental machine must be regulated because of internal grinding, that is, under conditions of a crisis, then we must relay on the power of one man and not interfere in his work.

I belong to those very strong individuals, and I would say that I have the gift of a strong character and the power to make decisions ... But still, having this exceptional power, I have gone through some strong vacillations, which have caused such monstrous pain that I thrashed about like a wild man, going through several rooms and nearly attacking everyone with my fists, anyone who in that moment would get in my way. So, what can be expected, when I have to deal with some scoundrel?

On 15 December 1930, a special salon rail car took Piłsudski from Warsaw to Lisbon. On 16 December, he went through Vienna, and on the next day, he was greeted at the French border by representatives of the government and Ambassador A. Chłapowski. Not stopping along the way and practically not leaving the rail car, he reached the Portuguese frontier where a representative of President Carmony greeted him. In Lisbon, which was the only place where an official visit took place, he was given the insignia of the order "Tower and Blade."[143] In the afternoon, he boarded the ship *Angola* and departed for the port and leisure town of Funchal on Madeira.

He was quartered in the in the single-level villa "Bettencourt" in the northwest suburb called Szo Martinho. In a beautifully kept garden, there was a gazebo, a favorite place for the Marshal, where he could play solitaire and chess with doctor Woyczyński. Outside of the doctor and Capt. Mieczysław Lepecki, Piłsudski had no entourage, because he was categorically opposed to having such. In front of the villa, the local constabulary placed a single policeman.

The Marshal would wear his favorite shooting jacket and led a very regular lifestyle. He rose earlier than before. At 8:00 am, he ate his breakfast and walked in the garden. At 11:00 am, he had his second meal and would read or dictated his last large work *Poprawki historyczne [Corrections to history]* to Dr. Woyczyński until 3:00 pm. After dinner, which he ate at 3:00 pm, he would walk about the garden and spend time in his favorite gazebo.

Konrad Wrzos, who was quoted earlier, was in Madeira after the Marshal's death and noted the following recollections from Emil Rodiriquez Doniz who, during Piłsudski's stay in Funchalu, was a gardener at the villa.

Sometimes I would see how the Marshal would walk on the path, this way and that, there and back. He had his hands in his pockets, his shoulders bent, rounded, and he seemed to be murmuring. I listened carefully, but what could I hear? The Marshal was talking to himself. He actually was having a conversation. Sometimes he raised his voice, but most of the time it was murmuring. ... Perhaps sometimes he was overly upset? ... Perhaps he devoted too much thought to his own country? When they left, I saw the Marshal wearing a small, round, blue cap. ... He was totally different. He put on the cap, saluted by placing two fingers to the visor, and left. The villa "Quinta Bettencourt" became empty.

In a letter to his daughters dated 31 December Piłsudski wrote:

My dear girls, my nice ladies and dearest daughters .... I am as if still in autumn, so that means there is winter to come, but the trees are blossoming. This I cannot stand, for flowers, let them do that, because even in our Sulejówek some dahlias or phlox or other awful things will flower even in October, but for entire trees to flower and give off aroma, this cannot be, cannot be. I tell you I don't like it, to have my reason turned upside down ... I cannot stand to look at the ocean and when I sit in the garden, I turn my back toward it, so it would not bother my eyes. I also cannot look at the mountains because they are constantly covered by clouds. Mostly I look in one direction, where there are no mountains, or clouds, or ocean. There I see two hills and there is a forest, very scruffy, tiny and thinned out, but still a forest where one can look, and your father named these hills – one is the Kościuszko Mound, the other Wanda's Mound, just as in Kraków.

The stay in Madeira lasted three and a half months and was the longest vacation Piłsudski took during his working life. His state of being and disposition quickly improved, so that he wrote to his daughters that "it frightened him." His breathing was regular, he rid himself of hoarseness and the tendencies to catch cold. To the Poprawki historyczne written on Madeira, he attached a long introduction and wrote a commentary for the memoirs of Ignacy Daszyński and Leon Biliński. He wrote:

With sadness I must say that all these works present myself, that is Józef Piłsudski, as a person unknown to me. It is a picture without resemblance, sometimes as stupid as a monkey, which for unknown reasons and for an undetermined purpose, became the central figure of a period that was most crucial to Poland ... I had planned to write a monograph about myself, but I don't know if I will be able to do it.

228

Finding the pages where his name was mentioned in those two memoirs, Piłsudski corrected and commented the errors and the false information regarding his person. In this way, the typed manuscript of *Poprawki do histori*, the last large work by the Marshal, came about.

Some of the difficult facets of Piłsudski's personality were revealed during the time that the Poprawki were being prepared for printing. It turned out that the Marshal's excellent memory was no longer as reliable as it seemed to him. In clarifying his own background and making corrections, he made several rather obvious errors himself, because he wrote the *Poprawki* without having books and sources on hand. Władysław Pobóg-Malinowski wrote about the "unauthorized" correction of the Marshal's errors, conducted in an atmosphere of fear, on the personal responsibility of General Julian Stachiewicz, in *Kultura* (no. 5, 1960). It is true that when the Marshal was approached on this subject, he muttered that the thing "was to be printed immediately without changing one letter" but this should not be taken too literally and used to demonize him as "an awful old man." In any case, Gen. Stachiewicz had clear power of attorney over Piłsudski's manuscripts, which, more or less, obligated him to "exercise oversight over the historical accuracy and consistency of the published texts."

The storm over the "unauthorized" corrections, whose frightful dimensions Pobóg-Malinowski describes in his memoir, never took place and this is much more likely in overview of the situation, rather than clearly exaggerated tale about the supposed intimidation under which Piłsudski's supporters lived during the final years of his life.

On 22 March 1931, the destroyer *Wicher* arrived in Funchal and took the Marshal back to Gdynia. After returning to Warsaw, he made a visit of President Mościcki and said that he cannot accept any great responsibilities, because this could lead to his complete exhaustion. *The matters that I need to order before my death will be completed, these are the army and international affairs. Please do not tire me with the economic situation, and mainly with the financial affairs.*

Piłsudski had bad premonitions not only in the case of his own death but also for the future of Poland. His pessimistic visions were noticed by many politicians and all the witnesses to history who had the opportunity to speak with the Marshal under unconventional circumstances.

Colonel Michałowski who visited Romania with Piłsudski in October 1931 recalled that: *During one of the night shifts I fell asleep, and on waking, heard the Marshal's voice ... I opened the door of the bedroom ... He was clearly deep in thought, and I interrupted him by entering. He said, "What do you need, my boy?" Before I had a chance to explain the reason for my interrupting his reverie, he continued his monologue while looking straight into my eyes. 'Yes, are you aware of the dangers facing Poland ... if Poles, all Poles, do you understand what I am saying, all Poles, will not work to defend the country's interests – and I am not here, then in ten years there will be no Poland.'* The Marshal threw the cards on the table, covered his face with his large hands and seemed to cry.

At the end of 1931, Piłsudski returned to the problem of his authentic biography. His confidant in this matter was Artur Śliwinski,[144] an old and trusted friend. During part of the time that the Marshal was also Head of State, Śliwinski was prime minister. After 1926, Piłsudski twice offered him the office of Minister of Education. He invited Śliwinski for the first private conversation on 4 November 1931.

He looked old, his face was sad and suffering, the eyes were tired. He spoke slowly, with long pauses, stuttering, something that never happened before. *I must die, and I know that I will die shortly ... We should have won the elections ... we must win. Otherwise I would have to go along with awful things ... Poland was in danger ... I had to use extraordinary means, even as that at Brześć ... I don't know why God had me live in Poland ... They will bury me on Wawel Hill, next to Kościuszko, and create another national hero.*

Then, Śliwinski recalls, he calmed down, took a breath, his tired eyes looked peaceful, and he moved on to "private matters."

I do not know the Piłsudski as described by his contemporaries. Often with surprise, I read what various people write. These are mostly lies and falsehoods, and it's done by both his enemies and his admirers. But I would like that at least some of this should reach our progeny. At one time, I wanted to write my own biography, so that none save one man knew the true author. Then after my death, the secret would be revealed. I had to abandon this idea, because writing and even dictation is too difficult for me.

Piłsudski asked Śliwinski if he was interested in writing a monograph about him, with his help. Śliwinski agreed. There were four or five conversations about Piłsudski's life, each lasted about three hours. They took place in the evenings, at the Marshal's office in the GISZ.

I have an incredible resistance to thinking, said Piłsudski. I can think about the one and the same thing continuously over several years and then return to it. I am faithful to my thoughts. I have not been discouraged by having to wait and I know how to wait. But, well, sometimes things get in the way.

Piłsudski did not adhere to doctrine. *Doctrine*, he said during one of his conversations, *gives one a peace with which people do not like to part. That is why so many are doctrinaire. But in life, all things change, and everything moves forward, while doctrine stays in place ... Doctrine is the death of thought, it is torpor, it is a separation from reality.* About his colleagues, he spoke perversely, *what can I do ... They can see ten meters ahead; I can see a thousand. So that even when we are looking in the same direction, we see the same things differently.*

Piłsudski spoke about the kind of socialist he was, that more important than this theory, very early on, was the idea of serving Poland. *To this idea, I was always faithful. Today, though I often say, "dumb Poland" and I curse at Poland and Poles, I still continue to serve only Poland... Socialism was a theory of social progress, or at least it passed for such. After the war, socialism started to lose out and will continue to lose. In Russia, it became a new form of bondage. Even in the west it created nothing new, it did not bring out anything from itself, something that would influence the fate of the world.*

Remembering the first months of Poland's independence, Piłsudski said: *I am still surprised today, how in those times, I could have received so many dumb people, listen to their nonsense, and still work and accomplish as much as I have ... After all, I had to deal with Poles.*

When Lewinski protested his negative comments about Poles, the Marshal grew happy and said: *The Poles have an internal instinct for freedom ... Poland cannot be ruled by terror. It will not work. I was allowed to do a lot and I took advantage of it, because I wanted to teach the Poles something. No one else could have done it. But one should not kill the instinct for freedom, and it cannot be killed. It is a quality that has a great price.*

According to Piłsudski, the negative qualities of the Poles were a certain kind of rowdiness and envy. *I often thought that, dying, I would curse the Poles. Today, I know that I will not do this. A man must serve someone or something.* The contact with Śliwinski was lost, and Poóg-Malinowski wrote that the Marshal, *waved his arm and said, 'he's too fragile and his reason can't absorb the flight of a predatory eagle'.* Poóg-Malinowski does not exclude the possibility that, *the Marshal was absorbed in matters of state, even to being buried in them, and simply did not have the time.* One of the obstacles to continuing the conversations with Śliwinski was undoubtedly the worsening state of the Marshal's health.

Preparations were underway for him to visit Egypt. A month in Cairo turned out to be very beneficial for his health. Returning through Romania, Piłsudski paid a visit to King Carol II[145] and conducted talks with Romanian ministers. The main topic was the Marshal's plan to form a block of countries stretching from the Baltic to the Mediterranean Sea (what he called "Międzymorze" or "Intersea"). Piłsudski tried to persuade the Romanians to start negotiations with Soviet Russia on the matter of a non-aggression pact. Poland's initiative on such a pact was already well underway and would lead to a signing in the near future.

Piłsudski thought that Polish foreign policy should be conducted using the principle of "balance" between its two powerful neighbors. Each of these neighbors was a major threat and it would have been a disaster to take either as a long-term ally. Polish foreign policy, as well as its armed forces, should not be subjected to much influence from public opinion and representative assemblies like the Sejm. Anti-German feeling was growing spontaneously and from grassroots, and this worried Piłsudski who thought that the greatest danger was from the east. This danger manifested itself in a catastrophic way through the Soviet-German Alliance (so-called spirit of the Rappallo Pact) and in Soviet pacts with the Western powers, directed against Germany. In the first example, the Russians and Germans would enter Poland together as her enemies; in the second example, they would come with the Allies as "friends." The effect of both these incursions, predicted clearly by Piłsudski, was dangerous and tragic for Poland – in September 1939 for the first example, and in 1944 for the second.

Piłsudski's ruminations about the danger posed by Russia were borne out by facts. Poland, at that time, had an army of over two hundred sixty thousand men, not counting the battalions of the Border Guard Corps. The German army was still only at around one hundred thousand men, as circumscribed by the Versailles Treaty. Meanwhile, Russia had over one hundred divisions of infantry under arms and a large cavalry.

Lt. Colonel Kazimierz Glabisz, an officer attached to the Marshal for special duties, recorded the following opinion issued by Piłsudski on the matter of foreign policy.

> It is Germany's fervent wish to establish cooperation with Russia – as it was during the time of Bismarck. The accomplishment of this goal is tantamount to our destruction. We cannot allow it. Despite the great differences in the systems and cultures of Russia and Germany, we must always be on guard for this. In this world, there have been stranger alliances than this. But how to prevent it? It will depend on the circumstances; by frightening the weaker party, or by defusing the situation. Since my plans for a federation failed and the West is shortsighted with its will paralyzed – the maneuvering will be difficult.

In accounting for these signals, Piłsudski concluded that a relaxation of tensions with Moscow was desirable and useful. The Poles initiated friendly contacts with the Soviet ambassador in Warsaw – Antonov Owsiejenko.[146] Along a parallel course acted the Polish ambassador in Moscow – Stanisław Patek.[147] The non-aggression pact between Soviet Russia and Poland was initialed on 25 January and signed on 25 July 1932. The pact obligated both sides to withhold from aggression and refrain from entering into agreements that would be detrimental to the other party. In a ceremony held during 1935, the pact was extended for an additional ten years.

It is now known that the Soviet Union did not treat this pact seriously, but it is baseless to accuse Piłsudski and the Sanacja government of naiveté. The attempts to guarantee Poland's independence through the signing of various pacts and agreements were the normal, wise, and principled means of international diplomacy. The ineffectiveness of this means was not a fault of the Poles, and the politicians who made these arrangements cannot be blamed. There is a large body of proof that Piłsudski mistrusted both the Germans and the Soviets, to the end of his days. An interesting item illustrating this mistrust is the Marshal's conversation with the Polish ambassador to Turkey – Jerzy Potocki (May 31, 1933).[148] Being familiar with the history of Polish-Turkish relations, Piłsudski asked at the start, if the last Polish representative to the Sublime Porte, Piotr Potocki, was related to Jerzy. Then moving on to the real subject of discussion, he stated that he wanted to give Jerzy a special mission to Turkey and have him meet with Kemal Ataturk[149] (in a private audience) to discover his stance toward Russia. Poland, despite stabilizing its border with the Soviets and signing a special non-aggression pact, had no trust in the Russians and considered them to be a very dangerous neighbor. If Kemal also held similar distrust toward the Russians, then an exchange of views would be necessary.

The "Keeper of the Privy Seal" of Great Britain (Anthony Eden), in reporting his conversation of April 1935 with Piłsudski, stated that the Marshal appeared to ignore Russia, commenting that one should not fear any aggressive actions from her during the next fifty years. It is difficult to determine whether Eden misunderstood or was consciously giving false information. However, from other sources (Szembek), we know that the meaning of Piłsudski's statement was totally different. The Marshal confirmed the negative stance of Poland toward the "Eastern Pact" that England was proposing, in which Russia would play a part. In addition, perhaps undiplomatically, but quite correctly for meritorious reasons, Piłsudski directly told the Western politicians that they did not know, nor did they understand, Russia. In this instance, the name of Lloyd George, who had stubbornly supported Denikin, was mentioned. When Eden, with near pride, stated that he personally met Stalin in Moscow, the Marshal riposted: *Congratulations, when I see his portrait, I believe that I see a bandit.* This generated an outburst of laughter.

The atmosphere of this meeting was not pleasant, Piłsudski was not in good shape. The deteriorating state of his health was a tightly guarded secret, but these were to be the last weeks of his life. Often, he was so weak that he could not turn from one side to the other in bed. One day, in late April 1935, he said to Lepecki: *There are such wheelchairs for the sick!* And when they started to wheel him about the apartment, *Once there was such a strong, magnificent Ziuk ... and now he's gone.*

During those times when he felt stronger, he tried to devote himself to the army and foreign affairs. On 29 April he had a forty-minute conversation with Beck on the subject of the last meeting of the League of Nations and the visit of French Foreign Minister Pierre Laval[150] in Warsaw. At that time, France signed a mutual assistance agreement with the Soviet Union. Piłsudski took this rapprochement between France and Soviet Russia as a weakening of the Franco-Polish Alliance and was critical of Laval's foreign policy.

The last conversation between Beck and Piłsudski was incredible. It took place on the day of the Marshal's death during the night of 10-11 May 1935. The Marshal was in near agony and mumbled to himself, *Ziuk, poor Ziuk ... I must, Laval. Russia ... I must talk to Beck. I must ... Beck.* Lepecki proposed that Beck be brought there. *Yes, yes, yes, bring Beck, my dear, my dear Beck.* A call was quickly placed to the Raczyński Palace where a reception to honor Laval was being held. Beck excused himself and came to the Belweder still in his formal clothes. Piłsudski was fully conscious, asked to be seated, and greeted Beck with the words, *What, you come to me like a dandy, in tails and with your medals.*

When Beck explained that he came straight from a reception, Piłsudski said,

> *Very well, I did want to speak to you. Laval must be made aware because they have no idea what Stalin is planning. Stalin wants a war of the West with the Germans. ... Listen to me, child, I am dying, and after my death, they will do everything to change our policy. This cannot be allowed to happen. One must maintain, as far as possible, the current relations with Germany. Many don't like this, but it must be done. At all cost, you must stay in alliance with France and what is more, bring Great Britain into this alliance. Today this seems impossible, but you must keep working diligently toward this goal. Don't let yourself be dragged into any internal conflicts.*

The conversation lasted for an hour, and at the end, Beck informed Aleksandra Piłsudski that the Marshal's mind was sharp as ever.

At this point, one should take a step back in time and consider the influence that Piłsudski had on relations between Poland and Germany, its other dangerous and grasping neighbor. The German state, during the years 1919-1933, existing as the Weimar Republic, was openly hostile toward Poland. Specific instances of this were visible in an unceasing tariff war and insistence on revisions to the Versailles Treaty, mainly to eliminate the "Polish Corridor" that separated East Prussia from the Reich.

A definite success in Germany's negotiations was the Locarno Pact of 1925, which differentiated Germany's borders. The western border was declared to be immutable, but the eastern border (with Poland and Czechoslovakia) did not receive such guarantees. German cooperation with the Soviet Union was dangerous for Poland, which was also carried on in the military sphere, on the basis of the Rapallo agreement of 1922. Piłsudski correctly evaluated the developments in Germany and therefore was not surprised when on 30 January 1933, he learned about the formation of a government under Hitler.

Having a good estimate as to the intentions of the Western powers, which were attempting to form a "Four Power Pact"[151] (England, France, Germany, Italy), Piłsudski decided to take firm action against this development and verify to what extent Poland would be able to count on its French ally support. He delegated Jerzy Potocki and General Wieniawa-Długoszowski to go on a special mission to Paris. This mission, conducted without any documents or protocols, is known to history as a proposal for a "preventive war." Preparations for such a war were being made on various levels and were not limited to diplomatic negotiations.

The West German historian Hans Roos, with some justification, points out the great military parade in Vilnius, passing in review before Marshal Piłsudski in April 1933. For several hours, various parts of the Polish armed forces marched down Mickiewicz Avenue in sections, none smaller than a corps. The Marshal was stooped and aged, but he tirelessly raised his arm to return, with definite satisfaction, the smart salutes given by consecutive commanders of companies, batteries, and squadrons. In addition to the two local divisions of infantry and brigade of cavalry, the Vilnius parade included the 1st Regiment of Light Cavalry and the 11th Uhlan Regiment together with many first-class elite units. Such a demonstration of strength, on territory close to the border with East Prussia, had a significance beyond that of a routine military celebration of the 14th anniversary of the capture of Vilnius.

Piłsudski showed decisiveness based on strength in dealing with the situation in Gdańsk. The Gdańsk Senate had passed a resolution, in a rather unilateral way, that it would now have total control of the city police, which earlier had ben under the authority of the Port Council. Piłsudski, considering this as a threat to Polish interests, increased the garrison on Westerplatte[152] by one hundred and twenty men. This elicited protests from Gdańsk and the High Commissioner of the League of Nations. Keeping a determined course, Piłsudski sent instructions to the Polish ambassador in Berlin (Wysocki) to demand a declaration from Hitler that Germany would not intervene against Polish interests in Gdańsk. The lack of such declaration would let Poland draw the obvious conclusions. The fact that this was merely a political ploy is confirmed by the report of Captain Lepecki. At this time, Piłsudski gave him, to reproduce, a draft of a decree from the President of Poland to create a Government of National Trust in case of war with Germany (the manuscript was signed by I. Mościcki). Taking advantage of the Marshal being in a good mood, Captain Lepecki asked him if Hitler intended to attack Poland. *Even if we had attacked him, then we would only be acting in self-defense.*

Hitler apparently did not yet have his full self-confidence, and as a result of the conversation with Wysocki, the Marshal issued a communiqué stating that the Chancellor of Germany wanted to maintain relations strictly within the framework of previous agreements. Meanwhile, France did not show any firmness toward Germany; and in the case of a Polish-German War, they declared help in the form of only arms and mobilizing public opinion. In regard to the situation in Gdańsk, France did not show any good will. The strong Polish stance in this situation cancelled any chances for the "Four Power Pact" becoming reality. German claims, among which the "elimination of the Polish Corridor" was first, suffered a setback. From then on, the Germans would speak mainly about removing obstacles for unification with Austria, the incorporation of Czech territories inhabited by a German majority, the reversal of the anti-militaristic clauses in the Treaty of Versailles, and recovery of German colonies.

In July 1933, Józef Lipski became Poland's ambassador in Berlin. In giving instructions to the new ambassador, Piłsudski said to Beck, *Well, let's give him a try.* Then he asked Lipski that, on meeting with Hitler, he should propose that the two countries sign a non-aggression pact.

On 6 October 1933, another great military parade, this time commemorating the 250th Anniversary of the Raising of the Siege of Vienna, was held on the fields outside Kraków. In addition to the military content, the celebration had a mythological component. Among the backstage commentators, some whispered that it was a "dress rehearsal for the Marshal's funeral." The following excerpt is from Jędrzejewicz's *Kronika życia* (vol. II, page 460), *The Marshal went to the Wawel, examined the*

236

*cathedral in detail together with St. Leonard's Crypt. Then he visited with
the Metropolitan Bishop Adam Sapiecha,[153] with whom he discussed details
of the ceremony.*

Piłsudski was in an excellent mood and spoke with his inborn
charm when he wanted to. At a certain moment, in conversing about the
burial vaults, he mentioned if there may be a place there for him.

In November, after Lipski had already met with Hitler, a communiqué was issued that both nations will conduct their business with negotiations and will forgo the use of armed force in their relations. Apparently
counting on establishing some kind of cooperation with Poland, Hitler
proposed a personal meeting with Piłsudski. It was to have taken place in
a railcar on the border. However, in accordance with his greater political
principles, Piłsudski considered such a meeting to be superfluous. *All we
need is a declaration of non-aggression.* This was signed in Berlin on 26
January 1934, for a duration of ten years.

The non-aggression pact between Poland and Germany created
much commotion among European diplomats. In a conversation with the
ambassadors of France (Laroche) and Romania (Cadere), Piłsudski explained that one should not look for any hidden motives; after all, the text
of the agreement is clear. Poland had a free hand within its alliances with
France and Romania. If there is anything to worry about, said Piłsudski, it
is France's unqualified complaisance regarding Germany.

In March 1934, there was a conference at the Belweder with all
the prime ministers since May 1929, President Mościcki, and Minister
Beck. Piłsudski presented his views on the international situation.

> *Poland knows too well from the past what it means for her two
> neighbors to be in an understanding. When they reach agreement,
> then we are in danger. ... I do not believe, and I do not think that the
> peace agreements with both of our neighbors will last forever. The
> good relations of Poland with Germany may last another four years
> because of the psychological changes that we see now happening to
> the German people.*

Piłsudski held a similar conference (April 1934) with his best
generals. Among them were Śmigły-Rydz, Sosnkowski, Osiński, Konarzewski, Kasprzycki, Fabrycy, Gąsiorowski, and several others. The Marshal
asked them to give him a written answer to the question: Which of the
countries, Russia or Germany, is a greater danger to Poland? Most of the
generals answered that Germany will become a greater danger first.

To continue study and analysis of the threats to Poland, Piłsudski
created a special unit within the GIS, which received the code name "Lab-

oratory." General Fabrycy became the commandant of this unit. *Much depends on the agility and autonomy of our foreign policy*, said Piłsudski. *The situation is such, that in case of war with Germany, we will most likely not be alone; but in a war with Russia, we may well be by ourselves.*

(Top Left) The Marshal, Józef Beck, Walery Sławek and Gen. Edward Śmigły-Rydz.
(Top Right) Ignacy Mościcki (1867 – 1946)
(Middle) Walery Sławek (1879 – 1939)
(Bottom Left) Gen. Edward Śmigły-Rydz (1886 – 1941)

Marshal Piłsudski saluting the tomb of Julisz Słowacki in Wawel, 1927.

Veterans of the January Uprising with the Marshal at Belweder Palace in 1933 at a gathering of about seventy people.

The Marshal playing "patience" in Madera, 1931

(Top) Meeting with Gen. Douglas MacArthur.

(Bottom) Presenting an infantry standard.

Chapter 26
The April Constitution and Post-Mortem Greatness

Piłsudski stated many times that one of the most important matters which remained to be accomplished in the sphere of internal relations (after May 1926) was the ratification of a new constitution. Poland had to be protected from a totalitarian system but had to work it out, and by constitutional means, accept a system of government that would not permit the excesses or catastrophic consequences of a badly functioning democratic system. This would have to be a system that would limit "sejmocracy" and the large number of potentially harmful parties. Such limitations cannot signify the elimination of the parliamentary system or any other democratic institution but should only form a reasonable framework for their functioning.

This task was not easy. To do a proper job, Piłsudski engaged his closest associates and most trusted persons; among them, his brother Jan, who was an excellent lawyer and knew the legislative systems used in the more important countries of Europe and North America. On the basis of proposals submitted, a first draft was formulated. The principles were accepted by the Marshal on 26 November 1930 (*Pisma Zbiorowe* vol. IX p. 259). The main pillars of the new Polish order were to be - the President, the Government, and the Sejm. The constitution was to be a type of agreement of understanding between the three centers of power in the state.

Piłsudski's views on constitutional principles as applied to regulating the state were widely known and accepted by society. But among people who practiced politics as a profession, they met with strong resistance. At the first meetings of the Sejm following the May events, there was absence of the necessary quorum to enact any changes to the constitution. Even after the elections in November 1930, the number of representatives supporting the Sanacja still hovered around the fifty percent mark. The entire process of preparing the new constitution was in the hands of Walery Sławek, but the content of the document was heavily influenced by the theories espoused by Stanisław Car.[154] These theories were in opposition to the classic three-part division of Montesquieu. Instead of using three divisions: Legislative, Executive, and Judicial, Car proposed six centers of authority: The President, the Government, the Commander-in-Chief, the Sejm, the Senate, and Department of Justice.

During this time, Piłsudski did not concern himself much with the constitution. He did not support Sławek's proposal that only recipients of decorations for merit, either the Virtuti Militari medal or the Independence Cross, be permitted to serve in the senate. Piłsudski's objections were supported by the commission in charge of preparing the constitution.

The opposition in the Sejm (the Nationalist Caucus, the Peasant Parties, and the Socialists) boycotted all preparations and Sejm discussions devoted to the constitution, as it often happens, fell into its own trap. Stanisław Car took advantage of the absence of most of the representatives in opposition. Since half of the Sejm was involved in deliberations over the constitution, he had the necessary quorum to conduct a valid vote. On Friday 26 January 1934, the Sejm voted in the new constitution. The enthusiasm of its supporters was met by protest from the opposition. Sławek wanted Piłsudski to referee the matter, but the Marshal cooled him off by having an adjutant inform him that a meeting could not be held until 31 January. On that day, Piłsudski carefully listened to Sławek and to Świtalski and asked a few questions concerning the legality of the proceedings. He then read Article 125 of the March Constitution and accepted the situation as a fait accompli.

The Constitution of 3 May was also ratified by this stratagem, but it is not a healthy phenomenon that such things be accomplished by trick and surprise. Further deliberations over the acceptance of the constitution by the Senate should have been made, more in keeping with the law.

The Senate deliberated over the constitution for a year and finally accepted it with several corrections. After this, the matter went back to the Sejm, under the rule that to accept this important law, only a majority of votes was necessary. On 20 March 1935, the Sejm voted, and the result was two hundred and sixty votes in favor and one hundred and thirty-nine against. Before the ceremonial signing of the new constitution by the President of the Polish Republic, the original document was signed by the speakers of the Sejm, Senate, and the Council of Ministers.

Piłsudski was not present at this signing ceremony, which took place on 23 April (when the constitution came into force). There are several versions of the circumstances under which Piłsudski signed this public document, the last he would sign in his lifetime. It is known that Walery Sławek took this matter to him several times, and each time, he was sent away. Most likely Józef Beck, who had the Marshal's greatest confidence in those final years, got him to do it. The April Constitution was sharply attacked both for its content and the way it was ratified. Communist and post-communist propaganda, up to present times, maintains that it came into being contrary to the provisions of the March Constitution of 1921 and ushered in a fascist state.

There is no need to debate such assertions of propaganda, but it must be stated that the April Constitution was in tune with the Marshal's views. It was also in agreement with the needs of the Polish State, which lived under the threat of war and was surrounded by totalitarian states. In the history of other countries, significant limitations on the parliament in favor of the president were justified and necessary, even under conditions much more favorable than those faced by Poland in 1935. It is sufficient to give the non-controversial example of France headed by Charles DeGaulle, where a constitution based in part on the Polish experience was adopted via a referendum in 1958.

The April constitution states: *At the head of the state stands the President of the Republic, who coordinates the activities of the main state organs, chooses the head of the Council of Ministers, presides over the opening, adjournment and closing of the Sejm and Senate sessions, and enters into agreements with other states.*

The role of the Sejm was limited by the April Constitution to legislative and regulatory activities over the government.

In connection with the outbreak of World War II, and its unfortunate results for Poland, the most important clauses of the constitution referred to the fact that the President of the Polish Republic could select his own successor and could sign a peace treaty. The legitimacy and continuity of the Polish government in exile up to the year 1990 rested on these clauses.

After being interned in Romania, President Ignacy Mościcki handed over the leadership of the government to Władysław Raczkiewicz. The legality of this act is not even questioned by the communists. In succession (by analogy) the office was filled by August Zaleski, Stanisław Ostrowski, and Edward Raczyński. During the years 1986-1989, the president was Kazimierz Sabbat, and after his death in July 1989, Ryszard Kaczorowski. At the election of Lech Walesa to the presidency in Poland, Kaczorowski declared his mission to be at an end, and according to Article 24 of the Constitution, on 9 December 1990, conveyed the seals and other insignia of office to the museum of the Royal Castle in Warsaw.

Fifty-one years after being outside the country, and nearly forty-six years after the western powers withdrew their recognition from the Polish Government in Exile in London, did it have legal and political significance to the continuity of authority and sovereignty of the Polish state? Undoubtedly, yes. The condition for Poland recovering its sovereignty was free elections. In tune with a greater political wisdom, the President and the Government in Exile should not give up its influence on the possibility of holding parliamentary elections shortly after the election of the president. Up to that time, it was necessary to hold onto the insignia of authority by the Polish Government in Exile, and by giving the greatest possible publicity to the matter, speed up the parliamentary elections. This would have been in agreement with Piłsudski's often repeated statement: "when the nation loses respect for its symbols of state, this is the symbol of its downfall." Walesa's postponement of the parliamentary elections to the Autumn of 1990 showed a lack of respect for these symbols and a harbinger, perhaps not of total downfall, but of great political losses by the Third Polish Republic, reborn after such massive struggles.

Piłsudski belongs to the leading group of heroes in the national pantheon, he has not gone, despite the fact that he died over seven decades ago.

In the autumn of 1934, the state of his health declined catastrophically. On 11 November, the sixteenth anniversary of regaining independence, the Marshal came to the Mokotowskie Field and viewed the parade but became weak while he was there and had to sit down until the end. On 20 March 1935, after a bout of vomiting, he heard the foreboding word "cancer" for the first time. *If it is cancer, then I have less time than I thought.* Then, after a while, without returning to the state of his health, he spoke only of Poland. *Why is it that here in our country, people consider those who fall under the influence of outside powers as realistic politicians, and not those who count on their own fellow countrymen. I am used to making clear and precise agreements, to respecting those agreements, but I also ask for respect for that which is honorable, with a sense of one's own worth.*

Despite the illness, and because of a bad diagnosis connected with the illness, Piłsudski devoted even more care to Poland which he raised to an independent state, and the Poland which was now facing so many dangers. *I am not eternal*, the words the Marshal repeated on many occasions now took on an unequivocal and totally concrete meaning. For several years he had tried to disabuse his coworkers from *attaching themselves too closely to his person*, but the effects turned out to be just the reverse of the intention.

Leon Kozłowski,[155] a brilliant professor of archeology but an unbalanced politician, became prime minister on 15 May 1934. After a long conversation on 28 May 1935, it was decided that Walery Sławek replace him as head of government. There is no doubt that Sławek was a close confidant, a man who would complete each task entrusted to him with diligence and honestly. In 1935, however, it was not the old Commandant Piłsudski who was discussing his ideas creatively with a true and tested friend.

A mark of the great confidence that Piłsudski had in Sławek was the dedication the Marshal wrote in his book *Rok 1920* to "my dear Gustav" which he gave to him on 24 December 1924.

Just yesterday, I saw in your eyes that you were exasperated with me and thought about how many times we both had such expressions in our eyes. We are like two tired old horses that walk across bumpy terrain alone but once in a while meet on the straight road of life to greet each other and pull the same carriage together. In the past, we have pulled surreys and carts, we pulled wagons often overloaded with mud – two old, tireless horses.

Unfortunately, both "horses" were already much changed and tired. The Marshal was at death's door. On 17 April, he tried to play a game of solitaire, but the cards spilled out of his hands. *I am weak, good for nothing,* he said starting a monologue with Captain Lepecki.

I want to go to Vilnius for the anniversary of its capture. ... It is because I feel unwell that I want to go to Vilnius. ... This year, Easter falls on the same date as it did in 1919. I want to review the Vilnius military parade just one more time in my life. But please do not try to console me. Please find out when the Vilnius garrison is going to celebrate the anniversary. Will it be on Holy Saturday or Easter Sunday?

Seeing the frightened expression on Lepecki's face, he gave him a kindly look and said, *What a madman I am, my child. This is but a natural thing.*

The vomiting episodes repeated with a vengeance and his body grew weaker. He would not consent to any testing or attempt any cures. His attitude toward physicians was not only suspicious but even hostile. Only after long and unrelenting coaxing by his family did the Marshal agree to have a specialist brought from Vienna. On Monday, 22 April, he decided that he would move to his apartment at the GISZ. *I don't want any lousy physicians fouling the atmosphere at the Belweder. My ladies always come up with God knows what.*

Professor Karol Frederic Weckenbach came from Vienna, but Piłsudski postponed his confrontation with medicine. *This Weckenbach of yours is probably as much a fool as other doctors - Wiseguys.* The tests took place on 25 April. On the next day, Prof. Weckenbach again examined Piłsudski and confirmed the diagnosis: ten percent possibility of necrosis of the liver, ninety percent possibility of cancer.

In the evening, Piłsudski received his first injection. It was very painful. *Why do they torture me like this, child,* he said to Lepecki. *I am going to my death most peacefully.* Lepecki tried to say something about the curative value of the injection, but Piłsudski cut him off, *I don't need you to advocate for the doctors. Careful that I don't call you a rascal.*

On the night of 3-4 May Piłsudski raised his hand and pointed to the photograph of his mother hanging above his bed. He said, *Madame Billewiczówna, my dear mother, waits for her Ziuk. And so, does Aunt Zula and Bronek, and so many soldiers are readying for the military parade. All must be "in order' as we said in the Legions.* Then he whispered something that Lepecki did not understand, and then he said, I *must go to the Belweder.* The physicians feared moving him, but the matter was taken in hand by his wife, and Piłsudski returned to spend his last days at the Belweder. On Wednesday 8 May Professor Weckenbach came to see him there.

Piłsudski felt no pain, for many hours he was in a semi-conscious state. From time to time, he recovered and amazed those present with his clarity of thought. After a conversation with Beck, on Saturday 11 May, he felt fairly well. Lepecki then asked him if he would receive Wieniawa, who had been coming by frequently and asking for a meeting. *Let him come, but quickly.* The Marshal's conversation with Wieniawa lasted for over an hour and he even smiled at the funny anecdotes told by his favorite. During one of his earlier meetings with Wieniawa he had said, I *fear for the fate of France in a war with Germany. France will not be victorious."* Referencing this statement, Wieniawa asked at the end, *Does the Marshal still think about France?*

Yes, well, and about this Poland that I'm leaving to you. These were probably his last conscious words. In the evening, there was a blood hemorrhage from his mouth that weakened him greatly. On Sunday, 12 May at 7:00 am blood again appeared.

Fr. Władysław Korniłowicz was a priest who was especially close to the Piłsudski family, and in a sense, filled the role of a chaplain at the Belweder Palace. He was called to administer the last sacraments. According to Fr. Korniłowicz's report, on hearing the loudly spoken words of a prayer the Marshal opened his eyes and understood clearly the significance of the moment. Then, without hurry, Fr. Korniłowicz applied the sacred oils and prayed until the moment of death.

The Marshal's wife and his daughters knelt at the side of the bed, holding her husband's hand. At his feet, next to Gen. Wieniawa-Długoszowski, stood the praying priest. The doctors, Mosołowski, and Stefanowski were leaning over from the right side and looking at the Marshal. His eyes were closed and his face, emaciated by the illness, was peaceful and beautiful. At one moment, he opened his eyes, coughed, and raised his arm energetically toward his lips. The arm fell back powerless. It was 8:45 pm.

One of the largest salons on the ground floor of the Belweder was turned into a funerary chapel. The Marshal's body, in uniform, rested on a catafalque. In his hands, folded as in prayer, was a gorget with the image of Our Lady of the Ostrobrama. Beside him were displayed three banners: from the 1831 and 1863 insurrections, and the Legion Standard.

Crowds gathered at the Belweder. It was a common expression of sorrow and grief, uniting all regardless of political or religious beliefs or national associations. Everyone felt pain knowing that the "Pater Patriae" had departed.

On 17 May 1935, a funeral service was held at the Warsaw Cathedral. At the same time, similar services for the repose of the Marshal's soul took place in Kraków, Vilnius, Katowice, Lodz, Poznań, Lwów, Toruń, Tarnów, and all other cities in Poland.

At the Cathedral in Warsaw, after the words "Requiescat in Pace," the Field Bishop of the Polish Armed Forces, Józef Gawlina, took the lectern.

Blessed is he who dies for justice's sake. ... And lasts for justice until death. This was the motto that guided Józef Piłsudski through his life. ... Vilnius, Siberia, the 10th Pavilion of the Citadel – those were on his journey. He wanted to free his homeland from oppression. And when the clock of history started to strike ... he took with him a handful of brave souls, soldiers without a homeland ... There were the walls of the fortress at Magdeburg, but the gates of the prison swung wide open, and the entire nation placed its fate in his hands. ... In the year 1920, the fate of Poland and the West hung in the balance. It was a monstrous time, of which Pope Pius XI said "the demon of darkness battled the angel of light" ... You organized Poland's future and accepted on your shoulders the weight of the times. You have endured moments of bitterness and pain, but you bore it all with the conviction that troubles are the food of the chosen ... Over your remains and ashes, on your spirit, marked with the sign of greatness, we pledge that we will love as you have loved Poland – our Homeland. So help us God.

During the time that the bishop stated the words of the pledge, all assembled in the cathedral stood up and raised their right hands, extending two fingers, which in the Polish tradition indicate God and Country.

Then Archbishop Kakowski, together with the Bishops and Monsignors, completed the funeral services. After the final "Requiescat in Pace," the generals raised the casket and carried it to a gun carriage in front of the cathedral. General Śmigły-Rydz marched behind the casket with the Marshal's widow, General Sosnkowski escorting daughter Wanda, and the Marshal's brother accompanying daughter Jadwiga. The family was followed by President Mościcki, senior marshals of the French, British, and Romanian armies with government delegations. The funeral cortege contained representatives from thirty divisions and thirty cavalry units, standard bearers of various military units, representatives of schools, government agencies, and institutions.

On Mokotowski Fields,[156] before the gun carriage bearing the Marshal's casket, the last military review under inspector general of the army Orlicz-Dreszetr took place. The orchestra played the proudest of Polish songs, the one that initiated the Legion movement, the *First Brigade*. Suddenly the skies in the east grew dark with threatening clouds, forecasting an approaching storm. The officers raised the casket, placed it together with wreaths upon the platform of a special train. The funeral train left Warsaw making its way south, the Marshal's last journey to Kraków and the Wawel Cathedral.

The train steamed slowly along a newly opened rail corridor through Radom, Skarżysko, Kielce, Jędrzejów, and Miechów. The route was lined by uncounted numbers of people. The casket was especially illuminated with searchlights. As it rode the rails, it received farewells and bade farewell to the mourners along the way. This funeral cortege closed an era. Kraków was overfilled with mourners and draped in funeral colors. Torches burned along the approach to Wawel Castle. As the casket was transferred onto the caisson, the cathedral bell "Zygmunt" began to peal. Soon, all the bells in churches across Kraków were ringing. At 10:30 am, the funeral cortege arrived in the Wawel courtyard. At the entrance to the cathedral, President Mościcki was the only speaker.

> *A new companion has arrived to join the shades of kings in their eternal repose. His brow never carried a crown, his hand held no scepter. Yet he was king of our hearts and commander of our will ... May the tribute we now give to the remains of this Great Pole turn into a pledge of faithfulness to His thoughts which peered into the far future. May they be forged into the duty to guard the pride and honor of the nation, may our will be turned toward the hard work and struggle with difficulties, and may our hearts burn with a great love, like His, toward the homeland.*

The pontifical service at Wawel cathedral was the last event in the funeral ceremonies. As loudly spoken prayers sounded, generals took the casket from the catafalque and carried it into the underground crypt. The last hymn played by the orchestra was the "First Brigade." An urn with the Marshal's heart was taken to Vilnius, to be placed among his soldiers in Rossa, at the feet of his mother's grave.

The League of Nations met in special session on 20 May, discussions being preceded by a commemoration of Marshal Piłsudski's memory. From the perspective of time and our experiences, it was rather ironic that this special session was led by the Commissar for Foreign Affairs of the Lithuanian Soviet, who said:

> *Marshal Piłsudski devoted his entire life to the rebirth of Poland and made great sacrifices to this cause. It is only fitting that he is proclaimed a national hero ... The recent funeral ceremonies gave testimony to the degree of how Marshal Piłsudski was beloved by his people, whom he guided in the effort to throw off foreign domination and in whom they saw a leader and a builder.*

The speakers that followed during the session who could voice, with undoubted sincerity, Piłsudski's accomplishments included the French representative Rene Massigli, the British Minister Anthony Eden, and representatives of Italy, Spain, Hungary, and Portugal. The international contributions of Józef Piłsudski were mentioned by representatives of both Americas and Asia. Yet the most eloquent and undoubtedly most sincere tributes came from the representatives of those nations which, through direct cooperation with Poland, during the Marshal's tenure in office, were able to gain their independence. The Romanian representative, Antomado, spoke in this spirit, as well as the Finnish representative, Holsti, and the Latvian representative, Feldmanis, who said:

> *The name of Marshal Piłsudski is known and valued in Latvia, not only because of the great role he played as a leader in his own country, but also and especially because of the heroic aid he rendered to my country at a difficult moment in its history.*

Thanking the gathering in the name of the Polish government, Minister Tytus Komarnicki said:

> *The Polish nation is deeply touched by the tribute given by the civilized nations to the one who was the maker of modern Poland. Eternal remembrance of him will guide the efforts of future generations to realize the flowering and greatness of Poland. In asking others to respect Poland's undeniable rights, Marshal Piłsudski aspired that international relations should be based on sincere respect for the rights of other nations. He was deeply convinced that this idea is an indispensable condition for true international cooperation and peace.*

(Left) One of the last photos of the Marshal at the railway station in Warsaw, bringing a coffin with the body of his sister Zofia Kadenac to a wagon before departure to Wilno, July 1935.
(Right) Bearing the body of the Marshal to the crypt in the Wawel.

(Left) The Coffin of Józef Piłsudski in Wawel Cathedral.
(Right) Piłsudski's Mound outside of Krakow.

Antoni Lenkiewicz

Chapter 27
Piłsudski's Last Will and Testament, His Mound, a Symbol of Independence

Piłsudski never wrote a formal last will and testament, neither in relation to passing on property rights, which he despised, nor in the area of political matters, to which he devoted his entire industrious life. One document that undoubtedly is an expression of his final will, is an undated sheet of official paper with the letterhead, "General Inspectorate of the Armed Forces, First Marshal of Poland." The writing is in ink, uneven and not very clear, without punctuation. The text is available in the form of photostatic copies. It is as follows:

> *I do not know if they will decide to bury me at the Wawel. Let them. But that only my heart be enclosed and hidden in Vilnius, where my soldiers are buried, those who in April of 1919, gave me, their commander, the city of Vilnius. On the headstone or marker engrave the motto I chose for myself during life:*

> *"When I could choose, I chose, instead of a home,*
> *a nest on the eagle's rock, may I be able*
> *to Sleep, when the eyes are red from thunder*
> *and I can hear the wails of devils in the rustle of the pines.*
> *Thus, I lived."*

> *And I entreat all those who loved me to bring the remains of my mother from Sugint in Wiłkomirski county to Vilnius and bury my mother (several intelligible words). May my proud heart rest at the feet of the proud mother. May my mother be buried with military honors: her body on a caisson and may all the cannon sound the salvo of farewell and welcome, so as the windowpanes in Vilnius shake. My mother raised me to take on a role such as mine. On the stone, engrave lines from Wacław by Słowacki, starting with "The proud cannot with misfortune..." Before her death, mother had me read this to her several times.*

According to Piłsudski's expectations, it was decided to bury him at the Wawel, and according to his wishes, his heart was placed at the Rossa in Vilnius, at the feet of his proud mother. Today, in both capitals of the Commonwealth of Two Nations, the memory of the creator of an independent Poland is honored daily with fresh flowers.

A measure of the general appreciation of Piłsudski's actions and service are not only the flowers but questions whose answers we seek of him. What awaits us? What to do? Which road to choose? The lack of a formal last will and testament and political directives does not present an obstacle in this regard. The answers to the above questions can be found in Piłsudski's life story. His political testament is contained in the twelve volumes of the *Collected Works*. In the same degree, just as the individual needs freedom – so said Piłsudski – then a nation needs independence. A basic condition for independence is the nation's will. For a nation to live and exist as a sovereign state and effectively care for the interests of its citizens, it must cultivate its own traditions and values. If Poland, despite oppression, despite the three partition zones, existed and lived, it owes that to the awareness and faith expressed in the words of its national anthem, "Poland has not perished, as long as we live."

The spirit of independence includes the feeling of a national dignity, the will to make independent decisions as to the future and the willingness to make sacrifices in the defense of common values. The nation must know and desire an independent existence, and in seeking it must, first, count on its own strength. We attribute our successes to spiritual strength, our failures to inadequate physical strength. The building of an independent state is the duty not of individuals, groups, classes, strata, or states, but should be the solidary activity of the entire society.

Poland is an important part of the Christian civilization and culture in Western Europe. A danger to this culture is the imperialism of Russia. Acting in well understood self-interest and society, one should support independence movements not only in the Baltic countries (Lithuania, Latvia, Estonia) but also in Byelorussia and most of all in Ukraine. Poland is quite obviously a part of the West but must remember that its ally in setting a political balance between the East and West is the United States of America.

The political system in the Polish Republic should be based on the division of power between the legislative, executive, and judicial branches, but it must be acknowledged that in addition to those centers of power, there are two more: finance and mass media. The Sejm is convened to legislate and control the business of government. The lack of majority rule with single mandate electoral districts and trustworthy political parties causes degeneration of democracy and parliamentary government. Participation in the governing of a nation must be treated as a service for the good of the whole.

The state and the nation which build political thought by negating the truth are doomed to failure. Those who build on lies and deceit are weak when compared to those who want to build upon the truth. Only society by itself can cure its own ills, repair a bad structure, and raise healthy things.

Part of Piłsudski's political legacy is his legend. As Witkiewicz wrote: *The legend is a treasure and a strength, a power mightier than history or reality*. Piłsudski is a symbol of the power and fitness of the nation, its possibilities and indestructible power.

Ziuk – Wiktor – Conspirator and Fighter – Commandant of the Riflemen's Groups and Legions – Grandpa – Resurrector of Independence – Head of State and Commander-in-Chief – Marshal – Victor of the Bolshevik War – the wise and steady hand at the wheel of the Polish ship of state – this is how the national consciousness has encoded the various phases in Piłsudski's life, and such are the chapters of his testament.

A nation is defended not only by soldiers and armed forces. A condition for an independent existence is faith in one's own potential, physical strength, and moral health. In his motivation for self and nation, Piłsudski reached for the imponderables, those things, phenomena and values that are beyond the realm of "practical reasoning."

In the year 1934, on the twentieth anniversary of the march-out of the First Cadre Brigade, it was decided to raise in Kraków a monumental funeral mound, that would memorialize all those who fought for the recovery of Poland's independence. The Marshal's death speeded up this initiative and gave it a name, "Józef Piłsudski's Mound." Without reserve, all Poland contributed deeds and finances to complete this undertaking. The soil used to build the mound came from all places connected to the history of Poland. Over three thousand urns of earth were brought. The work on the mound continued for three years and finished in 1939. Governor Hans Frank said, "we have no intention to have this Polish symbol visible from a distance." But, fortunately, the Germans did not carry through their destructive intentions.

Systematic destruction started during the times of the Polish Peoples Republic, in the so-called "Stalinist times." Using tanks, the huge granite boulder with the Cross of Independence and the initials "J.P." were dragged from the summit of the mound. From 1957, social efforts began to rebuild and maintain the mound. Letters and petitions addressed to the Kraków city administration, as well as to various branches of government including the Minister of Defense, went unanswered. Efforts at maintenance were carried out without official approval and were punished with repressions. In 1977, as the 60th Anniversary of the march-out of the First Cadre Brigade approached, the social efforts directed at maintaining the mound were given support by the Kraków archbishop – Cardinal Karol Wojtyła. He wrote:

I would like to express my full solidarity with the activities that have at its core the defense of our national dignity, the honor of the Polish soldier, especially the one to whom Poland owes the recovery of independence in 1918. ... The call for respect for the monuments of the past, among them the one to Piłsudski in Sowiniec, is fully justified. May it be effective.

Matters surrounding the renovation of the Piłsudski Mound were greatly improved after August 1980. During the months of Solidarity, the mound again became visible. Thanks to thousands of hours of donated labor, the surface of the mound was cleared of bushes and trees. The path leading to the summit was rebuilt. On 14 April 1981, the Piłsudski Mound was certified as a Monument of National Memory, and on June 22, it was registered as a historical place.

The new wave of political persecutions against Polish independence traditions that came after the declaration of Martial Law did not bypass the mound in Sowiniec. Harassment slowed down the tempo of maintenance work but did not stop it. During 1983-85, forty-five additional urns with earth from battlefields, graves, and places of national martyrdom were added.

After 1990, the Józef Piłsudski Mound, as the largest monument of its type, once again is a symbol of the struggle for independence in the past but also one for hope in the future. Many military units, as well as youths, who eagerly and generously come to Kraków, contribute their effort to maintain the mound. This confirms the longevity of the ideals which Józef Piłsudski served.

Important Dates in the Life of
Józef Piłsudski

1867
December 5 – born in Zułów in Lithuania.

1875
July – after the estate in Zułów burns, the Piłsudski family moves to Vilnius.

1877
September - Józef Piłsudski begins his studies at the Russian high-school located in a building formerly belonging to the University of Vilnius.

1880
Bronisław and Józef Piłsudski start to publish a conspiratorial publication, *Gołąb Zułowski*.

1882-1885
Conducts underground activities in the self-education group "Spójnia".

1884
September 1 – death of his mother Maria Piłsudska nee Bilewicz.

1885
Józef Piłsudski completes his high school studies and begins to study medicine in Kharkov.

1886
March – is arrested by the police for participation in a street protest on the occasion of the 25th anniversary of the Liberation of the Serfs and is held for six days.

1887
April 20 – sent into Siberian exile for five years. The Piłsudski brothers were implicated in a plot – Aleksander Ulianov (Lenin's brother) was sentenced to death, while Bronisław received a fifteen-year sentence.

1889
Piłsudski met his first love, Leonarda (Leosia) Lewandowska, whom he met during his time in exile.

1890
August 6 – Piłsudski relocates from Kiereńsk to Tunka, his new place of exile in the Sajański Mountains. Friendship with Bolesław Szwarc (1834-1904) who earlier was imprisoned in Szliisselburg, and he met Walerian Łukasiński there.

1892

July 1 – Piłsudski returns to Vilnius, after completing five years in exile in Kiereńsk and Tunka (one thousand and two hundred kilometers from Irkuck).

1893

Publishes in Przedświt (no. 8) an article entitled, "Our stance toward the Russian revolutionaries," which is the official policy of the Polish Socialist Party (PPS).

1894-1900

Piłsudski edits, prints, and distributes the periodical Robotnik [Worker] and is a member of the directorship of the Polish Socialist Party (PPS). Eventually, he comes out against the Marxist concepts of "class warfare" and stresses that "the national need is to prepare for an armed struggle for independence."

1895

May – travels to Kiev, St. Petersburg and other student centers of the Polish Socialist Party.

1896

Travels to London to participate in the Second Congress of the Socialist International.

1897

During Christmas time, Piłsudski is in Zurich and transforms the Union of Polish Socialists Abroad into the PPS.

1898

Returns to Poland in August. Stays mainly in Lwów and Kraków. He steers the PPS action connected to the 100th anniversary of the birth of Adam Mickiewicz, which the Russian authorities try to exploit for their own ends.

1899

15 July – marries Maria Juszkiewiczowa nee Koplewska in an Augusburg Evangelical church in the village of Paproć Duża near Łomża.

1900

February 22 – Maria and Józef are arrested while living in Łódź under the name Dąbrowski, while editing and printing the periodical Robotnik. April 17 – the pair is taken to the Tenth Pavilion of the Warsaw Citadel.

1901

14 May – makes his escape from a psychiatric hospital in St. Petersburg with the assistance of Psychiatrist Władysław Mazurkiewicz (1871-

1933) and Alexander Sulkiewicz (1867-1916).

1902

In mid-June, with Piłsudski's participation, the Sixth Congress of the PPS takes place in Lublin. A plan is accepted for reorganizing the party and publishing the periodical Walka [Struggle]. The first three issues (1902-1903) are printed in Kraków and are mainly filled with Piłsudski's writings.

1902-1903

Józef and Maria Piłsudski spend three winter months in Riga.

1903

During August, in Riga, Piłsudski writes an article reminiscing, "How I became a socialist". From August, he publishes (anonymously) in the journal Naprzód [Forward] consecutive segments of Bibuła. In the last segment (December 5), he reveals the name of the author.

1904

Travels to Tokyo in connection with the Russo-Japanese War.
November 13 – the first demonstration with armed protection on Grzybowski Square in Warsaw. Alexandra Szczerbińska is among the participants.

1905

January 22 – "Bloody Sunday" in St. Petersburg. On January 27, a general strike begins in all the Polish cities in the Russian zone of partition.

1906

Piłsudski manages to reconcile the differences between the "young" and "old" members of the PPS. He identifies with the "old" but is satisfied with autonomy for the Fighting Organization which he leads.

1907

After the breakup of the PPS into the PPS-Left Wing and PPS-Revolutionary Faction, Piłsudski concentrates on independence and insurrection-oriented activities, which he links to a future war between Poland's occupiers.

1908

September 26 – Piłsudski leads a successful action which results in the seizure of two hundred thousand rubles at the Bezdany railroad station. On the initiative of Piłsudski and Sosnkowski, the Union of Active Struggle is formed as a secret underground organization, with the goal of creating future leadership cadres for a future insurrection.

1909

The initiative of creating the Polish Military Fund begins.

1910

The Riflemen's Associations in the Austrian zone of partition are legalized.

1911

From January to March, Piłsudski and wife are in Nervi (twelve kilometers east of Genoa). The trip is for curative purposes.

1912

An initiative is put forward to create the Commission of Confederated Independence Parties and making Piłsudski the commandant of Polish forces in case a war with Russia breaks out.

1913

January 22 – Piłsudski speaks in Lwów at the commemoration of the 50th anniversary of the January Uprising, after which he leads a column of Riflemen through the city.

February 25 – the Kurier Litewski [Lithuanian Courier] publishes an interview conducted by Józef Hłasko with "Mr. Marian." It is Piłsudski under a false name. He predicts the outbreak and the course of a war, which would give Poland a chance to gain independence.

March 2 – The Commandant in Chief directs the first combined exercises of the Riflemen's units near the village of Stawczany-Basiówka near Lwów.

1914

August 6 – the First Cadre Company marches out and crosses the border into the Russian zone of partition as part of the Great War.

August 20 – the Polish Legions are organized, Piłsudski becomes commander of the First Brigade.

November 11 - a dangerous march between enemy forces ends successfully in Ulina Mała. Piłsudski enters Kraków at the head of the Legions.

1915

The Polish Military Organization expands into all the zones of partition, as the main force fighting for an independent Poland.

1916

From February 16 – the informal Colonels' Council is active in all three Legion brigades. This council strengthens Piłsudski's influence, but at the same time intensifies his disputes with the Military Department of the Main National Committee.

1917
January – Piłsudski becomes a member of the Provisional Council of State of the Polish Kingdom and takes over its Military Department.
July - the "Loyalty Oath" crisis. Piłsudski resigns in protest from the Provisional Council of State.
July 22 – Piłsudski and Sosnkowski are arrested by the Germans.

1918
November 8 – Piłsudski and Sosnkowski are taken from Magdeburg to Berlin for political discussions.
November 10 – Piłsudski arrives in Warsaw.
November 11 – the Regency Council makes Piłsudski Commander-in-Chief of the Polish armed forces.
November 22 – Piłsudski takes over the position of Provisional Head of State.

1919
January 16 – the government of Jędrzej Moraczewski is dissolved and Ignacy Paderewski is entrusted with the function of forming a new government.
February 20 – the Sejm entrusts Piłsudski with the position of Commander-in-Chief of the nation.
April 15-21 – the "Vilnius Expedition" is conducted under Piłsudski's personal command.

1920
March 19 – Piłsudski becomes the First Marshal of Poland.
April 25 – the "Kiev Expedition" begins.
June 10 – August 14 – the Polish army is forced back.
August 14-17 – the eighteenth most decisive battle in the history of the world (also known as the "Miracle on the Vistula") begins.
September 25-26 – beginning of the victorious and decisive battle for Poland on the Niemen River.
October 18 – an armistice is proclaimed along the entire front with Bolshevik Russia.

1921
February 3 – Piłsudski begins his official visit in Paris.
March 17 – the Sejm ratifies the Polish Republic's constitution.
March 18 – the Riga peace treaty is signed.
October 25 – Piłsudski marries Alexandra Szczerbińska in a Roman Catholic ceremony.

1922
Piłsudski rejects his nominaion as candidate for the position of President

of Poland.

December 14 – as Head of State, he transfers the office into the hands of President Gabriel Narutowicz but continues to be the Chief of the General Staff.

1923

June 9 – Piłsudski resigns from the position of Chief of the General Staff. He moves his family to Sulejówek and has no official position in the government.

1924

As a result of his lecture and writing activities, the following books are published:

Wspomnienie o Narutowiczu [Reminiscence about Narutowicz], O wartosci żołnierza Legionów, [The value of a soldier in the Legions] Rok 1863 [Year 1863], Rok 1920 [Year 1920].

1925

January – Piłsudski gives two important lectures in Warsaw: "O dowodzeniu" [On leadership] and "O psychologii więźnia" [On the psychology of a prisoner].

July – vacations in Druskienniki. There he meets Eugenia Lewicka.

1926

May 12-15 – military maneuvers, treated by Piłsudski as a show of strength and opposition to a government which does not have the support of the populace. The inability to reach an understanding with the President of Poland leads to fratricidal warfare. As a result, the government of Stanisław Wojciechowski dissolves and Wincenty Witos resigns from office.

May 31 – Piłsudski is chosen president but does not accept the office.

October 2 – Piłsudski becomes the Prime Minister.

1927

December 10 – Piłsudski takes part in the deliberations of the League of Nations in Geneva, addressing the increased tensions between Lithuania and Poland.

1928

June 28 – Piłsudski resigns from the office of Prime Minister.

1930

August 25 to December 3 – Piłsudski becomes Prime Minister again.

December 15 – Piłsudski travels to Madeira where he stays until 22 March 1931.

1931

During his stay in Madeira, Piłsudski writes his last book *Poprawki histo-ryczne [Corrections to history]*. He contemplates the problem of his own authentic biography. He entrusts this matter to Artur Śliwiński.

1932

January 25 – the initialing of a non-aggression pact with Soviet Russia, signed on July 25. In 1935, this pact was extended to 1945.

1933

Through special missions conducted by Jerzy Potocki and Bolesław Wie-niawa-Długoszowski, Piłsudski attempts to verify on the background of the "Gdańsk crisis," the effectiveness of French guarantees in a possible future conflict with Germany. This matter is known to history as the "Pro-posal of a Preventive War."

1934

January 26 – signing of a non-aggression declaration with Germany, dura-tion ten years. In this way, Poland blocks the so-called "Four Power Pact" (England, France, Italy, Germany).

1935

April – The Polish Sejm and Senate ratify the Constitution (dated April 23) signed by the President and Government.
May 12 at 8:45 pm – Józef Piłsudski dies.

Endnotes

[1] January Uprising (Polish: powstanie styczniowe) was an insurrection instigated principally in the Russian Partition of the former Polish–Lithuanian Commonwealth against its occupation by the Russian Empire. It began on January 22, 1863 spread to the other Partitions of Poland, and continued until the last insurgents were captured in 1864.

[2] A reference to the burial place of Roman Dmowski (Bródno). Józef Pilsuski's body is buried at the Wawel Catedral in Kraków, while his heart is in Vilnius.

[3] Currently Zalavas, Lithuania.

[4] Regarded as a national bard in Poland, Lithuania and Belarus, Adam Bernard Mickiewicz (24 December 1798 – 26 November 1855). Often compared to Byron and Goethe, he was a principal figure in the rise of Polish Romanticism. After spending five years of relatively benign political exile in Russia, where he was lionized for his poetic improvisations in the refined drawing rooms of St. Petersburg, Moscow and Odessa, he left Russia for a life of continued exile in Italy, France and Switzerland. For three years he lectured on Slavic literature at the Collège de France in Paris. He died in Constantinople after contracting cholera while helping to organize Polish and Jewish forces to fight against Tsarism in the Crimean War. In addition to his epic poem *Pan Tadeusz*, he is known for his poetic drama *Dziady* (*Forefathers' Eve*), the narrative poems *Grażyna* and *Konrad Wallenrod*, and his admirable *Crimean Sonnets*.

[5] Juliusz Słowacki (4 September 1809 – 3 April 1849) was a Polish Romantic poet. He is considered one of the three most important poets in Polish literature — a major figure of the Polish Romantic period, and the father of modern Polish drama. His works often feature elements of Slavic pagan traditions, Polish history, mysticism, and orientalism. His most popular works include the dramas *Kordian* and *Balladyna* and the poems *Beniowski* and *Testament mój*.

[6] This was the nickname Pilsudski had as a boy, possibly a distorted version of "żuk" – "little beetle."

[7] Henryk Adam Aleksander Pius Sienkiewicz, also known by the pseudonym "Litwos" (May 5, 1846 – November 15, 1916) was a Polish journalist, novelist, and Nobel Prize laureate. He is best remembered for his historical novels. His *Trilogy* set in the seventeenth-century Polish–Lithuanian Commonwealth consists of *With Fire and Sword*, *The Deluge*, and *Colonel Wołodyjowski*. He is internationally known for the best-seller *Quo Vadis* (1896).

[8] Vladimir L'vovich Burtsev (November 17, 1862 – August 21, 1942) was a revolutionary activist, scholar, publisher, and editor of several Russian language periodicals. He became famous by exposing a great number of agent provocateurs, notably Yevno Azef in 1908.

[9]Yevno Azef (1869–1918) was a Russian socialist revolutionary who was also a double agent and agent provocateur, working both as an organizer of assassinations for the Socialist-Revolutionary Party and a police spy for the Okhrana, the Imperial secret police. He rose in the ranks to become the leader of the party's terrorist branch, the SR Combat Organization, from 1904 to 1908.

[10]Bronisław Antoni Szwarce (October 7, 1834–February 18, 1904) was a Polish engineer and political activist. Born in France to Polish immigrants and educated there. He graduated from the Ecole Centrale des Arts et Manufactures in Paris in 1855. He returned to partitioned Poland and joined the radical democratic pro-independence underground. He became part of the Central National Committee but was arrested by the Russian authorities shortly before the January 1863 Uprising and exiled to Siberia.

[11]Stanisław Wojciechowski (15 March 1869 – 9 April 1953) was a Polish politician, scholar, and activist in the cooperative movement. In 1922, he was elected the second President of the Republic of Poland following the assassination of Gabriel Narutowicz. He was ousted by the May Coup d'État of 1926.

[12]A reference to Guiseppe Garibaldi, who joined the Carbonari revolutionary association, and in February 1834, participated in a failed Mazzinian insurrection in Piedmont.

[13]Stanisław Mateusz Ignacy Wyspiański (January 15, 1869 – November 28, 1907) was a Polish playwright, painter, and poet, as well as interior and furniture designer. A patriotic writer, he created a series of symbolic, national dramas within the artistic philosophy of the Young Poland Movement. Wyspiański was one of the most outstanding and multifaceted artists of his time in Poland under the foreign partitions.

[14]Wyspiański's widely acclaimed play *Wesele* (*The Wedding*) is a deeply critical yet sarcastic exposé of Polish society of the nineteenth century. *Wesele* transformed Wyspianski from a moderately successful visual and verbal artist associated with the Young Poland movement into a national dramatist-visionary of great significance in Poland. The drama made references to the contemporary situation in Poland and depicted a powerless society. Although censorship barred the sale of copies of *Wesele*, the play was staged in the theatre.

[15]Stefan Żeromski (14 October 1864 – 20 November 1925) was a Polish novelist and dramatist. He was called the "conscience of Polish literature". He also wrote under the pen names Maurycy Zych, Józef Katerla, and Stefan Iksmoreż. He was nominated four times for the Nobel Prize in Literature.

[16] The Racławice Panorama (Polish: Panorama Racławicka) is a monumental (15 × 114 meter) cycloramic painting depicting the Battle of Racławice, during the Kościuszko Uprising. It is located in Wrocław, Poland. The painting is one of only a few preserved relics of a genre of nineteenth-century mass culture, and the oldest in Poland.

[17]Stańczyks (Stańczycy) was a political grouping in Galicja that arose in the 1860s. Its name was inspired by Stańczyk (c. 1480–1560), the wise court jester of King Sigismund the Old.

[18]General Wacław Jędrzejewicz (29 January 1893 – 30 November 1993) was a Polish Army officer, diplomat, politician, and historian, and subsequently an American college professor. He was co-founder, president, and long-time executive director of the Józef Piłsudski Institute of America.

[19]Bolesław Berger (August 8, 1876 -1942 in Warsaw) was socialist activist, a founder of the Fighting Organization in the Polish Socialist Party (PPS).

[20]Józef Kwiatek (January 22, 1874 in Płock - 20 January 1910 in Kraków) was a socialist activist and journalist, of Jewish extraction.

[21]Adam Józef Borkiewicz (March 17, 1896 in Bąkowa Góra, - December 29, 1958 in Warsaw) was a soldier in the Polish Legions, Colonel of the Polish Infantry, a member of the General Staff of the Polish Army, and military historian.

[22]Wanda Juszkiewicz, (b. 1887 – d. 1908) twenty-one-year-old daughter of Maria Koplewski from an earlier marriage to Marian Juszkiewicz. Maria was later the first Mrs. Józef Pilsudski.

[23]Witold Tomasz Jodko-Narkiewicz (April 29, 1864 in Słuck - October 22, 1924 in Warsaw) was a socialist activist, publicist, and diplomat.

[24]This was probably Felicjan Sławoj-Składowski.

[25]Walery Jan Sławek (November 2, 1879 – April 3, 1939) was a Polish politician, freemason, military officer, and activist, who in the early 1930s served three times as Prime Minister of Poland. He was one of the closest aides of Józef Piłsudski.

[26] General Kazimierz Sosnkowski (November 19, 1885 in Warsaw – October 11, 1969) a Polish nobleman, independence fighter, diplomat, architect, politician, and a Polish Army general. An outstanding commander, an intellectual, and an artist; Sosnkowski was a key figure in Poland's twentieth century history. A lover of art, literature, and philosophy, a linguist who knew Latin, Greek, English, French, German, Italian, and Russian, Sosnkowski was a man of wide-ranging interests and talents.

[27]Ignacy Ewaryst Daszyński (October 26, 1866 – October 31, 1936) was a Polish socialist politician, journalist, and very briefly Prime Minister of the Second Polish Republic's first government, formed in Lublin in 1918.

[28]Adam Bernard Mickiewicz (December 24, 1798 – November 26, 1855) was a Polish poet, dramatist, essayist, publicist, translator, professor of Slavic literature, and political activist. He is regarded as national poet in Poland, Lithuania, and Belarus. A principal figure in Polish Romanticism, he is counted as one of Poland's greatest poets.

[29]Balkan Wars 1912-1913

[30]Zygmunt Balicki (December 30, 1858 in Lublin – September 12, 1916 in Saint Petersburg) was a Polish sociologist, publicist, and one of the first leading thinkers of the modern Polish nationalism in the late 19th century under the foreign Partitions of Poland. Balicki developed his original political thought inspired by the ideals of Aleksander Świętochowski from the movement of Positivism which was marked by the attempts at trying to stop the wholesale Russification and Germanization of the Poles.

[31]Tymczasowa Komisja Skonfederowanych Stronictw Niepodległościowych (TKSSN) – the Temporary Commision of Confederated Independence Parties

[32] Polonia refers to the Polish nation disbursedacross the partitioned areas and around the world

[33] "Our Bartek's" refer's to Polish soldiers in the Prussian army.

[34]Kazimierz Michał Władysław Wiktor Pułaski (Casimir Pulaski) (March 6, 1745 – October 11, 1779) was a Polish nobleman, soldier, and military commander who has been called, "the father of the American cavalry." Pułaski fought in the Bar Confederation to stop the Russian domination of Poland, implicated in a plot to abduct Poland's King Stanislaw August Poniatowski, and he departed for America where he died in the siege of Savannah, Georgia while making an attack on the British held city.

[35]Andrzej Tadeusz Bonawentura Kościuszko (February 4, 1746 – October 15, 1817) was a Polish military engineer, statesman, and military leader who became a national hero in Poland, Lithuania, Belarus, and the United States. He assisted George Washington in the American Revolutionary War. After returning to Poland he led, as Supreme Commander of the Polish National Armed Forces, the 1794 Kościuszko Uprising in the Polish–Lithuanian Commonwealth against Russia and Prussia.

[36]Jan Henryk Dąbrowski (29 August 1755 – 6 June 1818) was a Polish general and statesman, widely respected after his death for his patriotic attitude, and described as a national hero. He became actively involved in promoting the cause of Polish independence abroad. He was the founder of the Polish Legions in Italy serving under Napoleon from 1795.

[37]Prince Józef Antoni Poniatowski (May 7, 1763 – October 19, 1813) was a Polish leader, general, minister of war, and army chief who became a Marshal of the French Empire. He is greatly respected for his military prowess and patriotism.

[38]Józef Dwernicki (March 19, 1779 in Warsaw – November 23, 1857 in Lopatyn near Lwów) was a General of Cavalry in the Polish Army and a participant in the November Uprising (1830–1831).

[39]Józef Sowiński (1777–1831) was a Polish artillery general and one of the heroes of Poland's November 1830 Uprising.

[40]Zygmunt Erazm Gaspar Józef Sierakowski, (May 19, 1827 – June 27, 1863 in Vilnius) was a general, activist in the Polish independence movement, and commander in the January Uprising.

[41] Romuald Traugutt (January 16, 1826 – August 5, 1864 in Warsaw) was a general and commander-in-chief of the January Uprising. Captured, he would not break under interrogation. After his execution, he passed into history as a national hero and exemplary patriotic martyr.

[42]Gustaw Konstanty Orlicz-Dreszer (October 2, 1889 – July 16, 1936) was a Polish general, and a political and social activist. Before World War I, Orlicz-Dreszer was involved in pro-independence activities in partitioned Poland.

[43]General Michał Tadeusz Karaszewicz-Tokarzewski, (January 5, 1893 in Lwów – May 22, 1964 in Casablanca, Morocco) was a Polish general and founder of the resistance movement, "Polish Victory Service."

[44]Maciejówka (literally "Maciej's cap") is a type of headgear popular in late 19th and early 20th century Poland. It is a round, soft cap made of cloth, with a short-hardened peak, usually made of black or brown leather, often adorned with a decorative rope or braid. Originally part of traditional folk attire in many regions of Poland, during World War I it became part of military uniform of Riflemen's Association and the Polish Legions.

[45]Lubań Śląski was a train station in Lubań, in Lower Silesia. Per the Polish State Railways, it is classified as a local train station.

[46]Władysław Bandurski (May 25, 1865 – March 6, 1932 in Vilnius) was a Polish Roman Catholic Auxiliary Bishop in the Lwów archdiocese, an honorary chaplain of the Polish Legions, head chaplain of the Vilnius region Polish Scouting Organization, and recipient of the Virtuti Militari medal.

[47]Michał Sokolnicki (1880–1967) was a Polish diplomat and historian.

[48]Mieczysław Ryś-Trojanowski (October 21, 1881 – April 4, 1945 in Mauthausen) was a brigadier general in the Polish Army

[49]Brig. Gen. Bolesław Jerzy Roja (April 4, 1876 – May 27, 1940) - an officer of the Polish Legions in World War I, a general, and a politician in the Second Polish Republic, recipient of some of the highest Polish military awards including Virtuti Militari. He opposed Józef Piłsudski and his Sanacja regime in the 1920s. After the German invasion of Poland in 1939, he was arrested and murdered by the Nazis in Sachsenhausen concentration camp.

[50]Hans Hartwig von Beseler (April 27, 1850 – December 20, 1921) was a German Lt. General.
[51]Prince Zdzisław Lubomirski (1865–1943) was a Polish aristocrat, landowner, lawyer, a conservative politician, and social activist. The Prince was chairman of the "Central Civil Committee" (Centralny Komitet Obywatelski) in 1915. From 1916 to 1917, he was mayor of Warsaw. He was an activist of the "Real Politics Party" (Stronnictwo Polityki Realnej), and from 1917 to 1918, member of the Regency Council.

[52]Józef August Ostrowski (January 21, 1850 – June 20, 1923) was a Polish landowner and liberal-conservative politician, president of the "Real Politics Party", and a member of the Regency Council.

[53]Jan Kucharzewski (May 27, 1876 - July 4, 1952 in New York) was a historian, lawyer, politician, Prime Minister (1917–1918), and member of the Regency Council.

[54]Harry Clemens Ulrich Graf Kessler (May 23, 1868 – November 30, 1937) was an Anglo-German count, diplomat, writer, and patron of modern art.

[55]Unter den Linden ("under the linden trees") is a boulevard in the central Mitte district of Berlin, the capital of Germany. Running from the City Palace to Brandenburg Gate, it is named after the linden (lime) trees that line the grassed pedestrian mall on the median and the two broad carriageways.

[56]Tadeusz Szturm de Sztrem (October 18, 1892 – March 17, 1968 in Warsaw) was a Polish socialist and independence activist

[57]Jędrzej Moraczewski (January 13, 1870 – August 5, 1944) was Poland's Prime Minister and Minister of Transportation, railway engineer, Major in the transport corps of the Polish Army, union activist, politician and publicist, and one of the leaders in the Polish Social-Democratic Party and the Polish Socialist Party

[58]The Sejm of the Republic of Poland (Polish: Sejm Rzeczypospolitej Polskiej) is the larger, more powerful lower house of the Polish parliament. It consists of four hundred and sixty deputies (posłowie, literally "envoys", in Polish) elected

by universal ballot and is presided over by a speaker called the "Marshal of the Sejm of the Republic of Poland" (Marszałek Sejmu Rzeczypospolitej Polskiej).

[59]Stanisław Grabski (April 5, 1871 – May 6, 1949) was a Polish economist and politician, member of the Sejm, associated with the National Democracy political camp.

[60]Ignacy Jan Paderewski (November 18, 1860 – June 29, 1941) was a Polish pianist and composer, freemason, politician, statesman, and spokesman for Polish independence. He was a favorite of concert audiences around the world. His musical fame opened access to diplomacy and the media.

[61]Wojciech Korfanty (April 20, 1873 – August 17, 1939) was a Polish activist, journalist, and politician who served as a member of the German parliaments, the Reichstag, the Prussian Landtag, and later in the Polish Sejm. Briefly, he also was a paramilitary leader, known for organizing the Polish Silesian Uprisings in Upper Silesia, which after World War I was contested by Germany and Poland.

[62]Wincenty Witos (January 22, 1874 – October 31, 1945) was a prominent member of the Polish People's Party (PSL) from 1895 and leader of its "Piast" faction from 1913. He was a member of parliament in the Galician Sejm from 1908–1914 and an envoy to Reichsrat in Vienna from 1911 to 1918. Witos was also a leader of Polish Liquidation Committee (Polish: Polska Komisja Likwidacyjna) in 1918, head of the Piast party, and member of parliament in the Polish Sejm from 1919-1920. He served thrice as the premier of Poland, in 1920-1921, 1923 (Chjeno-Piast), and 1926.

[63]Greater Poland, often known by its Polish name Wielkopolska (German: Großpolen, Latin: Polonia Maior), is a historical region of west-central Poland. Its chief city is Poznań.

[64]Anton Ivanovich Denikin (December 16, 1872 – August 8, 1947) was a Russian Lieutenant General in the Imperial Russian Army (1916) and afterwards a leading general of the White movement in the Russian Civil War.

[65]Symon Vasylyovych Petliura (May 10, 1879 – May 25, 1926) was a Ukrainian politician and journalist. He became the Supreme Commander of the Ukrainian Army and the President of the Ukrainian National Republic during Ukraine's short-lived sovereignty in 1918–1921, leading Ukraine's struggle for independence following the fall of the Russian Empire in 1917.

[66]Leon Trotsky, born Lev Davidovich Bronstein (November 7, 1879 – August 21, 1940), was a Russian revolutionary, Marxist theorist, and Soviet politician whose particular strain of Marxist thought is known as Trotskyism. He joined the Bolsheviks ("majority") just before the 1917 October Revolution, immediately becoming a leader within the Communist Party. He would go on to become one

of the seven members of the first Politburo, founded in 1917 to manage the Bolshevik Revolution. During the early days of the Russian Soviet Federative Socialist Republic (RSFSR) and the Soviet Union, he served first as People's Commissar for Foreign Affairs and later as the founder and commander of the Red Army.

[67]Carl Philipp Gottfried (or Gottlieb) von Clausewitz (June 1, 1780 – November 16, 1831) was a Prussian general and military theorist who stressed the psychological and political aspects of war. His most notable work is *Vom Kriege (On War)*. Clausewitz was a realist in many different senses and, while in some respects a romantic, also drew heavily on the rationalist ideas of the European Enlightenment.

[68]David Lloyd George, 1st Earl Lloyd-George of Dwyfor, (January 17, 1863 – March 26, 1945) was a British statesman and Liberal Party politician. He was the last Liberal to serve as Prime Minister of the United Kingdom.

[69]Józef Dowbor-Muśnicki (October 25, 1867 – October 26, 1937) was a Russian military officer and Polish general, serving with the Imperial Russian and then Polish armies. He was also the military commander of the Greater Poland Uprising.

[70]General Michał Tadeusz Karaszewicz-Tokarzewski (January 5, 1893 in Lwów – May 22, 1964 in Casablanca, Morocco) was a Polish general and founder of the resistance movement "Polish Victory Service."

[71]Brigadier General Julian Stachiewicz (1890-1934) was a Polish Army officer, historian and writer

[72]Michał Grażyński (May 12, 1890, in Gdów – December 10, 1965, in London, United Kingdom) was a Polish military leader, social and political activist, Doctor of Philosophy and law, voivode of the Silesian Voivodeship, Scouting activist, and president of the Polish Scouting Organization.

[73]Jan Romer (1869 in Lwów – 1934 in Warsaw) was a Polish general and military commander. Studied in Mödling and joined the Austro-Hungarian Army. During the First World War, he fought at the battle of Limanowa (1914) and battle of Gorlice (1914), and he was wounded twice. Later, he joined the newly recreated Polish Army. During the Polish-Ukrainian War, he fought in the liberation of Lwów. In the Polish-Soviet War, he commanded the Cavalry Division at the Battle of Koziatyn (April 25-April 27, 1920), one of the most spectacular raids of the Polish cavalry, during the Polish advance towards Kiev. His troops fought against the Soviet cavalry elite Konarmia of Semyon Budyonny. He commanded the Polish 13th Infantry Division during the Battle of Komarów (August 31, 1920). Respected by Józef Piłsudski, he was among the first group military personas who received the decoration of Virtuti Militari, highest Polish military medal, restored after the recreation of the Second Polish Republic, and he himself re-

ceived the Commander's Cross of that award. He held position of Inspector of the Army after the war, and he was buried at Powązki Cemetery in Warsaw.

[74]Count Tadeusz Jordan-Rozwadowski (May 19, 1866 – October 18, 1928) was a Polish military commander, diplomat, and politician, a general of the Austro-Hungarian Army and then the Polish Army.

[75]Matka Boska Ostrobramska is the prominent Catholic painting of the Blessed Virgin Mary venerated by the faithful in the Chapel of the Gate of Dawn in Vilnius, Lithuania. The painting was historically displayed above the Vilnius city gate; city gates of the time often contained religious artifacts intended to ward off attacks and bless passing travelers.

[76]Maciej Stryjkowski (also referred to as Strykowski and Strycovius; c. 1547 — c. 1593) was a Polish and Lithuanian historian, writer, and a poet, notable as the author of Chronicle of Poland, Lithuania, Samogitia and all of Ruthenia (1582). The work is generally considered to be the first printed book on the history of the Grand Duchy of Lithuania.

[77]Władysław Zygmunt Belina-Prażmowski (1888 – 1936) organized the 1st Uhlan Regiment, former Mayor of Krakow and Woiwode of Lwów.

[78]Anton Ivanovich Denikin (December 16, 1872 – August 8, 1947) was a Russian Lieutenant General in the Imperial Russian Army (1916) and afterwards a leading general of the White movement in the Russian Civil War.

[79]Marian Włodzimierz Kukiel (May 15, 1885 in Dąbrowa Tarnowska – August 15, 1972 in London) was a Polish major general, historian, social and political activist. One of the founders of Union of Active Resistance in 1908 and prominent member of Riflemen's Societies; he fought in the Polish Legions in World War I. Kukiel served from 1919 until 1920 as Deputy Head of Section III, Polish General Staff and took part in the Polish-Soviet War.

[80]The Sich Riflemen Halych-Bukovyna Kurin were one of the first regular military units of the Army of the Ukrainian People's Republic. The unit operated from 1917 to 1919 and was formed from Ukrainian soldiers of the Austro-Hungarian army, local population and former commanders of the Ukrainian Sich Riflemen in Austria-Hungary.

[81]Count Tadeusz Jordan-Rozwadowski (May 19, 1866 – October 18, 1928) was a Polish military commander, diplomat, and politician, a general of the Austro-Hungarian Army and then the Polish Army.

[82]Wojciech Stefan Trąmpczyński (February 8, 1860 – March 2, 1953) was a Polish lawyer and National Democratic politician. Voivode of the Poznań Voivodeship in

1919. He served as marshal (speaker) of the Sejm of Poland from 1919–1922 and Senate of Poland from 1922 to 1928.

[83]Leopold Skulski (November 15, 1878, Zamość – Brest, June 11, 1940) served as prime minister of Poland for six months from December 13, 1919 until June 9, 1920 in the interim Legislative Sejm during the formation of sovereign Second Polish Republic following World War I.

[84]Ignacy Baliński (July 31, 1862 - March 11, 1951 in Sudbury) was a Polish writer, publicist, and social activist. Trained as a lawyer. A judge of the Supreme Court during the Second Polish Republic.

[85]Mychajło Wołodymyrowycz Omelianowycz-Pawlenko (December 8, 1878 in Tiflis - May 29, 1952 in Paris) was a Ukrainian general and independence activist.

[86]Bolesław I the Brave (Bolesław I Chrobry) (967 – June 17, 1025), also known as Bolesław I the Great (Bolesław I Wielki), was Duke of Poland from 992 to 1025, and the first King of Poland in 1025. As Boleslav IV, he was also Duke of Bohemia between 1002 and 1003. He was the son of Mieszko I of Poland by his wife, Dobrawa of Bohemia. According to a scholarly theory, Bolesław ruled Lesser Poland already during the last years of his father's reign. Mieszko I, who died in 992, divided Poland among his sons, but Bolesław expelled his father's last wife, Oda of Haldensleben, and his half-brothers and reunited Poland between 992 and 995. Fought a victorious battle at Chocim.

[87]Taczanki were two-wheeled horse-carts with a machine gun mounted on it for mobile attackes with the cavalry

[88]Count Stanisław Maria Szeptycki (November 3, 1867 – October 9, 1950) was a Polish aristocrat, general, and military commander.

[89]Józef Haller von Hallenburg (August 13, 1873 – June 4, 1960) was a lieutenant general of the Polish Army, a legionary in the Polish Legions, the president of the Polish Scouting and Guiding Association (ZHP), and a political and social activist.

[90]Gustaw Zygadłowicz (1869-1923) Officer in the Imperial Austrian Army and later General of Poland.

[91]The presidential residence in Warsaw.

[92]Fr. Stanisław Adamski (April 12, 1875 – November 12, 1967) was a Polish bishop, politician, and social and political activist of the Union of Catholic Societies of Polish Workers (Związek Katolickich Towarzystw Robotników Polskich), founder and editor of the Robotnik (Worker) weekly. Adamski was born in Zielonagóra. He was a Sejm deputy (1919–1922) and senator (1922–1927).

[93]Maxime Weygand (January 21, 1867 – January 28, 1965) was a French military commander in World War I and World War II. Weygand mainly served as a staff officer to Ferdinand Foch in World War I.

[94]Julian Baltazar Marchlewski (May 17, 1866 – March 22, 1925) was a Polish communist politician. He was born in Włocławek into a Polish family. In 1889, he co-founded the Polish Workers' Union. In 1893, he co-founded the Social Democratic Party of the Kingdom of Poland and Lithuania with Rosa Luxemburg.

[95]Feliks Dzierżyński (Russian: Dzerzhinsky) (September 11, 1877 – July 20, 1926), nicknamed Iron Felix, was a Bolshevik revolutionary and official. Born to ethnic Polish parents, from 1917 until his death in 1926, Dzierżyński led the first two Soviet state security organizations, the Cheka and the OGPU, establishing the secret police for the post-revolutionary Soviet government. He was one of the architects of the mass killings of hundreds of thousands of people during the Red Terror and Decossackization.

[96]Adam Feliks Próchnik (Lwów, August 21, 1892 – May 22, 1942, Warsaw) was a Polish socialist activist, politician, and historian.

[97]Feliks Yakovlevich Kon (May 18, 1864 – July 30, 1941) was a Polish communist activist.

[98]Józef Unszlicht (Stanislavovich Unshlikht) (December 31 1879 - July 28, 1938) was a Bolshevik revolutionary activist, one of the founders of the Cheka, and Soviet government official of Polish extraction from the Masovian region.

[99]Eustachy Kajetan Sapieha (August 2, 1881 – February 20, 1963) was a Polish nobleman, prince of the Sapieha family, politician, Polish Minister of Foreign Affairs, and deputy to the Polish parliament (Sejm).

[100]Władysław Dominik Grabski (July 7, 1874 – March 1, 1938) was a Polish National Democratic politician, economist, and historian. He was the main author of the currency reform in the Second Polish Republic and served as Prime Minister of Poland in 1920 and from 1923–1925. He was the brother of Stanisław Grabski and Zofia Kirkor-Kiedroniowa.

[101]Gabriel Narutowicz (March 17, 1865 – December 16, 1922) was a Polish professor of hydroelectric engineering, freemason, and politician who served as the 1st President of Poland from December 11, 1922 until his assassination on December 16, five days after assuming office. He previously served as the Minister of Public Works from 1920 to 1921 and briefly as Minister of Foreign Affairs in 1922. A renowned engineer and politically independent, Narutowicz was the first elected head of state following Poland's regained sovereignty from partitioning powers.

[102]Józef Krzysztof Leśniewski (September 26, 1867 - October 3, 1921 in Warsaw) was a Lt. General in the Polish Army.

[103]A Soviet organization that advocated world communism by any method that existed from 1919 to 1943.

[104]National Democracy, a nationalistic movement and political party ("en-decja" from the acronym ND), created at the end of the nineteenth century. Its chief ideologist and co-founder was Roman Dmowski.

[105]Adam Mickiewicz (1798 – 1855) was one of the three great bards of Polish literature and author of the romantic epic, *Pan Tadeusz*. (Also available from Winged Hussar Publishing)

[106]Marie Skłodowska Curie (1867 – 1934) was the multiple Nobel Prize award winning scientist.

[107]Norbert Barlicki (June 6, 1880 – September 27, 1941) was a Polish publicist, lawyer, and politician of the Polish Socialist Party (PPS). Barlicki was murdered during the Second World War in the German concentration camp Auschwitz.

[108]Witold Kamieniecki (March 9, 1883 - March 9, 1964) was a Polish historian, diplomat, senator, a lecturer at the University of Warsaw, member of the Warsaw Scientific Society, and freemason.

[109]Feliks Perl (April 26, 1871 – April 15, 1927) was a Polish socialist activist and publicist.

[110]Leon Wasilewski (August 24, 1870 - December 10, 1936) was an activist in the Polish Socialist Party (PPS), close associate of Józef Piłsudski, architect of Polish policy toward its eastern neighbors at the time of regaining independence. Father of writer Wanda Wasilewska.

[111]Jan Dąbski (April 10, 1880, Kukizów, Galicia – June 5, 1931, Warsaw, Poland) a Polish politician. Founder of Polish People's Party "Piast" (PSL Piast) in 1913. He was the chief negotiator for Poland at the peace negotiations in Riga after the Polish-Boleshevik War (1920–1921). Minister of Foreign Affairs of Poland in 1921. Deputy to Polish parliament (Sejm) until 1930, he was also an important politician in the PSL peasant party factions (PSL Piast, PSL Jedność Ludowa, Polish People's Party "Wyzwolenie", Peasant Party).

[112]Jakub Hanecki (March 15, 1879 in Warsaw - September 26, 1937 in Moscow) was a Polish communist activist, close associate, and treasurer for Lenin, participant in the Riga negotiations.

[113]Julian Leszczyński, (January 8, 1889 in Plock - September 27, 1937 in Moscow) was a Polish communist activist and publicist.

[114]Two operas by Stanisław Moniuszko.

[115]Jędrzej Edward Moraczewski (January 13, 1870 – August 5, 1944) was a Polish socialist politician who served as the first Prime Minister of the Second Polish Republic between November 1918 and January 1919. He had previously served as Minister of Communications. Subsequently, from 1925 to 1929, he served as Minister of Public Labor.

[116] Antoni Ponikowski (May 29, 1878 – December 27, 1949) was a Polish academician and politician who served as 7th Prime Minister of Poland in 1918 and from 1921 to 1922.

[117]Artur Śliwiński (August 17, 1877 – January 16, 1953) was the 8th Prime Minister of Poland from June 28 – July 7, 1922. In 1915, he had presided over the National Central Committee, which sought Polish independence from partitioning powers.

[118]Julian Ignacy Nowak (March 10, 1865 – November 7, 1946) was a Polish microbiologist and politician who served as 9th Prime Minister of Poland in 1922.

[119]The Sich Riflemen Halych-Bukovyna Kurin was one of the first regular military units of the Army of the Ukrainian People's Republic. The unit operated from 1917 to 1919 and was formed from Ukrainian soldiers of the Austro-Hungarian army, local population, and former commanders of the Ukrainian Sich Riflemen in Austria-Hungary.

[120]Marko Danylovych Bezruchko (1883–1944) was a Ukrainian military commander and a General of the Ukrainian National Republic.

[121]Bishop Franciszek Hodur (April 1, 1866 – February 16, 1953) was the founder and the first, and longtime, Prime Bishop of the Polish National Catholic Church.

[122]The Polish National Catholic Church (PNCC) is a Christian church based in the United States and founded in Scranton by Polish-Americans. The PNCC is not in full communion with the Roman Catholic Church; though it seeks full communion with the Holy See, it differs theologically in several important respects. The church has about twenty-six thousand members in five dioceses in the United States and Canada. The five dioceses are: Buffalo-Pittsburgh, Central, Eastern, Western, and Canada.

[123]Augustyn Łosiński (January 8, 1867 - Aril 30, 1937) was a Polish Roman Catholic priest, Bishop of Kielce 1910–1937.

[124]Maciej Rataj (19 February 1884 – 21 June 1940) a Polish politician and writer.

[125]Polish People's Party "Piast" or Polish Peasant Party "Piast" was a political party during the interwar period of the Second Polish Republic (1913–1931). Piast refers to the medieval Piast dynasty, Poland's founding royal house. It was created in 1913 and, after Poland regained independence in 1918, it formed a part of several governments.

[126]Dictator in the classical sense of Supreme Commander in times of emergency who returns powers to the state after the danger is past.

[127]Julian Tuwim (September 13, 1894 – December 27, 1953), was a Polish poet of Jewish descent, born in Łódź (then part of the Russian Partition). He was educated in Łódź and in Warsaw, where he studied law and philosophy at Warsaw University. After Poland's return to independence in 1919, Tuwim co-founded the Skamander group of experimental poets. He was a major figure in Polish literature, admired also for his contribution to children's literature.

[128]Gustav Ernst Stresemann (10 May 1878 – 3 October 1929) German statesman who served as Chancellor in 1923 (for a brief period of 102 days) and Foreign Minister 1923–1929.

[129]Gieorgij Wasyljewicz Chicherin (1872 - 1936) – Russian diplomat, lawyer, peoples' commissar for international relations in the Russian Soviet Federative Socialist Republic (1918-1923), as well as the Soviet Union (1922-1930).

[130]Lucjan Żeligowski (1865–1947) was a Polish general, politician, military commander and veteran of World War I, the Polish-Bolshevik War and World War II. He is mostly remembered for his role in Żeligowski's Mutiny and as head of a short-lived Republic of Central Lithuania.

[131]Bolesław Ignacy Florian Wieniawa-Długoszowski (July 22, 1881 – July 1, 1942) was a Polish general, adjutant to Chief of State Józef Piłsudski, politician, freemason, diplomat, poet, artist, and formally, for one day, President of the Republic of Poland. He was one of the generation that fought for, and saw, the rebirth of an independent Poland on Nov. 11, 1918 (Poland's National Independence Day) only to see that independence lost again, following the 1939 division of Poland between Germany and the Soviet Union pursuant to the Molotov–Ribbentrop Pact.

[132]Wilanów Palace (aka pałac w Wilanowie) is a royal palace located in the Wilanów district, Warsaw. Wilanów Palace survived Poland's partitions and both World Wars, and so serves as a reminder of the culture of the Polish state as it was before the misfortunes of the eighteenth century. It was built for King Jan III Sobieski in the last quarter of the seventeenth century and later enlarged

by other owners. It represents the characteristic type of baroque suburban residence built entre cour et jardin (between the entrance court and the garden). Its architecture is original, a merger of generally European art with distinctively Polish building traditions.

[133]Józef Beck (October 4, 1894 – June 5, 1944) was a Polish statesman who served the Second Republic of Poland as a diplomat and military officer and was a close associate of Józef Piłsudski. Beck is most famous for being Polish foreign minister in the 1930s, when he largely set Polish foreign policy.
[134]Ignacy Mościcki (December 1, 1867 – October 2, 1946) Polish chemist, politician, and President of Poland from 1926 to 1939. He was the longest serving President in Poland's history.

[135]Kazimierz Władysław Bartel (March 3, 1882 –July 26, 1941) was a Polish mathematician, freemason, scholar, diplomat, and politician who served as 15th, 17th, and 19th Prime Minister of Poland three times between 1926 and 1930, and the Senator of Poland from 1937 until the outbreak of World War II.

[136]Dr. Lenkiewicz writes - In the Lewicka matter I had a personal experience. In 1987, a female student from Warsaw told me that she was writing a doctoral dissertation on Eugenia Lewicka. She thought that I should not have left this matter out of my biography of Piłsudski and proposed a cooperation. When I told her that I had no time for such research, I was telling the truth. Years later, I checked the register of doctoral dissertations and did not find any that were devoted to Dr. Eugenia Lewicka (1896-1931).

[137]Wawel Castle is a walled royal compound located in central Kraków, Poland. Built at the behest of King Casimir III the Great, it consists of a number of structures situated around the Italian-styled main courtyard. The castle, being one of the largest in Poland, represents nearly all European architectural styles of medieval, renaissance, and baroque periods. In 1978, it was declared a UNESCO World Heritage Site. The Cathedral crypt is the final resting place of many Polish national heroes and kings.

[138]In the autumn of 1981, on the initiative of Solidarity, the crew of the Service Shipyard adopted the name of Józef Piłsudski for their workshops, when the Communist authorities refused to grant visas to the Marshal's daughters to enter their homeland. In a conversation with a Solidarity delegation, an irritated functionary of the government was heard to say, *But what was Piłsudski's connection to the sea?* There was a long moment of silence, while the fattened faces of the official and his retinue seemed to recover their former confidence. The silence continued, for how could one explain to them the history of the struggle for Gdańsk and the building and development of Gdynia, both of which were closely tied to the Marshal's plans for Poland. All this had been written into a proposal that was submitted several months earlier. *So, you gentlemen did not read our proposal?* But to the servants of the Soviet overlords in Poland, much stronger

than this question, was a retort by one of the workers.

And what connection does Lenin have to the Polish waterfront?
Listen here, comrade.
I am not one of your comrades, protested the Solidarity representative.

After the introduction of Martial Law, an attempt was made, just as before, to wipe out all the traces not only of the connection between the Service Shipyard in Gdańsk, but also all that the Marshal contributed to the development of the shipyards and the maritime economy for Poland. Unfortunately, the present situation of the Polish Shipyards and the state of the seafearing economy is not good. But one should know and remember the contributions he made, for this is a proud tradition, to which we must return.

[139]Eugeniusz Kwiatkowski (December 30, 1888, Kraków – August 22, 1974, Kraków) was a Polish politician and economist, Deputy Prime Minister of Poland, government minister, and manager of the Second Polish Republic.

[140]Front Morges was a political alliance of centrist political parties of interwar Poland (Polish Christian Democratic Party, National Workers' Party, Związek Hallerczyków). It was founded in 1936 in the Swiss village of Morges by General Władysław Sikorski and former Polish Prime Minister Ignacy Paderewski. Prominent activists included Józef Haller, Wojciech Korfanty, and Karol Popiel. They opposed the sanacja regime - which caused some of them to emigrate. They wanted to form a new government with Paderewski as the president and Wincenty Witos as the prime minister. They demanded democratization and closer ties with France.

[141]Prometheus Movement was a political and intellectual movement in Europe during the inter-war period (1921–1939) politically directed against the USSR, aimed at bringing about a transformation of independence within this state, effected by the nations which during 1918-1921 were brought into the Soviet system by force. In effect, the Soviet Union would be split up into independent nations.

[142]Felicjan Sławoj Składkowski (June 9, 1885 in Gąbin – August 31, 1962 in London) was a Polish physician, general, freemason, and politician who served as Minister of Internal Affairs and is 28th Prime Minister of Poland before World War II.

[143]The Military Order of the Tower and of the Sword, of Valour, Loyalty, and Merit (Portuguese: Ordem Militar da Torre e Espada do Valor, Lealdade, e Mérito) is a Portuguese order of knighthood and the pinnacle of the Portuguese honors system. It was created by King Afonso V in 1459. The order may be bestowed on people or on Portuguese municipalities.

[144]Artur Śliwiński (August 17, 1877–January 16, 1953) was the 8th Prime Minister of Poland from June 28 – July 7, 1922. In 1915, he had presided over the National Central Committee, which sought Polish independence from partitioning powers.

[145]Carol II of Romania (October 15, 1893 – April 4, 1953) reigned as king from June 8, 1930 until his abdication on September 6, 1940.

[146]Władimir Owsiejenko, (b. 1883, shot February 10, 1938) was a Soviet leader, Communist politician, and journalist.

[147]Stanisław Jan Patek (May 1, 1866 – August 25, 1944) was a Polish lawyer, freemason, and diplomat, served as Polish Minister of Foreign Affairs from 1919 to 1920.

[148]Count Jerzy Józef Potocki (January 29, 1889 – September 10, 1961) was a Polish nobleman, captain of the cavalry, and diplomat. On January 8, 1919 he joined the Polish Army after the dissolution of the Austro-Hungarian Empire and Army, was assigned to the General Staff, and appointed military attaché in Budapest.

[149]Mustafa Kemal Atatürk (May 19, 1881 – November 10, 1938) Turkish field marshal, revolutionary statesman, author, and founder of the Republic of Turkey, serving as its first President from 1923 until his death in 1938. Ideologically a secularist and nationalist, his policies and theories became known as *Kemalism*.

[150]Pierre Jean-Marie Laval (June 28, 1883 – October 15, 1945) was a French politician. During the time of the Third Republic, he served as Prime Minister of France from January 27, 1931 to February 20, 1932, and a second time from June 7, 1935 to January 24, 1936.

[151]The Four-Power Pact, also known as a Quadripartite Agreement, was an international treaty initialed on June 7, 1933, and signed on July 15, 1933, in the Palazzo Venezia, Rome. The pact was not ratified by France's Parliament.

[152]The Polish Military Transit Depot established on the Westterplatte Penninsula of Gdansk in 1925. Poland was required to remove the extra garrison shortly after increasing it. It was the object of the opening attacks of World War II, holding out for seven days against land, sea, and air attacks.

[153]Prince Adam Stefan Stanisław Bonifacy Józef Sapieha (May 14, 1867 – July 23, 1951) was a Polish cardinal of the Roman Catholic Church who served as Archbishop of Kraków. Between 1922–1923 he was a senator of the Second Polish Republic. In 1946, Pope Pius XII elevated him Cardinal.

[154]Stanisław Car was a Polish politician, lawyer, Marshal of the Sejm, deputy Prime Minister and the Minister of Justice. In 1915, he became a judge, and a member of the Commission of Civil Law of the Provisional Council of State.

[155]Leon Tadeusz Kozłowski (6 June 1892 – 11 May 1944) was a Polish archaeologist, freemason and politician who served as Prime Minister of Poland from 1934 to 1935.

[156] Pole Mokotowskie ("Mokotów Field") is a large park in Warsaw. Part of it is now called "Józef Piłsudski Park." Located between Warsaw's Mokotów district and the city center, the park is one of the largest in Warsaw. Until World War II, a major part was occupied by an airfield and the Warsaw Polytechnic aircraft works.

Index of Names

About the Translator

Peter J. Obst was born in Poznan, Poland; he came to the United States in 1963 and later became an American citizen. He attended Holy Ghost Prep, and then Drexel University in Philadelphia, graduating with a bachelor's degree in Commerce and Engineering in 1977. That summer he participated in the Kosciuszko Foundation session at the Jagiellonian University.

He started writing free-lance articles that appeared in *The Wall Street Journal Europe, Private Pilot* magazine, *The Polish-American Journal* and other publications. His travels to Poland and familiarity with the Polish language led to a translation of Jaroslaw Kurski's book Wódz, which was published in 1993 under the title *Lech Walesa: Democrat or Dictator?* by Westview Press of Boulder, Colorado.

In 1994 he started a home-based business, preparing books for publication. Over the next five years he completed publishing assignments for Westview Press, the University of California, the Polish Embassy in Washington, Princeton University, and many other customers.

He is currently employed by Mr. Edward Pinkowski, a Polish-American Historian, as researcher and translator working on many projects, including research into the life of Kazimierz Pulaski.

In addition to his writing and publishing activities he also designs and maintains websites for several Polonia organizations and the Pinkowski Institute. He is a member of The Polish Heritage Society of Philadelphia and for two years (2000-2001) was the Editor-in-Chief of Polish Heritage, the American Council for Polish Culture (ACPC) quarterly newsletter. He is active in both the ACPC and the Kosciuszko Foundation where for over five years he had served as president of the Philadelphia Chapter. He is also active with the Pulaski Jubilee Committee in Savannah, Georgia. In 2001 he was awarded the Cavalier's Cross of the Order of Merit by decree of the President of Poland.

During 2002 three more his translations from Polish were published: *My Flights to Freedom, A Family from Sosnowiec,* and *A Man Who Spanned Two Eras, the Biography of Bridge Engineer Ralph Modjeski.*

About the Author

Antoni Lenkiewicz (born October 25, 1934 in Ostrołęka) - Polish historian, lawyer, publicist, activist of the anti-communist opposition.

In the years 1952-1956 he was imprisoned for belonging to the Polish Fighting Scouts Union. In 1963 he graduated from the Faculty of History and the Faculty of Law and Administration of the University of Wrocław. In 1970 he obtained a doctoral degree. Starting in 1963 he worked for social causes.

In the 1970s, he worked with the Human Rights and Citizens' Defense Movement and the Student Solidarity Committee and published in magazines that appeared outside of censorship. In 1980 he co-organized NSZZ "Solidarność" in Wrocław. He was the head of legal advisors of the union in Lower Silesia. He then became a contributor to *Tygodnik Solidarność*. From December 13, 1981 to December 23, 1982, he was interned and then deprived of his job. On November 11, 1985 after a lecture at the Church of St. Charles Borromeo in Wroclaw he was kidnapped by civilian officers of the SB and was sentenced to one-year imprisonment for calling for civil unrest. He spent nine months in prison. He was

active in the Confederation of Independent Poland and in Fighting Solidarity.

In the years 1990-1994, he was a counselor and chairman of the Audit Committee of the City Council of Wrocław. He presented his socio-political experience from that period in the book, *A Parade in the Municipality of Wroclaw*. He then became the editor-in-chief of *Wrocławska Gazeta Polska*.

He was one of the first people to apply for compensation for the period of internment under martial law. In January 2008, the court awarded him twenty-three thousand zlotys in damages.

Find out more about Pike & Powder Publishing Group, LLC and Winged Hussar Publishing at:

https://www.wingedhussarpublishing.com

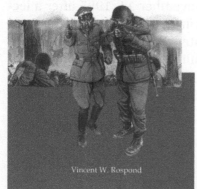

The Polish Army in 1939

Vincent W. Rospond

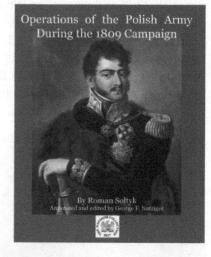

Operations of the Polish Army During the 1809 Campaign

By Roman Soltyk
Annotated and edited by George F. Nafziger

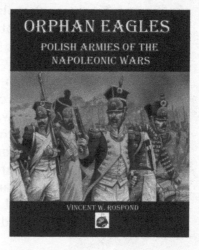

ORPHAN EAGLES

POLISH ARMIES OF THE NAPOLEONIC WARS

VINCENT W. ROSPOND

This publication has been supported by the © POLAND Translation Program

BOOK INSTITUTE

©POLAND

This publication has been supported by the ©POLAND Translation Program